# You Are The Music

# Praise for *You Are the Music*

'[D]eep yet accessible … a manual for the successful use of music for the benefit of self and others.'    *Science*

'An excellent starting point for anyone wanting to know more about the role of music in human experience.'
*Psychologist*

'An insightful book on a fascinating subject.'    *The Lady*

'A fascinating insight into our relationship with music.'
Waterstones.com

# You Are The Music

## How Music Reveals What It Means To Be Human

Victoria Williamson

ICON

First published in the UK in 2014 by
Icon Books Ltd, Omnibus Business Centre,
39–41 North Road, London N7 9DP
email: info@iconbooks.net
www.iconbooks.net

This edition published in the UK in 2014 by Icon Books Ltd

Sold in the UK, Europe and Asia
by Faber & Faber Ltd, Bloomsbury House,
74–77 Great Russell Street,
London WC1B 3DA or their agents

Distributed in the UK, Europe and Asia
by TBS Ltd, TBS Distribution Centre, Colchester Road,
Frating Green, Colchester CO7 7DW

Distributed in India by Penguin Books India,
7th Floor, Infinity Tower – C, DLF Cyber City,
Gurgaon 122002, Haryana

Distributed in South Africa by
Jonathan Ball, Office B4, The District,
41 Sir Lowry Road, Woodstock 7925

Distributed in Australia and New Zealand
by Allen & Unwin Pty Ltd,
PO Box 8500, 83 Alexander Street,
Crows Nest, NSW 2065

Distributed in Canada by Publishers Group Canada,
76 Stafford Street, Unit 300
Toronto, Ontario M6J 2S1

ISBN: 978-184831-743-7

Typeset in Dante by Marie Doherty

Printed and bound in the UK by
Clays Ltd, St Ives plc

# Contents

Acknowledgements                                                vii

Introduction                                                      1

**Part I: Music in early life**
Chapter 1      First musical steps                               11
Chapter 2      Music in childhood                                31
Chapter 3      Music for adolescent years                        53

**Part II: Music in adult life**
Chapter 4      The musical adult                                 79
Chapter 5      Music at work                                    111
Chapter 6      Music at play                                    139

**Part III: Music across the lifespan**
Chapter 7      Music and memory                                 169
Chapter 8      Music and lifelong well-being                    197

Notes                                                           225
Index                                                           257

Contents

# Acknowledgements

It all started about five years ago. I did not know quite what to think when my partner Oscar gave me musicpsychology. co.uk as a birthday present. He explained himself quickly: I loved talking about the psychology of music and this was a chance to discuss my passion with the whole world. He was right (yes, I said it). The blog soon became my baby and this book is the culmination of over a decade's exploration into the wonderful world of music psychology. So thank you Oscar, for everything.

I am hugely grateful to all the magnificent people at Icon Books, especially to Duncan Heath, who supported me throughout the writing process, to Andrew Furlow and Henry Lord for their enthusiasm and creativity, and to Robert Sharman for his keen and careful eye. I am grateful, too, to the talented Richard Green for his striking cover design. I consider myself very lucky to have had such a great team behind my book.

Many students, colleagues and friends have been generous with their time in discussing both this book and the psychological impact of writing it upon the author. I could not possibly name all these kind souls but I want to make special mention to Joydeep Bhattacharya, Rhiannon Jones, Pamela Heaton, Daniel Müllensiefen, Georgina Floridou, Maurice Douglas, Danielle Richardson and Team Barcelona.

Dad, thank you for the baby taming, the music lessons, the instruments, the lifts to music centres, the speakers, the vinyl, the music-filled holidays, and for reading every chapter of this book with the same vigour and humour that you once reserved for my maths homework. You are my hero.

Finally, this book is dedicated to my amazing, supportive, enthusiastic, loving, one-of-a-kind family.

# Introduction

Since you have been so kind as to consider reading this book I am going to assume that you have an interest in music; why we love it so much and how it affects us. Me too!

I promise to assume nothing else about you. To read this book requires no expert knowledge of or training in music, psychology, brain science, or any other kind of academic discipline. All you need with you on this journey is your curiosity about music.

The reason for this book, and for my career, is a passion for music. I am, at best, an amateur musician. I love my classical guitar ('The Professor') but we see each other rarely these days what with work demands, so my musical interests don't come from the viewpoint of a skilled performer. Nor would I consider myself to be particularly knowledgeable about music. I am not a sophisticated listener; more a musical chameleon. I rarely come across music that I don't enjoy on some level.

I put the blame for my music addiction squarely on my dad. When I was born he acquired a lovely book called *Baby Taming*[1] (seriously), which stated that playing loud music at bedtime helps a child to sleep deeply and with less disruption. I have no idea whether this pop psychology contains any truth – as far as I know the claim has never been tested – but my dad needed little encouragement to fire up his Celestion Ditton 66 speakers and crank out the vinyl every night.

As a result of this baby book and my dad's love of vinyl I have been surrounded by music from day one. Not music practice or performance so much, as neither of my parents could play an instrument. Rather, in my family music was in the air.

I was fortunate to go to a primary school that offered free instrument lessons for a time and I chose to play the guitar, though I also dabbled in mandolin, recorder and flute. I had formal music lessons on classical guitar, with a charming teacher named Andrew Forrest who instilled in me a love of Spanish music, especially Fernando Sor, Francisco Tárrega and Isaac Albéniz. I enjoyed my formal lessons until the age of eighteen but took few music exams as I found them too stressful.

Alongside my formal music education I had increasing access to my favourite music as I grew up thanks to the explosion in the availability of compressed music and portable devices. And the music listening revolution has continued in my adult life with developments like cloud-based systems for musical storage. Today this means that people need never be far away from their top tunes. And I never am. I am listening to the wonderful Three Tenors as I write this introduction. I had BBC music radio playing in my car on the way to work this morning. My dad's beloved Celestion Ditton 66 speakers now take pride of place in my living room.

Not only am I addicted to music, I am also addicted to working out why I am addicted to music. (I believe that is what is known as an over-analytical mind.) I blame my passion for studying my musical addiction on a handful of inspirational academics that I have been lucky enough to meet on my journey as I studied psychology, the psychology of music, and finally as I began my research career. There are too many people to name individually, though deserving of special mention are my 'academic fathers' and inspirations, Professors Alan Baddeley and Graham Hitch.

I have devoted my research career to understanding how and why music is so much a part of our everyday lives. There are already many technical books out there that explore aspects of music psychology – a young and vibrant science that examines the relationship between music and our mind, brain, and body. There are also excellent compilations, essay collections and student guides, for which I am hugely grateful as a lecturer. But I wanted a book that I could recommend to a friend who was keen to learn about the impact of music on everyday life: the person who listens to their iPod on their way to work and who refuses to contemplate a long car journey without music; the parent who takes their child to musical activity classes or pays for formal music lessons; the person who owns a shower radio, looks forward to concerts and gigs, shops to a soundtrack, and who carefully selects music for a romantic night to ensure maximum seduction; the person who can't help but be transported back to that one perfect evening when they hear 'that song'. I wanted an easy-to-access guide book that explained everyday music psychology for everyone – so I decided to write it.

This book contains a selection of the findings and theories through which researchers have sought to tell the story of our lives with music. My aim in this book is to consider why we live this way. In terms of music's power over us I want to have a go at revealing 'the wizard behind the curtain'.

As we shall see in more detail in the pages to come, music can trigger growth in the brain at any age, a fact which has been linked to enhancement of hearing acuity, language learning and motor control. In children, music lessons have been associated with the advanced development of many physiological, social and cognitive skills and in adults music can boost sports performance by up to 15 per cent. Music provides a source of communication for those who struggle with language and it can provide significant comfort from both physical and mental pain. It can help improve recovery from illness and injury, and support and guide transitions through life stages. Finally, it provides a personal soundtrack and an instant memory passport.

Just about everyone is exposed to music every day, whether voluntarily or not. People dedicate their time to its production, performance and consumption. There are national music days, where countries celebrate their musical heritage, talents and passions. So the issue is not whether we are engaging with music; in fact, we are gorging on it. The secrets of music psychology can help solve the question of why music has such an effect upon us. Why do we love it so much? Why is it everywhere? And how does it have so many effects on our brains, bodies and behaviours?

The underlying concept for the book is 'the music of our lives': from the time we are born to later adulthood. The mapping of music through life in this way allows a journey to unfold and means that there will, I hope, be something in the book for everyone.

But before we begin, there are some fundamental questions we need to consider.

### What is music?

I was once asked this intriguing question as part of a radio programme hosted by Professor Lord Robert Winston. I froze completely. What could I say? Over a decade of focused study behind me and I could not think of a single decent response. I kicked myself the whole way home from the recording studio, and for several days afterwards.

I have since forgiven Professor Winston for his excellent question and have considered what my answer might be, given what I have learned so far. I have come up with the following definition: *Music is a universal, human, dynamic, multi-purpose, sound signalling system*. That description is not set in stone; it is a work in progress. For now it gives us something to work with for the purpose of this book.

### Where did music come from?

There are many theories about how music became part of our world. Charles Darwin's theory of sexual selection posits that music evolved as a form of fitness display to attract potential mates. Or maybe we developed music as a way to soothe and educate our infants. It might have provided a valuable medium for tribes and families to identify themselves and communicate their social cooperation. Or maybe music evolved from a proto-language that allowed our ancestors to communicate crucial signals before they developed words and sentences.

I have been a firm believer in all these theories of music's origin, and more, at various points in my career. That is the best way to be as a scientist. There is nothing more boring than someone who sticks to the same tired old ideas for years, refusing to budge or admit they may need a rethink.

My preferred explanation at the time of writing comes from Mark Changizi, who muses about the origins of music and language in his fantastic book *Harnessed*.[2] He suggests that our obsession with music arose because it 'harnessed' so much of nature around us and because it used existing and ancient brain mechanisms for new and exciting purposes.

Music in this sense is not a fundamental part of human life because it's a part of our souls or the 'language of love', tempting as it is to fall back on such romantic notions. Changizi's argument stresses that music is a part of us because we designed it based on who we were and what we needed as humans. The human animal, our evolving brains and bodies, were the blueprint for music.

I like the idea that music is part of what turned us into the modern human that we recognise today. Changizi suggests that music, along with language and reading, is what turned apes into humans. We, by this definition, are the musical animal.

### Are we the only musical animal?

We are not the only animal to make musical sounds, although you could argue that we have a tendency to anthropomorphise such behaviours. Birds, mice and whales sing, gorillas duet, seals and elephants move to the beat, and so on (see Chapter 6).

Despite these examples, to my knowledge there is no other animal on earth that is as driven by, obsessed with, and vulnerable to the strains of music as humans. No other animal invests as much in the creation or acquisition of musical sound; we devote precious energy to making instruments, constructing and maintaining music ensembles, producing music for easy consumption, and aspiring to solo musical performance perfection.

I do not mean to say that other animals can't share in aspects of musical perception, production or enjoyment. It would be a pretty strange world if we humans had developed a skill that did not exist in any form in any other animal – that would make us a musical alien. My premise for this book is instead that we are far and away the most musical animal this planet has ever seen. In this sense our musical lives provide a unique glimpse into what it means to be human.

♪

The book is divided into three sections. **The first section** deals with music as we grow up. **Chapter 1** begins at the start, with the music we hear before we are even born. We see that babies come into the world with an impressive catalogue of musical skills that lay the foundation for their musical adulthood. Through **Chapters 2 and 3** we explore the effects of music in childhood through to adolescence, including the link between music and IQ, the ingredients for a successful musical education, and the role that music plays in our personal, emotional and social development.

The **second section** takes a look at music in the adult world: the true hidden musical talents within us and the transformations that occur in the brain when an individual trains as a musician (**Chapter 4**). We will also take a look at individuals who struggle with music their whole lives and find out what it is to be 'tone deaf'. We then take a tour through the music in our modern adult world, at work (**Chapter 5**) and at play (**Chapter 6**).

The **third and final section** takes a reflective journey through the importance of music across the whole of the human lifespan. **Chapter 7** is devoted to musical memory, my personal academic passion. We look at feats of musical memory and explore cases of musical memory surviving extensive brain damage. Then there is the intriguing question of why musical memories get stuck in our heads. Finally, we build on these and other studies in **Chapter 8** to explore how music can help support health and well-being at all life stages.

I can appreciate that this looks like quite a journey – after all, it's a whole human life – but you are free to dip in and out of the book as you like. The chapters are designed to be largely self-contained so you can jump right to your personal interest, whether it's musical babies, music lessons, music for romance, music for work, music for exercise, or music for stress relief.

So, my fellow musical animal, let's begin our exploration of what the world of science and psychology can tell us about our day-to-day, lifelong, love of music.

# PART I

# Music in early life

Chapter 1
# First musical steps

*'I was born with music inside me. Music was one*
*of my parts. Like my ribs, my kidneys, my liver,*
*my heart. Like my blood. It was a force already*
*within me when I arrived on the scene.'*

Wolfgang Amadeus Mozart was born in Salzburg in 1756 and went on to become one of the world's most prolific and influential composers. Although he lived for only 35 years and died over 200 years ago, sales of his exquisite music regularly top the classical music charts and he is frequently voted in the top five composers of all time.

Mozart was playing and composing music by the age of five. Because of this he is often cited as the prime example of a human being who was 'born musical' – far more musical, in fact, than the rest of us. But was he?

There is no doubt that Wolfgang Amadeus Mozart had a very early start to his musical career and that he had a 'pushy parent'. Johann Georg Leopold Mozart was one of Europe's leading music teachers and in the year of his seventh child's birth he published his dense textbook *Versuch einer gründlichen Violinschule* ('A Treatise on the Fundamental Principles of Violin Playing'). According to reports, little Mozart received intensive musical instruction from his father before he could even speak.

There is such a thing as talent and there are such things as prodigies, though our present understanding of both concepts is still hotly debated.[1] Perhaps because of this fact I am inclined to believe that it was mostly Mozart's unique upbringing that set him apart musically from the rest of us. Whether Mozart possessed advanced natural musical ability or not, the point I want to make here is that all babies are born musical, not just our finest composers.

We are born musical because our first experiences of music are pre-birth, as the womb is flooded with the music-like sounds of our world: the pitch glides, the melodies and the beats of body movements, voices, natural and artificial sounds. As a result of this early exposure, newborns come into this world possessing an impressive set of basic musical skills that play an important role in general development, quite aside from the issue of whether or not the child goes on to learn how to play a piano or pluck a violin.

When it comes to musicality, everyone had to start somewhere, including Mozart. And as we shall see we all have something in common with Ray Charles: we were born with music already inside of us.

## Music in the womb

I have never seen a 'prega-phone' but I remember the first time I was told about their existence. I was giving a lecture on music psychology for the Open University, during which I discussed the origins of musical skills. A member of the audience raised their hand to point out that you could improve a baby's lifelong musical skills by playing them music through a microphone strapped to a pregnant woman's tummy: the aptly named prega-phone. It turns out that you can buy all sorts of similar devices

Given what I knew about music and brain development I thought it unlikely that intensive prenatal music exposure could benefit later musical development but I set out to investigate this question anyway. If nothing else, then the next time I was faced with a similar comment I could be a little more useful to the audience than simply playing devil's advocate.

Before we look at the effect of prenatal music listening on development, let's deal with the first important physiological question: what does music sound like before we are born?

Music doesn't sound like anything until about the fourth month of pregnancy, the stage at which human hearing begins to function. It then takes about another two months for the fine structures of the ear that detect frequencies (for example, the cochlea) to fully form.[2] At this point an *in utero* baby becomes aware of a range of auditory stimulation from the environment. What they actually hear is a matter very much open to debate.

Given that a foetus is surrounded by amniotic fluid, we can assume that they perceive sounds a little like when they are played under water. Not many swimming pools are fitted with underwater speakers and there is a good reason for this; in this submarine environment you may be aware of pitch movements in the low register, changes in volume and maybe a strong beat, but the fine detail is largely lost. Picking out instruments or singers can be almost impossible, because of the loss of high frequencies, and finer points of melody are also hard to detect.

A developing foetus would find it even harder to follow the exact detail of music early on, as they will be hearing other sounds much closer to them, such as the mother's digestive system, air movements through her lungs, and the activity of her heart and blood vessels.

At the time of writing there are no known studies of musical sound in the human womb (recordings are only really possible during labour) but recordings in pregnant sheep have found at least a 10-decibel reduction in external sound within the womb,[3] with less reduction in low frequency sounds compared to higher frequencies. If you tried to identify words in this kind of environment you would probably get about 40 per cent of them right.[4]

What does all this mean for our prega-phone? I have seen no evidence that *in utero* hearing devices offer anything more in terms of sound transmission than a pair of headphones over the abdomen or a seat close to a speaker, although I'm assured that they offer some ergonomic comfort for the mother. What is undeniable is that a typically developing foetus can hear what is going on in their external world during the last trimester.

Although we can't know exactly what a foetus hears in the womb, their brain responses to sound can be studied using a specially adapted form of fMEG (foetal magnetoencephalography). This kind of scan requires a mother to kneel with her tummy enclosed with a specially adapted series of sensors (known as a SQUID array) that pick up the minute magnetic changes around the foetal head caused by brain activity.

Using the SQUID array device researchers have shown that from around 28 weeks gestation the majority of foetuses can detect frequency changes in the range of 250Hz, equivalent to the gap across five white notes in the upper middle section of a piano (octave five).[5] What is more, research conducted during labour using a hydrophone has found that foetal hearing reaches impressive levels, being described in some studies as near perfect.[6]

I have often been asked whether a foetus enjoys music in the womb; for example, when a baby kicks in response to music I have heard it said that this is because they like the sound. I'm sure I don't have to tell you that it's not possible to determine the aesthetic preferences of a foetus: in terms of their movement and heart rate, being asleep probably appears similar to being bored, and being excited probably appears similar to annoyance. That is assuming, of course, that such emotional states are possible in one so young.

And while a foetus can certainly respond to music, there is no suggestion that this is in any way different to how they respond to all manner of external auditory stimuli, including sirens, animal cries or, as we shall see in a minute, aircraft take-off. So let's leave the point of musical preference on one side for now.

Whether or not unborn babies have a preference for sound has little bearing on the question of whether they remember what they hear. We have known for a long time that babies can remember sounds that they have experienced *in utero* because of their behaviour once they are born. Newborns respond more frequently and regularly to their mother's voice, the voice with which they are undoubtedly most familiar because of the direct transmission it gets through her body.

A great example of foetal memory for other sounds was a study conducted with babies whose mothers had lived near Osaka International Airport, Japan during pregnancy. After they were born these infants were not woken by, and had little or no discernible brain wave reaction to, recorded aircraft noise. By comparison they were awakened and disturbed by a music sequence that had similar characteristics to the sound of planes taking off.[7]

In theory therefore a foetus can become accustomed to and remember musical sounds if they hear them as frequently as those babies heard aircraft take-off – but can newborns really remember complex music, given the increased difficulties with the muffled nature of the sound?

In my previous research post I spent many a happy coffee break chatting about life with our head technician, Maurice, a good friend of mine. When I mentioned I was writing this chapter he told me a story about one of his wife's pregnancies. At the time she was a fan of *Neighbours*, the long-running

Australian soap opera. The show had had the same theme tune for years, marked by large pitch leaps and a steady beat, two musical features that have a good chance of getting through to a foetus. Maurice says that when little Matthew was born he would react strongly to the *Neighbours* theme: his face lit up, he searched around for the source of the sound, and he made animated noises. Maurice is convinced that Matthew remembered the *Neighbours* theme tune from his time in the womb, as he didn't react this way to other music.

This everyday anecdotal experience of infant response to *in utero* music is supported by science. In 2011, Carolyn Granier-Deferre and her team played women a novel descending piano melody twice daily during the 35th, 36th, and 37th weeks of their pregnancy.[8] At six weeks old the newborn babies were played these melodies again while they were asleep, along with a similar control melody that went up instead of down. The researchers measured the heart rates of these 25 babies and compared them to the responses of 25 'control' babies who had not heard any of the tunes before.

All the tunes triggered a decrease in the babies' heart rates (by about five to six beats per minute) but the familiar tunes had twice the relaxing effect on the 25 babies who had heard them in the womb.

This extra deceleration in heart rate in response to the downward melodies is a remarkable finding when you consider that the babies had not really heard the melodies very often – probably less frequently than little Matthew had heard the *Neighbours* theme tune over the course of his mum's pregnancy and certainly less than the Osaka babies had heard aircraft taking off – but still their sleeping heart rate responses gave away the fact that they remembered this musical shape.

*In utero* exposure to music may be limited and missing the full complexity that we hear outside the womb, but the fact that babies are sensitive to and can learn to recognise musical sounds means that by the time they are born they have had months of exposure to some of the basic features of music (rhythms and contours) and thereby months of opportunities to learn about musical sound.

This finding leads to a series of interesting questions, that take me right back to the comment made by my Open University student: does prenatal exposure impact on later musical skills? Will increasing foetal exposure to music make for a more musical baby or, even more controversially, a smarter baby?

The majority of the evidence says 'no'. Not a single study to date has convincingly demonstrated that increasing prenatal music exposure above the typical amount heard in everyday life improves later musical perception or production. It's not the case, for example, that parents who are both musicians always produce a child who is interested in or skilled in music.

I doubt that we will ever see evidence for a direct effect of prenatal music on musical skill either, for one good reason: what happens *after* a child is born, as with young Mozart, is lilkely to be far more important to musical development than degree of exposure in the womb.

It's important to emphasise that all sounds, whether we think of them as musical or not, will transmit 'musical' information to a foetus due to the qualities of the womb environment. In the final trimester a foetus hears the sounds of voices, industry, and nature as a series of beats and movements in pitch. It's not clear how or why flooding the foetus with extra music makes any difference – if anything, such a strategy may block exposure to the wide variety of useful sounds that they might otherwise hear, such as familiar voices.

I will leave it to my next chapter to get into the debate about whether musical exposure can boost intelligence – suffice to say there is no evidence that *prenatal* musical exposure improves intelligence in *newborns*. And while it may be possible to create a musical memory for a newborn that they associate with beneficial relaxation responses, we now know that familiar voices, a human heartbeat and even planes taking off can all have similar effects.

Prenatal music intervention may not lead to a more musical baby or a smarter baby but the sounds that babies hear in the womb are still important. In the next section we see how our young are born with some pretty impressive basic musical skills – partly due to typical *in utero* sound exposure.

There will always be a debate about nature and nurture when it comes to newborns' abilities, but exposure to musical aspects of sound in the womb influences the development of the building blocks for later musical skills. The crucial thing about building blocks, though, is that they are basic and can go only so far – if you don't continue to build with them, they will stay at the same level.

## Newborn rhythm

A newborn's experience is not the coherent assemblage of sensory streams, neatly knitted together into a thread of consciousness, which we take for granted as an adult. The American philosopher and psychologist William James famously stated that the newborn infant perceives their new world 'as one great blooming, buzzing confusion'.[9] When you think about it, it's no wonder they cry.

In spite of this sensory chaos, newborns are attracted to and can respond to sound patterns that already make a degree of sense to them, and we have just seen how they remember sensory experiences from their time in the womb, particularly ones involving sound.

One of the consequences of the early development of hearing in humans, compared to other senses such as vision, is that babies are born primed with skills that they can use to learn about musical patterns in their environment. One of the most important is their sense of 'the beat'.

Rhythms are perhaps the strongest and most coherent low-frequency auditory messages that a foetus experiences regularly, hearing as they do the rhythms of speech, the rhythms of musical and environmental sounds, and the rhythm of their mother's walk and heartbeat. One might suppose, therefore, that if we were to be born with any musical skills then we must be born with an idea of the beat. This appears to be the case.

In 2009, István Winkler and colleagues published a landmark paper called 'Newborn infants detect the beat in music'.[10] They studied musical skill in infants that were only two to three days old – while they were asleep.

The researchers took advantage of a feature of our brain responses known as the 'mismatch negativity', or MMN, which is measured using electroencephalography, or EEG. An EEG scan measures the minute electrical activity across the scalp caused by brain activity, usually by means of a person wearing what looks like a shower cap covered in wires.

The MMN is a particular brain wave pattern that happens in response to a change in an otherwise consistent sequence of environmental events. MMN responses occur in all the senses but of course we are interested in sound. If you hear ten beeps of a certain note and the eleventh note changes, then your brain will give an MMN response. The MMN is the neural signature that your brain has spotted the 'oddball', the deviation in your expectation of what should come next. The interesting thing is that your brain will show an MMN response whether or not you are paying attention to the sounds – and this makes it an ideal brain response to study in sleeping babies.

Winkler and his colleagues used a specially adapted EEG system to measure MMN responses in newborns, smaller and more delicate than the adult version, accounting for infants' fine skin and petite features. The researchers fitted the baby EEG and waited until the babies had a nice big meal and fell asleep.

Once the babies were sleeping, they were played sound sequences based on a typical rock drum accompaniment pattern, featuring a snare, bass and hi-hat. Occasionally the pattern missed a downbeat, the first strong beat of a unit of music, which adults hear as a rhythm break or a moment of strong syncopation. The dropped downbeat creates a rhythmic 'oddball'. Would two- to three-day-old babies be aware of this oddball, and show an MMN response?

The answer is 'yes'. Even when asleep the newborns gave an MMN reaction to the dropped beat. Importantly, this reaction wasn't simply triggered by the missing note; dropped notes at non-rhythmic points did not trigger an MMN. This evidence shows that newborn babies can extract the beat from musical sequences. That is pretty impressive for a two-day-old brain, and strongly implies that infants are born with sensitivity for rhythmical sounds.

The researchers of this study suggest that newborns' beat detection skills may have been learned partly because of hearing rhythms *in utero* and partly due to an innate drive. More specifically, newborns may apply their innate sensitivity for patterns in order to assemble rhythms and generate expectations in sound sequences. This makes them capable of basic beat induction, which, as we shall see in Chapter 6, is a skill missing in nearly all other animals on the planet.

Beat induction is an example of a basic music building block that is essential for later musical behaviours such as playing in synchrony and dancing, and which appears to be ready and willing to go right from the start of our lives.

## Newborn name that tune

Newborns' musical skills extend beyond detecting the beat to include sound discrimination based on features such as volume, duration and pitch.[11] Not only this, newborns can discriminate between different contours, the equivalent to spotting the difference between two melodies, and they can use this information when listening to speech.

Thiery Nazzi and colleagues[12] tested French newborns' ability to discriminate between two lists of Japanese words that differed only in their contour, either going up or down. The researchers used a measurement technique that takes advantage of newborns' natural inclination to suck. They gave them a special pacifier that measured every suck, noting its strength and time of occurrence. They started testing with 121 newborns but, as is often the case with infant research, they had a few drop-outs: 34 fell asleep (awww), fifteen rejected the special pacifier, seventeen committed the crime of 'irregular or insufficient sucking', and fifteen did not settle. That leaves us with 40 willing and able babies.

These 40 babies were played one of two word lists for a few minutes; one list contained words that went up in sound and one comprised words where the contour went down. During this familiarisation period the baby gets used to the sound and their sucking rate steadies to a consistent rate. Then half the babies – the experimental group – were played a different list while half – the control group – continued to hear the same list as before.

If the babies were capable of discriminating a change to the contour, it was predicted that their sucking rate would change – they would suck more as they became alert to and interested in the new sound. The control babies, who were hearing the same sound, were expected to continue on at a steady suck.

This is exactly what happened. The babies in the experimental group clearly noticed the change in the contour of the Japanese speech, the melody of the words, before they then settled down to a familiar sucking pattern again.

Importantly, all the babies in this study came from French-speaking homes, so it's almost impossible that their responses could have arisen from prior exposure to Japanese. This result shows newborns' ability to not only spot differences in contour but to do so in unfamiliar speech, hinting at a flexible sound learning system that could potentially form an important basis for language development.

I mentioned earlier how the womb structure fosters the transmission of the musical aspects of speech as a result of the loss of higher frequencies (the speech detail). These musical aspects of speech include the pattern of contour stresses that we naturally use when we speak our native language. The study above shows that newborns can detect these contour changes in unfamiliar speech. Babies can also go one step beyond and use the familiar aspects of musical speech contour in their own vocalisations. It might even be the case that newborns cry in their native language.[13]

Birgit Mampe and colleagues analysed the crying patterns of 30 French and 30 German newborns. They studied the ups and downs of their natural cries and it turns out that French babies produce more rising pitches, whereas German babies cry more with falling contours. The same patterns were revealed in intensity: volume went from low to high in French babies while the reverse was found in German babies. This difference between a rising and a falling sound mirrors the speech contours used by native adult speakers of French and German, respectively.

The study by Birgit Mampe suggests that babies can not only perceive and remember the musical patterns of the speech they hear *in utero* but that they also mimic these familiar patterns when making their first cries. This is probably the earliest evidence of the impact of our native language on our vocalisations – and it's the musical features of communication that are the first to develop.

All of these studies support the idea that infants are born with a high level of sensitivity to the musical aspects of their sonic world; the beats and the contours that they have heard so far in their young lives. In the next section we will see how this sensitivity is fed and developed by the uniquely musical world that our young inhabit.

## Baby talk – music to their ears

When my best friend from school had her first baby I couldn't wait to see pictures. She lives hundreds of miles from me now and I didn't have time to make the long trip to see her, so I waited anxiously for an image of her bundle of joy. When I finally saw the photos I was overwhelmed with joy; Isobel was completely adorable, with her mum's eyes too.

Then I started talking to the photo. 'Aren't you the most gorgeous little thing? Oh my goodness, look at you with your little hands and tiny fingers all tucked up! You are such a sweet little angel, just like your mummy, yes you are, yes you are …' Thankfully, no one was in the room with me at the time. Not only was I talking to a photo; even stranger was the voice I was using to address the image.

My voice would start really low, then shoot up high through the words and rapidly back down again. I was speaking much faster than normal, apart from long, high-energy pauses on the start and end of phrases ('yes' and 'are'). At some points I was almost squeaking the words.

I'm sure you recognise the phenomenon I'm describing – we have all either done this or heard it done. This kind of vocalisation is known colloquially as 'motherese' or more formally as infant directed speech (IDS), and it differs significantly from adult directed speech (ADS).

IDS has been reported in every known language tested to date.[14] IDS has basic sound features that make it unique: a higher fundamental frequency (basic pitch level), more intense and exaggerated contours and slides, and more repetitive and rhythmical elements. It's also frequently accompanied by rhythmic body movements to the beat of the speech sounds, like nodding or shaking the head, clapping or bouncing. If you spoke this way to an adult then they would likely view you with suspicion. So why do we speak this way to babies?

Here we encounter a chicken and egg problem. Who started doing IDS first, and why? There are two possibilities: either adults started to mimic the natural sounds that babies can make and found this to be beneficial, or babies were naturally drawn to more musical vocalisations that adults can make.

Like all evolutionary arguments, we will probably never solve this riddle to everyone's satisfaction: all evidence for the origins of IDS is lost to the mists of time. However, finding an answer to this conundrum is not as crucial as the recognition that IDS suits both adults and babies for different reasons, and that this is probably why it still exists in all known forms of human culture.

Babies prefer to listen to IDS compared to ADS almost as soon as they are born (a strong preference emerges within one month),[15] irrespective of whether it's spoken by a man or woman.[16] This preference for IDS has even been found in infants born to deaf parents.[17] IDS provides a reliable way for adults all over the world to trigger a positive reciprocal response from their young. It's a method by which we can attract their attention and potentially modify their behaviour, at a developmental stage when verbally reasoning with a baby is tempting but largely pointless.

Another main advantage of IDS for adults is that we get a smile. When we speak to a baby in musical tones, we often get positive feedback that is, frankly, adorable. Their eyes widen, they wave their arms, blow bubbles, giggle and bounce their cute chubby little legs.

This happy response has the benefit that the baby is not crying. Scientific evidence shows that parents experience a release of stress hormones in the brain on hearing a baby crying, resulting in an increased heartbeat, raised blood pressure and a cold sweat.[18] It's extremely beneficial therefore to have a technique that can minimise these negative effects on our own physical state.

As much as a baby's cry can be emotionally and physically distressing, once upon a time it was downright dangerous. A screaming baby would have been no good to our ancestors if they were trying to hide from predators or allow their community to get valuable rest in order to restore energy levels. As such, it's an extremely useful survival skill to be able to create a state of calm in a baby by low-energy methods that require only our own voices.

In modern times this calming technique remains useful in situations where the baby's natural response is not necessarily productive or desirable, such as when they must have a vaccination or try a new food. The use of IDS can distract a baby from responses that might be automatic and based on sound evolutionary survival principles, such as spitting out an unfamiliar taste, but which may not actually be beneficial for the baby – or the care-giver in the clean white shirt.

## IDS for learning

I said before that the benefits of IDS were a two-way street, and that means there is something in this for babies too. In fact, when we look closely at the benefits we see that babies probably get directly useful input from musical IDS, and it may be that IDS has developed as a crucial learning tool for the preverbal stages of human life.

The first obvious benefit of IDS is that babies can respond to adults using these sounds. They can't talk back to us yet but they can soon produce coos, pitch glides, and rhythmic responses. When we interact with babies they mimic our IDS, and in so doing the baby guarantees a safe and nurturing environment that is low-threat.

Research even suggests that a baby's engaging behaviour in response to IDS can make them more attractive to adults who are not their parents.[19] A human baby can't hope to survive without the help and support of adults therefore it's in their interests to attract and maintain our attention, and to stimulate positive responses. When you are largely immobile, your voice is one of your best tools.

In learning how to mimic, babies also build one of their first communicative skills that will become valuable both in their behaviour and speech: the concept of turn-taking. You speak, and then I speak in response to your message. This way we form an understanding, we develop ideas and we effectively transmit information.

One of the oldest functions of musical IDS was probably to communicate emotional state. IDS exaggerates the features of our own emotional speech, such as high-pitched, fast sounds when we are happy and low-pitched, slow sounds when we are sad. Not only do caregivers use these features of IDS to communicate emotional information to babies, they also use them to modify a baby's emotional state.[20]

In 2002, Laurel Trainor and Renée Desjardins defined another linguistic benefit of IDS. They were interested in the way that IDS exaggerates 'formant frequencies' – the frequencies that emerge as a consequence of the way we use our vocal tract to produce different vowel sounds.[21] They hypothesised that these special pitch contours in IDS may serve as a clue to the location of vowels in speech and may therefore help babies to learn and discriminate these crucial language sounds.

One of the great pieces of anecdotal evidence that the researchers cited in support of this idea was a study showing that 'pet directed speech' contains many of the features of IDS (such as high pitch) but not the IDS focus on vowel differences.[22] After all, there's little point in trying to teach your favourite pooch to speak.

Trainor and Desjardins tested 96 babies between the ages of six and seven months and looked at their ability to discriminate between two English vowels, /i/ as in *heed* and /I/ as in *hid*.[23] The crucial comparison for our interests was between the steady state and pitch contour versions of these sounds, which are equivalent to the sounds made by ADS and IDS respectively.

The method they used to measure the babies' responses was the 'conditioned head turn procedure'. This method is based on the premise that once a baby is used to a sound it will then only turn its head if it hears a different sound. Therefore, if the baby turns its head then this is an indication that it is able to discriminate two sounds. In the IDS study, everyone but the baby wore headphones, so there could be no question of adult influence on the baby's response.

The researchers found that the babies were much better at recognising a change to a vowel when they heard IDS as compared to ADS. They concluded that IDS contains musical features that can help babies to learn about different vowel types long before they are able to make use of this information. Our musical speech may therefore help our young to build the foundations of their language learning.

## Musical meaning

You might think that learning about vowels is sophisticated enough for a six-month-old but musical IDS may serve an even higher function in language learning: the ability to communicate the meaning of a message.

As an adult we are blessed with syntax, semantics and prosody (pitch movements, points of focus and rhythm) with which to convey meaning. When trying to communicate with preverbal infants, we are limited to prosody cues so we tend to exaggerate them; hence musical IDS. This allows us to quickly get across basic intention messages such as a prohibitive gesture ('No, don't touch'), approval ('Aren't you a clever baby!'), direction ('Lie down, it's sleepy time now') and comfort ('It's okay, it's okay, daddy's here').

There is an interesting developmental trajectory to babies' liking for IDS, which mirrors their mental and physical development over the first year of life. Christine Kitamura and Christa Lam studied three-, six- and nine-month-old infants and looked at their preferences for IDS that communicated different intentions; whether a mother was attempting to communicate comfort, approval or directive intent.[24]

They found that babies go through stages of preferring comfort messages when they are youngest, to then responding more to approval, and finally, around nine months, being more attracted to directive communications. The conclusion was that as a baby learns more about language they are more drawn to IDS that has phonetic and instructive content as opposed to simple, repeating sounds.

It's one thing to show that babies can respond to the meaning and intentions of musical IDS; it's quite another thing to show that these intentions are actually understood.

Elena Sakkalou and Merideth Gattis studied the effect of prosody on young infants' (average age sixteen months) ability to distinguish whether an adult action was intentional or accidental.[25] In their experiment, an adult performed two versions of an action, such as dropping a toy, one with intention ('There') and one with accidental speech ('Whoops'). The actor kept a neutral face and posture so the sound of the utterance was the only clue to their intention. It turns out the infants were significantly more likely to respond and copy the intentional action compared to the accidental one, indicating that they had understood the core meaning of the musical IDS.

Taking everything into account, it appears that IDS has

multiple uses, which is no doubt the main reason why it exists all over the world. Although studies of language acquisition in babies are appealing, it's probably stretching things to claim that IDS is a vital language-learning tool. One argument against this idea is that children will pick up language almost irrespective of how much adults speak to them[26] (except in rare cases of extreme neglect). In my opinion, however, the research presented here supports the idea that the musical features of IDS have an important role to play in our preverbal development.

Verbal development is not the only potential benefit of IDS. In our evolutionary past IDS likely provided a valuable way to stimulate pair-bonding, facilitate behavioural learning and modulate stress responses. IDS also provides adults with an invaluable way to interact with babies in the period before they can speak – when they are at their most physically vulnerable and when it's most crucial for us to communicate basic intentions and feelings.

In this chapter I wanted to tackle a few urban myths about the idea that only a few of us are really born musical. We have seen that just about every baby is born with the building blocks of musical skills, thanks to the early development of our hearing system and our ability to detect a good proportion of the sound from the outer and inner world. No evidence that I have ever seen has convinced me flooding this early environment with extra music is beneficial.

Babies learn and remember musical patterns that they hear as part of everyday *in utero* life whether we, as adults, consider those sounds to be music or not. These everyday tunes of life trigger happy and relaxed responses after birth, especially the music that newborns have heard most often: their mother's voice and heartbeat.

Babies' memories of womb music influence their new-born perception of patterns in sound, drive their interest in melodic patterns, and influence their first attempts at vocalisations. No doubt the musical nature of our newborns is one of the reasons why we developed a musical way to communicate with them in the form of IDS. We don't yet fully understand why we instinctively speak to our young in this musical way but there's no doubt that IDS benefits both adults and babies by stimulating early interactions, promoting care-giving, and providing a few early lessons in the nature of complex cognitions like emotion and language.

In the next chapter we move on from babies to consider the musical world of our children. We break a few more urban myths, such as the idea that listening to music (and in particular our friend Mozart) can help make children smarter. We also look at some of the potential developmental benefits of engaging in musical activities and show how the building blocks of musical understanding that we have seen in babies continue to take shape in our children through simple every-day musical exposure.

## Chapter 2
# Music in childhood

*'Kids: they dance before they learn there is
anything that isn't music'*
WILLIAM STAFFORD

Time flies. One minute your little bundle of joy is producing their first babbles, cautiously lifting their head from their blanket and perfecting their gummy smile. Then before you can blink they are mobile and everything must be swiftly babyproofed. You must keep a sharp eye out for their passionate desire to put anything and everything into their mouth. Curious coos become first babbled words and that firm, unyielding grasp reflex evolves into delicate, intentional movements. Booties become shoes and we all emerge triumphant from the potty training trials. The baby is becoming a child.

In this chapter we will look at some of the burning questions that parents encounter when considering the role that music might play in their child's life. Behind most of these queries is a single, simple, need-to-know: will music improve my child's life?

One frequently asked version of this question is whether music makes a child smarter. I will start by facing up to that thorny issue. Another related question: what skills will music lessons give my child, other than the ability to sing or play their chosen instrument? Music performance is a valuable ability, but we are talking about investment here. Very few children go on to make their living via music performance or composition and for the investment it takes to become a professional musician many a parent would hope that you get some side bonuses. We will look at the evidence for such 'transfer' benefits.

Then we will dive into music education research to tackle the question of what makes for a successful musical education. What instrument is right for my child? What makes one child press on with their lessons while another loses interest?

Finally, we will consider the impact of music on childhood outside the world of formal training. A child's world is even more musical than that of your average adult: young children still hear musical IDS, many attend music groups that may or may not teach instruments, and general education often features music as well. Songs are used to teach social etiquette and community values, as well as maths, languages and physical education. On top of this, children's television is crammed full of music that children seem to love but which often drives adults crazy. How is all this exposure to music impacting on the way our children develop?

## Mozart for a smarter child?

In childhood we can begin to assess the question posed in Chapter 1 regarding the effects of music on intelligence. In babies this is almost impossible to measure; IQ tests for babies make little sense given their limited ability to respond. However, once a child begins to reliably communicate their intentions and understanding of the world then we can begin to assess their cognitive strengths.

The question of a link between music and intellect is also important in a practical sense as a child starts to show an active interest in engaging with music: dancing, singing, and playing instruments. At this point parents are likely to think about whether to involve their child in music groups or music lessons, or to invest in a music player for their room. Perhaps a few Mozart CDs? Hang on ... hold that thought. Let's take a look at the evidence.

A friend recently told me that he has taken to playing Mozart CDs to his young daughter while she is falling asleep in the hope of invoking the 'Mozart effect'.[1] He hopes that listening to Mozart's music will trigger a boost in his child's intelligence, an idea that has now firmly made its way into pop psychology legend.

In fact, the Mozart effect is often one of the first things people ask me about when I tell them that I'm a music psychologist. It has its own Wikipedia page and a substantial industry has grown up around the idea that playing a certain kind of music has benefits for IQ. A well-balanced glance through the literature, however, reveals that all is not what it seems.

It all started innocently enough in 1993, with a one-page paper in the journal *Nature* by Frances Rauscher and colleagues.[2] They conducted an experiment where US college students were played either ten minutes of Mozart's Sonata for two Pianos in D major (KV448), or listened to relaxation instructions or sat in silence. The researchers then asked the students to complete a test of spatial-temporal reasoning. This type of task (paper-folding, matrices, or pattern analysis) requires you to think in your mind's eye about shapes and how they might fit together. The researchers found a significantly higher score on the test only after listening to the Mozart piece, which translated to a boost of between eight and nine IQ points.

The researchers went on to replicate their findings but found no similar boost effects after ten minutes of music by Philip Glass, British trance music, relaxation instructions or an audio book.[3] The Mozart effect seemed like a very exciting and important finding that might suggest a particular type of music has a positive effect on our ability to think.

How might this effect work? Rauscher and her colleagues

speculated that hearing Mozart's music might strengthen neural firing in an area of the brain that also supports performance on spatial-temporal tasks.

It all seemed too good to be true: a simple solution (listen to music) to a complex problem (boost mental power). Sure enough, all was not what it appeared.

The first issue is the temporary nature of the effect. To be fair, the original authors stated that the effect only lasts approximately ten minutes so we were never talking about any permanent boost to thinking. The problem is that in wider pop science culture you often lose an important bit of information like this from the original research, which in fact points to a key limitation with the effect.

A second issue with the effect is its specificity. In a subsequent article the original authors suggested that a researcher needed to use exactly their experimental conditions in order to have a hope of getting an effect.[4] This limitation suggests that the effect is not a very general one.

On top of all this, more recent studies have shown that you can get a similar boost effect if you play Schubert's piano music, when people prefer Schubert to Mozart.[5] You can also get the boost effect when you read people a bit of Stephen King, if they enjoy his writing.[6] Following such results, researchers have proposed that the Mozart effect actually relies on a temporary improvement to our mood and arousal states (how awake we feel),[7] which then has a positive effect on our task performance. And you don't necessarily need Mozart to boost your mood.

The final big issue with the Mozart effect is the failure to replicate. The numbers of studies I know about that have failed to replicate this effect now outweigh those that have worked.[8] I even have personal experience of trying to replicate the original paradigm. I followed the recipe of the original study to the letter with high hopes. It didn't work.

Taking all the evidence from the Mozart effect into account over the years, it is now largely accepted that simple passive (listening) exposure to music does not boost IQ, cognitive function, or reasoning ability in the long term,[9] and that any temporary small boosts to task performance are due to a concurrent increase in mood and arousal.[10]

So by all means, buy a child a Mozart CD if they like listening to his music, enjoy twirling and swaying to the sounds, find it relaxing as part of a sleep routine, or perhaps soothing in times of illness. The lesson from the research in this area is that we must not expect a child's IQ to grow in response to hearing music as if we were feeding fertiliser to a rose.

The Mozart effect story may not meet all the hype and false promise that has surrounded it over the years but it does have a positive ending. Thanks to the exposure of this science story in the media there has been a renewed interest in engaging children with music across the world and several industries have developed that use musical games and activities as part of playgroups and educational settings. As we'll see later, these alternative forms of active musical engagement (rather than just passive listening), while not as influential as music lessons, can have positive effects on child development.

## Music lessons for a smarter child?

Passive listening to music may only ever have temporary effects on our mental processing power but active musical involvement can have long-term effects. To paraphrase Nina Kraus, of whom we will hear more in a moment: you won't get fit watching sports on TV – you will get fit if you work out.

Let me be blunt to begin with. If performing music made more intelligent human beings then all professional musicians should have consistently higher IQs than similarly educated non-musicians. Put simply, they don't. Musicians do better on certain tests of cognitive function (more on this in Chapter 4) but not on general IQ tests. In one study musicians even performed worse.[11]

When is anything in life ever that simple? If playing music automatically made us smarter, then scientists would have shouted it from the rooftops long ago. So let's put that idea aside and get more specific. Maybe an effect of music on IQ is harder to find in adults because so many other things come into play – a lifetime of education and experience in other domains. How about children who take music lessons: do they have higher IQs?

A comprehensive series of studies on the link between music lessons and IQ in children has been conducted by Glenn Schellenberg. In 2004 Schellenberg randomly assigned 144 six-year-old children from Toronto to one of four groups: keyboard or singing lessons, drama lessons, or a control group who had no extra lessons.[12] In order to be fair, the control group were offered the same lessons as the other children after the trial period was over.

Lessons ran for 36 weeks at a dedicated school in group sizes of around six pupils. All the children completed IQ tests in the summer break before they began their lessons and at the end of the study. Matched measures of age and socioeconomic status were taken.

After one year the vast majority of the children got better at the IQ test, which makes sense as they were a year older. However, the two music groups showed larger IQ improvements compared to the drama or control group. The IQ increase was small – equivalent to three or four IQ points – but it was there, and this effect was replicated in a similar study two years later.[13] In both studies the achievements on the IQ tests were mirrored in classroom performance.

Does this small difference in childhood IQ really mean anything, given the lack of a similar IQ difference between adult musicians and non-musicians?

On the positive side, it may be that a childhood boost in IQ helps or reflects development in other areas of the brain that may aid later mental function. For example, adult musicians show improved verbal learning and memory compared to similarly educated people with no musical training (more on this in Chapter 4). It could be that these early childhood IQ differences are an early marker of later adult differences in cognitive ability.

On the negative side, we are talking about three to four IQ points here for a year of lessons. Is that really worth writing home about? It's interesting for psychologists but in a practical sense it doesn't seem fair to put a child through a year of lessons for such a gain, especially if they aren't enjoying themselves. And psychologists are not even convinced that music lessons actually *cause* IQ boosts. All that the above research establishes is that a relationship exists between music lessons and IQ, not that one leads to other. It does not rule out all possible other 'hidden' variables that might be driving the difference. And it may be that those children who are predisposed to higher IQ gains at younger ages are more likely to choose and/or respond well to music lessons.[14]

After all that, maybe it's not wise to treat IQ as the be all and end all of child development. There are other potential 'transfer' benefits from music lessons that, for my money, are more direct and more interesting. So let's focus on them now.

## Benefits of music lessons

Musical performance ability can be defined as a 'super skill' because it makes many varying demands on the mind and body. To achieve this ability requires long periods of concentrated attention and learning in areas such as auditory focus and direction, motor movement and coordination, pattern recognition and decoding (plus learning to read music in the first place), sensory integration, and emotional communication.

On top of that, a child must absorb the rules of musical styles, structures and cultural traditions of performance.

All told, learning how to play an instrument or perform with one's voice is an extremely complicated business and because of this there is a list of related skills that may receive a boost along the way.

What follows is not an exhaustive list of the possible transfer benefits of music lessons; these are too wide-ranging to discuss in depth and often lack clear evidence. Instead I focus on two areas where a positive impact of music lessons on a child's development has been reported and, importantly, replicated: hearing and listening, and language and reading.

### Hearing and listening

The first benefit of music lessons, most obviously, is that children's hearing skills tend to get better. This boost happens quickly and studies have reported effects of training on hearing within one year.[15] This improvement in hearing skills has direct benefits for tests of musical ability[16] but can also extend into more general listening tasks. Here we will turn to the work of Nina Kraus.

Kraus runs an auditory neuroscience lab at Northwestern University, USA. Over the last few years her research group has conducted many studies of hearing skills in children who take music lessons. Her team believes that music lessons can help shape the brain for hearing tasks in ways that extend beyond the immediate demands of their musical education. Kraus refers to this concept as 'music for a smarter ear',[17] a phrase that sums up her lab's findings rather nicely.

In particular, her group has found an advantage for musical children when it comes to hearing speech in noise. Hearing in noise (HIN) is an important ability in younger years as children often find themselves trying to understand and learn words in noisy environments like classrooms or playgrounds. HIN requires a child to focus on certain characteristics of a sound, such as its pitch, timbre and rhythmic patterns, in order to isolate, lock in on and track its development in a complex soundscape.

Dana Strait, Kraus and their colleagues[18] reported that a group of children (aged seven to thirteen) who were taking music lessons showed superior HIN ability compared to their non-musician classmates who were matched on IQ and basic hearing skills. Furthermore, the ability of the musical children on HIN tests was significantly related to hours of weekly practice; more music practice equals better HIN ability.

How might musical training help to boost hearing skills? According to Bharath Chandrasekaran and Kraus,[19] this effect is due to the plastic (i.e. malleable) nature of the brain. The auditory system has 'feedforward' neurons that transmit information about sound to the brain but it also has lots of 'feedback' neurons that carry information backwards from the brain to the ears. The higher centres of the brain use these feedback pathways to provide guidance for the auditory system on how to focus and track sounds. This process refines our everyday perception of sound – it tunes our ears. Again I will quote Kraus: 'What we do with what we hear changes the way our nervous system responds to sound.'[20]

Of course, there is always the question of whether musical training *causes* improvement to listening skills or whether these improved systems are in place to start with in children who choose to take music lessons; you will recall this issue of causality from our discussion on music and IQ. Kraus argues for an influence of musical training on listening ability rather than vice versa, based on the strong and consistent relationship between the number of years that a child has been training and their task performance.

A child's ability to process spoken language is undoubtedly connected to the types of listening skills I have been describing. And children who take music lessons show an above-average boost in related areas such as memory for sound, a skill that may contribute to the improvement of HIN.[21] But there are some skills that are not so directly related to basic sound processing that also appear to receive a boost related to music lessons – namely language processing and reading.

### Language and reading

Sylvain Moreno has looked into the effects of musical training on children's development for many years and has frequently found a boost in the way that they process language. In 2006 he and Mireille Besson conducted an experiment to determine whether short-term musical training (eight weeks) would help eight-year-old children to detect pitch changes in language.[22]

All the children were tested beforehand on their ability to detect pitch changes in simple spoken sentences. The researchers looked at their accuracy and response times, and their brain responses. To assess brain responses they used EEG as described in the previous chapter, a contraption resembling a swimming cap covered in wires, which registers the brain's electrical activity. In this case the researchers were interested to measure brain responses to pitch changes.

After all the initial language measures were collected, ten of the children started eight weeks of music lessons while ten began eight weeks of painting lessons. When all the children took the language test again, the researchers found no difference in their performance but they did see a difference in the brain activity of the children who had taken music lessons. Their brain responses were stronger when pitch changed compared to the children who had enjoyed the painting lessons. In this case it appears that only eight weeks of music lessons had modified the way that the brain responds to language sounds.

The authors followed up: what happens after more long-term training? How about six months? The idea was the same: divide the children into two matched groups, one that takes music lessons and one that takes painting lessons. In this case the sample was slightly larger, 32 children from two elementary schools in northern Portugal, all of whom had similar socioeconomic backgrounds.[23]

Before the training began the two groups showed no difference in a number of standard tests including memory and reading ability. They also showed no difference in pitch discrimination.

The musical classes included lessons about rhythm, melody, harmony and timbre.[24] In the painting lessons the children were taught to distinguish and create different colours, about form and space perception, linear perspectives and the nature of different materials and textures. At the end of the year the children in the music group gave a public performance and the children in the painting group had a show of their best creations.

This time, after a longer period of lessons, the researchers found a much bigger group difference. The children who took music training now had significantly better scores on sentence discrimination (as well as pitch discrimination) and were also faster at the tests compared to the children who had taken painting lessons. The researchers replicated their earlier result with the brain EEG: musical children showed a stronger and more robust brain response to pitch changes in language.

Together these studies imply that a relatively short period of time spent on music lessons can have a positive influence on the way that a child processes words and that this effect gets stronger as a child continues their lessons.

As yet we do not know whether these effects are sustained if a child stops their lessons or if there is a continued 'dose effect' whereby more lessons, or lessons on more instruments, produces a stronger result. What is clear is that music lessons appear to have a significant effect on the way that a child's brain responds to language and that after only a few months this development will have consequences for the way they react to sound in the real world.

Another interesting result in the six-month study was an improvement in reading ability within the music group but not the painting group. This result suggests that music lessons can improve the development of the word representations in the mind that are necessary for reading.[25]

These language learning findings may be partly linked back to the responses of the auditory brainstem – the way that musical training tunes the ears. Dana Strait, Jane Hornickel and Nina Kraus[26] reported relationships between brain responses, musical aptitude and reading ability in 42 children. The poorer readers in their study showed less robust brainstem responses to various aspects of speech sounds.

Overall, the story of transfer effects from music lessons is still one where the most convincing positive evidence relates to skills that are trained as part and parcel of the music lessons. We have looked at hearing and the musical aspects of language processing, up to more complex cognitive skills such as reading. There are a number of possible transfer effects that I have not mentioned here where the evidence is more variable, including visual, motor and spatial skills as well as concentration, emotional senstitivity, creativity and self-confidence. An excellent review on this vast area of literature has been written by Susan Hallam.[27]

The take-away message when it comes to transfer effects is not to get carried away in assuming that musical lessons will boost the brain and behaviour in every sense. Having said this, there is now little doubt that musical training, being a 'super skill', brings rewards and benefits beyond those directly related to musical performance.

## Effective musical education

We've established that music lessons can bring benefits during development so let's look at the nature of music lessons themselves. I am not a professional musician but I taught music for thirteen years. I was lucky enough to teach a number of wonderful children who were keen to play the classical guitar, and who typically started lessons between the ages of five and ten. I taught boys and girls, individually and in groups, in schools and at home.

Over the years I saw some children struggle, some flourish, some fade in interest, and one – my star pupil Patrick – overtake me. One of the best days of my life was when I had to tell his father that I simply could not take his money for lessons any more, as Paddy could do everything that I could do ... and more!

There are countless individual differences and situational factors that play into whether a child responds well to their music lessons or loses interest. But there are also several aspects to music education that can predict whether lessons are likely to be effective and over which parents/carers and teachers have a degree of control: here I will tell you about choice of instrument, teacher selection, degree of reward and motivation, and practice strategies.

I am not presenting myself as a music education guru here and it's not my aim to compare or rate different musical education techniques. What I'd like to give you is the evidence regarding some of the general factors that contribute to a successful musical education that can be adopted and used by anyone.

### Choosing an instrument

Let's start at the beginning. What instrument would I recommend for a child? I have been asked this question many times, mostly by friends when their child reaches about five years old. Studies have shown that instrument choice, and more specifically who makes that choice, can influence the success of musical education. When it comes to instrument selection a child should have a strong say, if not the complete say, in what they want to learn.[28]

Ask yourself, what sounds does your child enjoy hearing? What type of music gets them up and dancing? What shape/ colour/feel of instrument do they get excited about? These may seem like trivial concerns but giving a child the choice over their musical instrument (or voice) has a big impact on their drive to get involved in their lessons, which in itself will have positive consequences for later development in motivation.

There is a proviso when it comes to instrument choice: a parent should try to match the demands of the instrument to the child's development so as not to put them off by giving them too great a physical challenge at the start. This could seriously damage their motivation before it has even got going. There are many options, so for example you could try a recorder for a child who is interested in the flute but who struggles with breathing difficulties. Playing the recorder will teach them the basic fingering they need for the flute and help them work on their breathing.

Another consideration with instrument choice is size. You might go for a keyboard or a smaller brass instrument for a child who has their heart set on a grand piano or a tuba but needs time to grow a little first. When my pupil Patrick started learning guitar at the tender age of five he played the sweetest little quarter-size guitar. At the beginning of our time together he often tried to get hold of my full-size guitar but soon realised that he could make much better noises on his own as he could reach all the strings.

A music teacher will be able to give advice on the ideal starter instrument for a child and you never know, they may end up loving it and never moving on! I still have a soft spot for the recorder and have three in the spare room that I enjoy playing now and again. Another plus point of this strategy to bear in mind is that diversity of instrument experience is associated with later musical excellence.

### Choosing a teacher

So, you've chosen the instrument – now what about the teacher? A child's first teacher can exert a powerful influence on future musical development but this depends much more on the match between personality and temperament in the child and teacher, in the dynamics of their relationship, than in the teacher's level of technical ability or performance credentials.[29]

I was only fifteen when I began teaching; neither technically advanced nor concert-experienced. I now know however, that those things are not so important when a child is just beginning their lessons and needs to learn the basics of making sounds, reading music and/or ear-training skills. You can afford to save the expert teachers for later when specialist skills are more important in a musical role model; this is about getting started and gaining motivation momentum.

When asked about their first teacher, young expert conservatoire musicians reported that they remembered them as warm, friendly, and encouraging; in some cases the teacher was even seen as a member of the family.[30] Able young performers often change teachers within two or three years and some have lots of different music teachers: their band, orchestra or choir leader, their school/theory music teacher, and eventually their instrument/voice specialist.

Successful musicians tend to report having had more teachers than those who do not achieve such a high standard.[31] That first relationship is all-important, however, so a keen-eyed parent should observe a few lessons to check out the dynamics of the relationship and ask the child how they feel about the teacher.

Are there any differences between boys and girls? Jane Davidson and colleagues carried out an interview study of 257 children to determine how they saw their teachers and how this related to their later level of musical achievement.[32] The researchers found no gender differences in the ratings of first teachers – encouragement and friendly, relaxed support were important for all.

### Maintaining motivation

It goes without saying that lessons must be seen as enjoyable by a child in order to maintain their interest in this extra form of education, but what might be less obvious is the level on which it should be a rewarding experience. There is an important shift that must happen within musical and indeed any form of education – that from external to internal (or intrinsic) motivation.[33]

External motivators tend to come first and they can be anything from a token-based reward system (for example, ten minutes on a favourite computer game at the end of each lesson) to a performance achievement (for example, an exam certificate or applause in the school assembly) or simply the smile and attention of a parent. These are all crucial in the early stages of learning when the benefits of music lessons, other than making an enjoyable sound, may be somewhat lost on a young child.

Performers who continue on to high standards will then develop their own internal motivation to practise and perform. They carry out these activities because it makes them feel good, gives them a sense of achievement and drives them to reach higher goals. This process shift from external to internal motivation is not something that you can influence directly, but it won't happen at all without effective early external motivation. And internal motivation is something that you can look out for and praise when you start to recognise the signs.

### Practice

Effective music lessons are nothing without effective practice.[34] This was the one major stumbling block that I experienced during my teaching career and one that was common in children who ended up giving up on their lessons. No effective practice between lessons means little if any progress in general. In fact, as a teacher you often find yourself having to go backwards at the start of a lesson to get to the level that you reached at the end of the last session.

We have talked about music lessons in terms of making them enjoyable (helped by choice of instrument and teacher), stimulating reward, and the transition to self-motivated, internal reward systems. The same all goes for practice. There is an additional secret to practice strategy in music – it must be 'deliberate'.

'Deliberate practice' is a term that comes from the literature on the psychology of expertise.[35] In musical terms deliberate practice is defined as the ability to imagine, monitor and control performance, and the use of optimal strategies to aid progress. Rather than playing or singing at the same level for a long period of time because you are good at it, repeating pieces that you can perform well already, deliberate practice requires a constant self-evaluation, focusing on weaknesses.[36]

Instead of playing or singing pieces from start to end, a musician should aim to develop their own strategies for identifying and correcting mistakes. One of the key factors here is the development of self-regulation.[37] Musical practice that targets weaknesses and develops mental strategies of self-regulation is a better predictor of success than just the number of hours spent playing or singing.[38]

Another important factor in effective practice is getting a balance between formal and informal strategies. Simply repeating technical exercises over and over again is a less successful strategy than balancing this necessity with time for improvising and experimentation on the instrument or with the voice.[39] By a similar notion, routine is very important for lessons and practice structure but so is the occasional surprise task or reward that can refresh interest and encourage confidence to improve further.[40]

One of the unsung heroes in the development of effective practice, and an indispensible source of that all-important external motivation for early days, is, of course, the parent/carer. Many studies of young successful musicians have pointed out that support in the home is absolutely essential in terms of encouraging regular, deliberate and effective practice.[41] Motivation to please a parent/carer can predict early progress and even once the transition to internal motivation has kicked in, many conservatoire students still report a desire to inspire pride in their elders.[42]

For parents/carers there has to be a degree of tough love for those occasions in the early days when a child does not want to practise as well as do their homework, as long as the child is still enjoying their instrument and lessons in general. A regularly present and consistently supportive parent/carer may not be able to advise directly on the technical aspects of playing or practice strategy but their presence is eventually worth its weight in music education gold.

Getting the most from an effective musical education requires time and effort from all the key stakeholders (child, parent/carer and teacher), especially at the beginning. A child's enjoyment, motivation and sense of achievement with music may come from many different sources but in the early stages all these factors must be fed and encouraged by friendly and supportive adults. In time, as self-regulation, internal motivation and effective deliberate practice strategies develop, both parents and teachers will be able to take a step back and the child will emerge with all the right sustainable tools to push themselves through their education as far as they desire.

And if they are anything like my pupil Patrick, then they will surpass your hopes and never look back. Paddy was not one of the very few who go on to become a world-class professional musician but he is a skilled guitarist and a sensitive performer with a talent for composition. The CDs and MP3s I have of him playing his own music are among my most prized possessions.

## Music for general development

At the beginning of this chapter we looked at the evidence for the Mozart effect and concluded that passive exposure to music (listening alone) is unlikely to result in significant improvements to IQ or cognitive skills. I would like to end the chapter by making clear that I do not mean to say that music activities have no benefit for children. There are a number of areas in development where engagement with music that falls short of formal training can play a substantial positive role and promote learning about the world.

Engaging with music is not limited to learning how to play an instrument or sing. In recent years I have been lucky enough to be involved in a research project with a pre-school active music class provider in the UK. These types of sessions are becoming more common all over the world. The classes do not aim to teach children a specific instrument or voice skills, although they often involve singing. The musical activities and games that these classes involve are largely for pleasure without any aim of improving performance.

Classes such as these provide a fun atmosphere for socialising with other children, teach songs that can help simple behavioural routines (such as going to bed or brushing teeth), and communicate social skills, such as turn-taking, imitation and bonding. Because they often involve moving to music or playing drums, the classes also promote motor coordination, synchronisation and development.

Music is not an essential component for all these cognitive, social and motor developmental processes. There are many cultures in the world that do not use anywhere near as much music in the early stages of a child's life as we do in Western society and this fact does not seem to impair their children's development. Probably the most important role of music in these kinds of music activity classes is as a facilitator: music creates an environment where the rules of social interactions are framed in a simple and engaging way.

Music is not the only way to do this, of course, but it is often an enjoyable way. The reason it tends to be fun is that children react well to music. This harks back to what we discussed in Chapter 1 about their natural attraction towards musical sounds. And a happy, engaged child makes for a happy, engaged parent, a situation which is likely to promote learning and stimulate bonding for both.

Laurel Trainor and her colleagues conducted some of the first studies to systematically investigate the effects of active music participation classes. In their first study[43] they assigned six-month-old infants to either an active musical class or a similar class where the children just listened to music (the Baby Einstein™ CD series) and occasionally played along (the 'passive' group). The theory was that the active music classes featured a greater amount of social interaction and participation in music-making and that these two factors are beneficial for development.

All the classes were weekly and one hour long. The musical teachers from each group were blind to the nature of the experiment and classes took place both within lower- and middle-class socioeconomic areas. After six months of classes, the children were measured on sensitivity to musical structure and expression. The active class kids showed higher levels of sensitivity to pitch and rhythmic structure than the passive class kids, although no group differences were found in reactions to musical expressivity.

The researchers then looked at brain development using EEG (the swimming cap with the wires again). Before training, the infants from the two groups did not differ in their responses to piano tones, but after the six months of classes, the active group kids showed stronger and earlier responses to musical tones than the passive group kids.

Finally, the researchers looked at social development using the Infant Behaviour Questionnaire. Once again there were no differences before the classes started but after six months the active class showed less distress to novel stimuli, more smiling and laughter, and were easier to soothe than those who had taken part in the passive group.

Overall, it appears that the more active music classes helped to boost the development of many cognitive and behavioural characteristics that could reasonably be related to the nature of the lessons. It is interesting to see, however, that not all musical skills were improved in the active class (reactions to musical expressivity). Some types of musical learning in children seem to carry on regardless of the type of engagement they encounter.

This final important point from the music class study is one on which I would like to conclude this chapter. Musical engagement in childhood exists on a continuum: from passive listening to active engagement, informal playing and singing through to formal music lessons and training. All of this exposure to music influences the way that the brain and behaviours develop, just in different ways and by different degrees.

Musical listening is an important part of our childhood, not because it makes us smarter, better readers or faster socialisers but because we learn about music itself, a process known as musical enculturation.[44] When we are young children we do not understand what music is all about, any more than we understand our native language. We need to be exposed to these uniquely human sounds and their structures over a period of years in order to be able to comprehend and respond to them.

It's hard to imagine that listening to music is a complex skill but it is, in the same way as listening to your friend talk is a skill. We don't think of these things as difficult; mostly because we can't really remember what it was like not to be able to do them. A child, however, is learning about the nature of both of these complex sound systems (language and music) through every single exposure. In the case of musical enculturation they are learning about the rules of melody and rhythm construction, performance expression and style that are common to their musical world.

♪

The building blocks of musical understanding, constructed quietly and behind the scenes in a child's mind as they hear music, form the basis for their development of individual tastes, preferences and reactions to music that will become very much a part of who they are as a person. Some of that person's individual tastes in music might come as quite a surprise to their parents when the child hits the next stage of their development – the adolescent years.

So let's leave childhood for now and move on to the teens and early adulthood, and talk about how the music of this unique period shapes our musical future as well as influencing our personal and social development.

# Chapter 3
# Music for adolescent years

*'There is nothing stable in the world;*
*uproar's your only music'*
JOHN KEATS

Like many people I have rather sketchy memory of what it really felt like to transition from a child to an adolescent. I don't recall the day I certainly left my childhood behind but I remember the hallmarks of my adolescent life: my first crush on TV and in life (David Duchovny and a boy called Keith), my first heartbreak, my first and only real argument with my loving father, my brilliant first car (a sixteen-year-old silver Nissan Micra that I named Ruprect[1]) and my first long, lost summer.

More importantly I remember the soundtrack to each of those experiences. Keith has a song, as does Ruprect, and the boy who broke my heart. I can't hear 'Kiss Me' by Sixpence None The Richer without being taken right back to that long fantastic summer that I spent running through the sweet-smelling yellow oilseed fields at the back of my village with one of my best friends, Owen. Ah, to be fifteen again …

By the time we reach our teens some of us have had musical training and some not, but just about everyone is still learning about the world through music. Our childhood spent overhearing musical sounds has been well spent as we can now easily listen to multilayered complex rhythmic and pitch structures with minimal effort such that the lyrics, chords and instrumentation wash over us, stirring up the teenage whirl-wind of emotions, anxiety, confusion and excitement – not to mention hormones.

Music, by association and absorption, is becoming part of us. In this chapter we will see that the music of our teenage years and early adult life comes to frame a great deal of our musical future and identity in later adulthood.

In this period of life we first start to regularly use music as a tonic, a kind of self-mediation. We learn about the music that makes us feel good and the music that makes us feel ter-rible, and we begin to experiment with emotions through music.[2] Music also mirrors and perhaps even helps to shape the development of our personal and social identity. Through these and other processes that we will discuss in this chapter, the music of this unique life period becomes heavy with nos-talgia and, as a consequence, is thought by many people to be the very best music of their life.

## Music for moods and emotions

Before we dive into the murky world of adolescence let's talk briefly about how music is connected to our moods and emotions, as this is an important factor when thinking about adolescence.

It will come as no surprise that mood and emotion regu-lation is consistently identified as one of the main reasons that we listen to music: survey after survey and test after test, music psychologists report on the influence that music can have on our feelings of happiness, sadness, excitement, peace, and so on. One study reported that an average 64 per cent of everyday music listening in a two-week period was associated with emotions.[3] In my life it is more.

Some of the most highly cited scholars in this area (there are many, so apologies that I can't include everyone) include Tia DeNora,[4] Alf Gabrielsson,[5] David Hargreaves and Adrian

North[6] who have all collected large amounts of data exploring the effect of music on mood and emotion as we go about our everyday lives as well as in our peak moments.

The ultimate encyclopaedia of research into music and emotion was compiled in 2010 by Patrik Juslin and John Sloboda: the *Handbook of Music and Emotion: Theory, Research, Applications*. This is a huge book by any standards; I do not use the word encyclopaedia lightly. I often place this compendium on my desk if I feel an immediate need to look scholarly. It is a super read even though it is very dense, and much of this chapter draws inspiration from its pages.

The existence of many large, well-known studies tells us that there have been decades of research in this area carried out by some of the best in the business. This gives us a rich base with which to explore the effects of music on one of the most moody and emotional times of our lives: our teenage years through to early adulthood.

At this point I should say a brief word about the difference between 'mood' and 'emotion'. Many of the same words can be used to describe both an emotion and a mood, like 'happy', 'sad', and 'angry'. The generally accepted difference is that an emotion has a clear trigger, something tangible or a thought that induces a change in our state. Emotions also tend to be short lived. So a nice piece of dark chocolate at the end of a long day can trigger happy emotions for me that may soon dissipate after the treat is gone. A mood, by contrast, does not need to have a trigger; we can all wake up in a happy mood with a bounce in our step for no particular reason. Plus a mood can last.

What is emotion and why does it happen? According to the James–Lange theory, proposed way back in the 1890s, emotions are a result of the way we interpret our bodily reactions. For example, if we are surprised by a lion (hopefully not too common an occurrence for you) our physiology changes as a result of chemicals triggered by our brain and released in our glands, and the subsequent reaction of our autonomic nervous system. Our pulse races, we begin to sweat and our breathing becomes shallow. This is all part of a well-tuned evolutionary response to danger as our body prepares optimal conditions for 'fight or flight'. William James and Carl Lange proposed that emotions like fear were a result of our head trying to make sense of what was happening to our body.

The James–Lange theory is convincing on first read and there is certainly a component of bodily reactions in our moods and emotions. It is hard to imagine being really frightened without the racing heart and cold sweat – such sensations are why people go on rollercoasters and watch really scary films. However, the James–Lange theory turns out to be too simplistic in reality to explain all emotional reactions. Not all our emotions have a bodily response and many of them overlap (our hearts race for many reasons) but we don't regularly confuse our emotions. On top of this, emotions can be experienced before the onset of a full bodily reaction.

Despite these issues, aspects of the James–Lange theory are important because they help us understand why our teenage years are hyper-emotional, as our body undergoes a vast number of uncontrollable hormonal changes in a short period of time. This fact, combined with the first exposure to so many emotionally charged situations (first love, leaving home, financial freedom) means things are bound to get rocky and that emotions will be all over the place at times. No wonder it is at this stage of life that we start to explore different ways to modulate, control and enhance our emotions and moods. For many people, this is the time when music really comes alive.

There are many theories as to how music influences our emotions[7] and regulates our moods: in fact, current understanding is that there are at least six different psychological mechanisms* that are responsible for triggering emotion-like states in music.[8] I don't intend to go into too much depth about these debates and mechanisms (the music and emotion encyclopaedia does that far better than I ever could) but it is useful for us to summarise some of the main theoretical players here:

### Musical mirror

Plato was perhaps the first to note that aspects of music mimic the sounds that we make in different emotional states. When we are happy we talk faster, in a higher pitch and with bigger leaps in sound, whereas when we are feeling sad we talk slower, in a lower register and with not much vocal movement. If you map out the characteristics of happy and sad music they look very similar. Patrik Juslin and Petri Laukka[9] conducted a thorough examination of a range of different emotions and found many similarities between the sounds we make normally with our voices and the sounds we hear in emotionally matched music.

### Expectation

In the 1950s the composer and author Leonard B. Meyer gave a series of lectures where he outlined his theory as to why music is emotional. He said that we have expectations as we listen to music – we expect the next note to go down or up or for a phrase to end in certain ways. Our expectations are based on the enculturation of music that we talked about at the end of the last chapter, which happens through normal exposure to musical sound.

According to Meyer, composers are aware of these expectation effects (they sense them as well) and they both satisfy

---

* Brainstem reflexes, conditioning, emotional contagion, expectancy, memory and visual imagery.

and thwart them in order to trigger different emotions. This theory was later expanded by Ray Jackendoff and Fred Lerdahl as part of their seminal work, *A Generative Theory of Tonal Music*,[10] and was most recently explored in the award-winning book *Sweet Anticipation* by David Huron.

### Deep brain stimulation

We must not leave the brain out of this discussion. Many of the complex appraisal reactions from recognition of emotion in music and calculations of musical expectations rely on the higher centres of the brain such as the frontal cortex. However, evidence from Valarie Salimpoor and Robert Zatorre suggests that peak emotional music, music that we associate with 'chills' down the spine, can also trigger responses in the much older and subconscious areas of our brain which are closer to the emotion centre, or amygdala, and reward systems.[11] These brain responses appear to be much earlier than those which we could associate with a conscious evaluation, suggesting that some music can touch us very deeply although we do not yet fully understand why.

### 'Darling, they're playing our tune'

I love that this term in used in the scientific literature, firstly by John Booth Davies back in 1978.[12] This phrase captures the sense that music can be emotional because we attach emotion to it as it makes connections within our life memories. This is also known as the effect of nostalgic familiarity.

These piggybacking music memory emotions can be both happy and sad, and very powerful. I can't listen to Ray Charles sing 'Take These Chains From My Heart' very often – it is my heartbreak song. If you just listen to the music then it should be a happy song as it has all the ingredients of a happy musical structure. But then there are the lyrics, the aching way it is sung by Ray Charles and, most importantly, the image in my head of my first love walking away from me, as fresh and raw as if it had happened yesterday.

I listened to this song many times in the days after he left, hence it became a strong part of that memory. Many years later, the visual memory of that day is not that upsetting; the music, however, opens the floodgates.

Emotional memory attachments are often formed most strongly during adolescence. Our emotions are all over the place and anything that can help settle them or even exaggerate them in an attempt to reach a cathartic resolution is bound to have an appeal. It is at this time that many of us come to appreciate that music is a comparatively safe option for emotion and mood expression and regulation compared to some of the other substances on offer. So we start to experiment and the result is a pair bonding between us and the music that touches us.

I should point out before I go any further that music is not necessarily used in this way by all adolescents. I certainly used it this way, without understanding how or why at the time, and I know many people who have had similar experiences. My partner on the other hand navigated his teenage tempests by getting lost in the world of Spanish classical literature and he maintains that music was, by comparison, not that important for his emotional development. While music is not a teenage tonic for everyone, it is enough of a universal agent to trigger a significant scientific literature of its own, so is worth our while trying to understand why it is so popular and effective.

## Adolescent experiments with music

It should come as no surprise that adolescents who listen to music do so for a significant proportion of their time and consider it to be a very important part of their life. A ten year old but substantial UK survey of music listening in this age group put the figure at between two and three hours every day[13]. My guess is that this figure is much higher nowadays thanks to a substantial increase in personal control orientated music technology in the last decade.[14]

Music listening is a popular method for emotion and mood regulation in adolescence[15] and younger people use music for this reason more than adults.[16] In these years we are still learning how to regulate physical and mental state; unfortunately we have to learn these skills quickly as developmental changes put sudden demands on us to grow up. Some studies put the age of fifteen as a turning point in the use of coping strategies, including music listening, to self-regulate[17] – that fits in nicely with my strong personal memories of the song 'Kiss Me' during my long, lost summer.

Suvi Saarikallio has devoted many years to studying music for adolescent state regulation. Her research confirms that regular listening for mood and emotion regulation is both deliberate and unconsciously motivated, and that some of it is really quite effective.

In 2007[18] Saarikallio carried out a large study aimed at categorising the psychological meaning of music for adolescents. She conducted a meta-analysis, essentially a study of lots of other studies. This type of analysis allows scientists to synthesise findings from different labs to determine the consistent results, thereby locating the strongest effects. Saarikallio noted four main functions of music: *identity*, *interpersonal relationships*, *emotion* and *agency*.

*Agency* describes gaining a sense of control, competence and self-esteem from music listening. *Emotion* describes how young people use music to both express and learn about emotional reactions, especially negative types, in what Saarikallio calls a 'safe and acceptable expression of difficult, violent, or disapproved thoughts and feelings'. We will discuss *identity* and *interpersonal relationships* in the next section.

Saarikallio used this research to develop a scale for measuring mood regulation with music. She tested 1,515 adolescents and found that girls use music in this way more than boys and that older adolescents use it more than younger ones; this latter result makes sense as we tend to use strategies more as we learn and get better at using them.

In addition, Saarikallio showed that greater life involvement with music predicts greater use of music for mood regulation but, perhaps surprisingly, this link was not limited to formal musical training; it included how important someone thought music was in their life and how much they heard music in their home. She also found that music listening for mood regulation tends to occur more in private than in public.

Adolescents who used music successfully for music regulation tended to have a wider variety of tastes – in Saarikallio's study they were better able to choose from a large selection of music that they liked for just about any mood. Having said this, the use of music in mood regulation was most strongly connected to a preference for rock and heavy metal music. Saarikallio suggested that the strong intensity, volume, and 'roughness' of these styles may reflect the emotional experience of youth and therefore enable better reflective coping.

### Music to aid coping

There are two ways in which music helps coping. The first is the behavioural response. That can be anything from dancing and singing to laughing or crying (as in my Ray Charles example). Music helps with mood regulation by stimulating physical behaviours that have a positive effect on a person's ability to regulate how they feel; to maintain a desired mood, make it more intense, or change it depending on the demands of the situation.

The second mechanism of music coping is cognitive, where music stimulates thoughts and memories that help us review experiences, link the meanings together in our minds, and learn for future occasions.

This two-part model (physical and cognitive mechanisms) gives us a framework to understand how music has its effect and how, in our adolescence, it becomes a 'tool' for us to use to stimulate body and/or mind in order to get us to where we want to be in terms of our physical or mental state.

Dave Miranda and Michel Claes[19] collected questionnaires from 418 French-Canadian adolescents to assess musical preferences, depression levels, and styles of coping by music listening (emotion oriented, problem oriented or avoidance/disengagement). They were also interested in the importance of lyrics and peer reactions.

They found that social peer groups agreed strongly on the types of music that they used for coping with emotions, supporting the idea that music is an important factor in social relationships in adolescence. They also showed that problem-oriented coping when listening to music was associated with lower depression levels in girls. This finding sits well with the idea proposed by Amiram Raviv and colleagues that female adolescents identify with song lyrics and artists for solace and advice about personal problems.[20]

By contrast, emotional coping with music was more associated with depressive symptoms in boys. This was not a strong relationship, however, nor did it represent severe depressive symptoms; this may reflect a type of maladaptive 'venting' of emotions through music that is more common in male adolescents.

An important caveat with this last finding is the influence of time. Adolescents who listen to music in order to relieve negative moods tend to feel worse initially but then after some time has elapsed they often feel better.[21] This was definitely my experience when I was trying to cure my heartbreak with Ray Charles. I felt rotten at the time but the catharsis was an important part of the healing process. And even though the song still makes me cry I tend to feel better quickly as the song reminds me that I got through that difficult time and everything worked out for the best.

The study of French-Canadian teenagers combined with Saarikallio's work shows us that adolescents who are surrounded by and enjoy music use listening to cope with the stresses that they experience as they encounter personal problems and emotional challenges for the first time. Some of the music coping strategies may be more helpful than others, especially at first, but this is all a learning experience and must be considered in terms of long-term outcomes. The adolescents in these studies are learning to use music to regulate their moods and emotions in a way that many of them will go on to dip into throughout their lives.

## Can some music be bad?

At this point I would like to make a comment or two about the idea that music (in particular songs from certain genres) can 'corrupt' a young person; the idea that music can do damage to emotional development that may lead to problem thoughts and/or behaviours.

Adrian North and David Hargreaves published an excellent review of this thorny issue[22] wherein they pointed out that this idea is nothing new; in 1951 a number of radio stations banned Dean Martin's 'Wham! Bam! Thank You, Ma'am' because of the apparent salacious nature of the lyrics. And a Florida judge famously threatened to arrest Elvis Presley in 1956 if he shook his body during his upcoming performance at a local theatre.

As strange as it may seem to us now, the Florida judge was quite justified in his desire not to offend the older audience and parents/carers, many of whom thought that Elvis's music had a bad effect on young people. One of the quotes about Elvis's music at the time was made by Frank Sinatra:

> It fosters almost totally negative and destructive reactions in young people ... It is sung, played and written for the most part by cretinous goons and by means of its almost imbecilic reiterations and sly, lewd – in plain fact dirty – lyrics, and as I said before, it manages to be the martial music of every sideburned delinquent on the face of the earth.[23]

The debate about whether or not adults should protect young people from music modified over the years but certainly did not disappear, as many might believe, in the swinging sixties. In 1985 the US senate held a debate on the morality of music, one outcome of which was the famous 'Parental Advisory' sticker. Among the first albums to feature the sticker were Soundgarden's *Louder Than Love* and Guns N' Roses' *Appetite for Destruction*. The sale of a CD with this sticker to a minor in parts of the US can still result in prosecution and albums with the label can be banned from sale in some countries.

Is there any science to support the notion that music, as well as aiding emotional and mood regulation, could in some cases be harmful to coping styles and/or behaviours?

Research has established relationships between many music genres such as rap, heavy metal – even classical and country music[24] – and problem adolescent coping (depression, anxiety and anger) and behaviours (violence and substance abuse).[25] As such it is not wise to brush aside the idea that some music might contribute to harm. If we want to make the argument that music can be powerful enough to do some good then we must accept that in some cases it may contribute to problems.

A pinch of salt is required, however, as the majority of studies in this area are correlational in nature.[26] This means that the researchers measure music listening and problem behaviour or coping separately, and then use statistics to look for a relationship between the two things. Now, you can get a nice significant relationship between hours of sunshine and ice cream eating behaviour, but that doesn't mean that eating ice cream makes the sun come out. What a correlation study can never establish is a direct *cause*.

The main problem with a correlation finding is that there could be any number of additional factors involved in the relationship between music and problem coping/behaviours. So, for example, one study found that adolescents who feel sadder after listening to heavy metal music have more depressive symptoms.[27] This result can be accounted for by maladaptive coping behaviours that could have developed entirely separately from the music. The important caveat is that music does not necessarily *cause* whatever coping style a person is using, though it can become part and parcel of the whole thing.

Another issue with studies that *have* found an effect of music on maladaptive coping, meaning they played music and measured how it made people feel, is that the majority employ music videos.[28] This is legitimate and interesting scientific investigation but I wonder why most studies in this area use videos and not just a CD or MP3 track. The evidence (or lack of it) in this area seems to suggest that maladaptive responses to music are weaker in the absence of visual images, though this is an idea that remains to be tested.

Finally with regards to maladaptive responses to music, we must accept a lack of knowledge at present on two important issues: long-term effects and placebo effects. One series of experiments that found short-term effects of listening to music with violent lyrics on ratings of aggression[29] concluded that comparable direct long-term effects were unlikely; such feelings could easily dissipate if exposure to violent lyrics was interrupted by non-violent music or a positive event. And one study found that teenagers' impressions of the same piece of music (either 'suicide-inducing' or 'life-affirming') were driven by what they were told about its meaning.[30] This last finding suggests that responses to music are sometimes less about the music itself and more about how it is marketed.

In conclusion, we must be careful not to label any one musical song, artist or genre as simply 'bad'; rather we need to look more carefully at how particular music, lyrics, and visual media influence young people, and at the effects of how the artists and their materials are presented to and interpreted by the adolescent listener.

We also need to look more at the link to long-term behaviours[31] and not so much at immediate reactions – many of us might fill in a questionnaire to say that we feel temporarily more aggressive after listening to heavy metal but that doesn't mean we intend to go out and indulge in violence. Future studies will hopefully narrow down any potential direct negative influence of music on behaviour, if any exists, and thereby enable us to offer more useful guidance than just a roughly drawn idea of what adults think is 'safe music'.

## My music, my self

Music becomes an important part of who we are and how we want other people to see us during our adolescence. Music can provide a group identity; my brother was a skater boy in his teens and this defined the music that he listened to as well as his 'look' (including exaggerated moptop) and aspects of his behaviour as he strived to be part of an in-group.

Remember the research by Miranda and Claes, who found that the French-Canadian teenagers all tended to agree about the music that their close friends liked? And remember Saarikallio's finding that listening to music in adolescence is linked to *identity* and *interpersonal relationships*? This is the section of this chapter where all that comes together as we explore how music becomes not only a tool in our box of coping mechanisms but a part of who we are as adolescents.

The concepts of self-identity and social (or group) identity are linked. It is often by asserting our self-identity that we clarify our social identity. And we gain important components of our self-identity, such as self-esteem, through other people's evaluations of our social identity. While they are entwined concepts, music contributes selectively to self- and social identity, so we will deal with them one at a time, starting with the self.

### Self-identity

Learning about ourselves (what is important to us, how we think, our morals and sense of justice) is one of the most difficult but important psychological transitions that we face in adolescence. Many individuals seek to understand themselves better through their reactions to the world: what they like or don't like; what seems right and what seems wrong; what moves them and what leaves them cold. The reflective nature of music explains why it is such a useful medium for learning about self-identity in this way. It is not strictly right or wrong in and of itself, but it can be evaluated in this way depending on each person.

A conductor once told me that a great piece of music is like a mirror and everyone sees themselves. We can add anything we like to music and it will still make sense. Music is therefore one of the greatest recipes for self-definition – just add meaning as required!

Some people, like my partner, find their personal inspiration and ideals in reflective literature. Some will find them through visual arts. It is fair to say that most of us find them through music.

I will use myself as an example. As a teenager and into my twenties I spent hours listening to the music of John Lennon. His music taught me a lot about how I felt with regards to human nature and the world. I didn't need anyone to tell me, 'You need to listen to this music and appreciate and learn from the sentiment.' In fact, my parents were not Beatles fans, though their taste did go to sixties music. My peers were mostly into modern music, to which I had little access. I found Lennon all by myself and I loved him right from the start.

He was different, and in my young eyes so was I. His journey, the things he sang about and the way he composed music all triggered reflective thoughts in my head that encouraged me to think about both the fun and the difficult things in life. I learned from his good and bad examples, and through his music I was able to interpret for myself where I had come from, how I wanted to be seen by others, and where I wanted to go with my life. Of course, this was partly to do with my interpretation of him as a person but I did not spend hours reading books about him or watching his films. I wanted to listen to his music.

Suvi Saarikallio's research suggests that I am not alone in my experience. She found that adolescents use music to promote self-exploration, to gain self-knowledge and to strengthen and reinforce their growing conception of themselves as people.

In their book *Musical Identities*,[32] Raymond MacDonald, David Hargreaves and Dorothy Miell discuss the many self-identities that can reflect and develop through music, including national identity and gender identity. There are also self-identities that develop through musical education, such as the performer's persona. Important concepts for young musicians include their self-assessed level of competency, natural ability (or perception of talent) and degree of independence in their musical development.[33]

All this evidence leads to the inevitable conclusion that music is a useful and powerful vehicle for the development of our idea of 'self'.[34] In the next section we will see how we go on to use that musical identity in our social environment, like a badge or cover, to quickly indicate to other people who we are and what we are all about. Music can be a much more effective communicator of this kind of information during adolescence than taste in clothing, films, books or other hobbies.[35]

### Group identity

Our private identity may be something we only ever reveal to a select few people in our lives; our social identity, on the other hand, is out there for all to see. Everyday life requires us to interact with others and we develop a persona that is, to a degree, a reflection of our self-identity but can also partly be purely for social purposes. Our adolescent years are most strongly identified with the development of our social selves as we strive to be part of an in-group.

Achieving a sense of belonging and support through membership of a social in-group can not only boost our own sense of self-identity but it can facilitate an unconscious mental process by which we learn to engage in social comparisons with other people. We define ourselves partly in response to how we see ourselves against other people and music becomes a powerful definer for many people in adolescence.[36]

We have all heard of social in-group labels that are defined by musical genres. We have emos (emotional hardcore rock/ punk), goths (gothic rock), new romantics, mods (ska, soul and R&B), rockers, beatniks, and so on. Within these social groups people like to assimilate the characteristics of those who share similar musical tastes.[37]

Adolescents draw on common social musical identity to create a sense of group cohesion (peer bonding) where they view their own in-group more positively compared to other groups. This in turn promotes a level of optimal distinctiveness[38] in the social world. This is an important concept in adolescent socialisation: we seek out a position where we are not too isolated but at the same time retain a sense of self-identity. Achieving optimal distinctiveness becomes a crucial source of positive self-esteem.[39]

This process is all part of learning how to interact with wider society, something that children are often shielded from in small families and schools but a valuable skill that they must learn before heading out into the wide world. Dolf Zillmann and Su-lin Gan[40] suggest that music listening and fan culture in adolescence is all part of the natural transition from socialisation with parents to socialisation with peers. They agree that small peer groups can gain significant gratification from belonging to a 'musical elite'.

Our musical social identity not only impacts on the way we behave in the world but it can have an effect on the way people view us. For example, if I tell you that a new acquaintance of mine shares your musical tastes then you are significantly more likely to appraise them positively and to want to become their friend than if they don't share your musical tastes.[41]

Music can also have a positive impact on appraisals of social 'out-groups'; in other words, it can have a pro-social effect. In one study, Spanish participants were asked to listen to either flamenco or classical music. This was followed by a subconscious test of their attitudes towards Gypsy groups. Those who heard the flamenco music before the test showed less prejudiced attitudes towards Gypsies compared to those who heard classical music.[42]

Exploring musical identity in adolescence from both inside and outside social groups gives an important insight into the nature of the more subtle appraisals that are made in social situations and which are a feature of adult life in all cultures.

In adolescence our musical taste narrows to perhaps the smallest range it will ever be in our lifetime. During this period we focus on the music that speaks to us, reflects who we want to be, and through association with that music we learn about our self-identity and how our social world works. One consequence of this focus is that we listen to the same sorts of music over and over again. Because it becomes such an integral part of our development, this music invariably becomes 'the best music ever made' – in our humble opinion.

## The best music of my life

In our adolescent years we create matches between music and our forming identities (both self and social) with the result that the music we hear at this time eventually becomes part of us and our reflection. This process has been termed the cohesion or crystallisation of musical tastes[43] – the idea that the music we hear in our teens and early twenties becomes a large part of the music that we will enjoy for the rest of our lives.

But why does the music of our adolescence so often become our favourite? We don't seem to have such consistent, strong associations with the food we tasted in young adulthood, the clothes we wore or the places where we lived.

### Frozen in time

The first reason is that while all those other things can change (quality of ingredients, fabrics, and buildings) music stays exactly the same, frozen in time. Otis Redding, Amy Winehouse, Johnny Cash, Luciano Pavarotti, and Ella Fitzgerald may all have left this earth but at the flick of the switch I can hear their voices as if they were recorded yesterday. Music is so effectively frozen in time that it makes a perfect stimulant for mental time travel.

When I say mental time travel I don't necessarily mean to say that we journey to a specific point in time. Hearing a favourite piece of music from our youth *can* transport you to a certain time and place but it can also simply take you back to a time period. This is often the case with our favourite songs, when we have heard them so often that they are not really attached to a specific event. Rather these pieces represent a symbolic concatenation of the youth experience – 'this song reminds me of what it was like to be 21'.

Our minds are capable of specific time travel as well, thanks to a special form of memory known as episodic auto-biographical memory (the 'self-memory' system), which is your memory for your life episodes (more on this in Chapter 7). Very often our memories can become foggy and need a jump-start to trigger the recollection of a particular event. Music is a great cue as it is reliable over time and per-sonal to us. This means we end up using it more as a mental time-travel device than other things in life, such as food or locations, and because of this regular use, music is more likely to end up tied to our best and worst times from growing up and by association becomes part of our favourite music.

### Emotional jolt

The second reason why we become so attached to the music of our youth is the emotional ingredient, which again is hard to recreate with a good sandwich or a pretty park. Our adolescent experiments with music, mood and emotion stand us in good stead for the emotional journeys we will go on as adults but they also lay down deep markers that stay within us.

Most of the really strong emotional experiences that we have with music occur in our adolescence.[44] The music that is most effective in touching us emotionally in this way is very often the music that will touch us for the rest of our days because it becomes so psychologically and physically significant in our life story.[45]

### Unique brain signature

Both the strong link to memory and the special ingredient of emotion mean that our brain reacts differently when it hears our favourite life music compared to when it hears music that is not in our personal hit parade. We talked at the start of this chapter (*see page 58*) about how music that gives us a physical sensation of chills can stimulate deep areas in the brain associated with emotion and reward. But this is not the only brain area to react to our top memory tunes.[46]

Petr Janata studies the brain signatures of music-evoked life memories. He believes that this type of memory is unique and may hold promise as a way to stimulate memory in medical conditions such as dementia (see Chapter 8).

In 2007 Janata and his colleagues tested the musical memories of 329 students in their early twenties at the University of California, Davis.[47] His team downloaded 1,515 different songs from the Top 100 pop and R&B lists and trimmed them to 30-second samples. Each participant heard a selection of songs that were in the charts when they were aged between seven and nineteen years old. The students were asked if they had any personal memory recollection in response to each song clip.

Janata found that a life memory was associated with at least one of the music clips in 96 per cent of cases. Most of the songs triggered memories from the last five years for the students, putting those memories in early adolescence as opposed to childhood. The most common memories were of friends (47 per cent of songs) and partners (28 per cent of songs), and in around 50 per cent of cases the participants provided detailed descriptions of the memory, proving just how vivid they were.

Importantly, the emotional rating given to the music-evoked memories were significantly higher than neutral and the most common emotion words selected were 'happy', 'youthful' and 'nostalgic'. This preliminary study confirms just how intricately music gets knitted into emotional memories of our adolescent life.

In a follow-up, Janata used this kind of music to trigger life memories of thirteen adolescents (average age of twenty) in an fMRI scanner, which measures brain activity by analysing the way that the brain uses oxygen in the blood.[48] In response to musically related life memories he found unique activations in a distributed network of brain areas including the medial prefrontal cortex (MPFC). This part of the brain is located in the middle of the head, just behind the frontal cortex (the bit of the brain encased by the forehead – see diagram on *page 83*). These MPFC activations were stronger in response to the most salient and favourite adolescent life memories.

Janata concluded that this brain network is involved in music life memories because so many different memory systems (emotion, knowledge, recollection, etc.) are triggered by hearing the music and all fire together in order to make a stronger and more vivid memory for the person. That brain activation signature is unlikely to be unique to adolescence but the research we have seen in this chapter suggests that the types of music that trigger this brain response are more than likely going to be those that we heard during that period.

All this evidence suggests that we enjoy the music of our adolescence in a special way, in a way that no other music we will ever hear in our lives will inspire. During these years our mind and body face a unique set of stressors (hormones, personal and social challenges, rapid physical growth) that mean the way we take in music, weave it around our memories and sense of self, and the frequency with which we recall it for the rest of our days, will always give that music a special place in our hearts … and in our brain.

♪

Ask yourself, what are my top five favourite songs or pieces of music? I would bet good money that most of what you come up with will be the music that you were listening to in your adolescence. Out of my top five, four songs are from that period[49] and I know that all six of my dad's (yes, I asked him for a top five and he gave me six)[50] are from that time. Two of mine are connected to specific people or events from that time period while the rest, and all of my dad's, are simply the soundtracks of our youth.

This chapter has thrown some scientific light on why this brief but unique period of life can be so very important to the growth of our musical ideals and tastes, and how through emotional support, memory prompts, self assurance and social facilitation the music of this period becomes an integral part of our lives. This is no doubt why we choose to take it with us as we journey on to the next life period – adulthood.

# PART II

# Music in adult life

Chapter 4
# The musical adult

*'Most people live and die with their music still
unplayed. They never dare to try.'*
MARY KAY ASH

The next three chapters of the book explore the role of music in adult life. Wherever we go and whatever we do with our adult life, music will be there playing an often subtle but important role, whether we choose to play it or not. We will explore how this blanket of music impacts on our working life and our reactions to the commercial world (Chapter 5) as well as our hobbies, pastimes, and romantic life (Chapter 6). These two chapters will show how music can change the way we feel about, react to and interpret the world around us.

First I will lay the groundwork for an exploration of musical adulthood by taking a look at the full spectrum of adult musical ability from high expertise through to those individuals who live with a specific music learning difficulty, and finally the majority of us, who would not think of ourselves as 'experts' but who enjoy music and who are, in fact, incredibly musical.

We will explore the relationship between normal music exposure and subsequent learning (including after lessons) and brain/behaviour development. In reviewing the full spectrum of the adult musical brain we will see that music learning does not stop once we reach adulthood; it goes on and can be boosted for as long as we live, whether you are a famous concert pianist, an enthusiastic music listener, a new learner, or simply an occasional radio surfer. This chapter will reveal the musical adult in all its variety.

## Music changes the brain

At the time of writing I teach at a university in London on a course that explores 'Music, Mind and the Brain'. Of all the lectures I give, the most eagerly anticipated is about how musical training may change the brain – I think that this particular lecture is so popular because many of my students are musicians and they want to hear all about their special brains!

You might fall into that category too, and if so then you are about to hear all about the kind of changes that may have happened to your brain as a result of your hours of hard work. Even if you are not a musician, the story of how musicianship realtes to the brain is still fascinating because it is symptomatic of a remarkable faculty that we all share: our brain's ability to change, grow and heal throughout our lives.

Plasticity is one of the best tricks that our brain possesses; the ability to reorganise pathways and synapses in response to environmental pressures and biological needs. This ability explains how we survived as a species for so long, as brain plasticity is essential for learning from experience and for recovery from brain illness and injury.

We do not yet know exactly how brain plasticity occurs: it could be that neurons get bigger, synapses get denser, cell support structures grow, cells die more slowly than usual, nerve conduction speeds increase, and so on and so forth.[1] Any or all of these mechanisms could be behind each example of brain plasticity. What matters is that the brain is incredibly flexible and continues to develop all the time.

We have a critical period of maximal brain plasticity when we are young, where we learn the most we will ever learn in such a small period of time. We now know, however, that the idea that our minds become rigid and set in stone after this point is simply untrue; your brain remains plastic for your entire life. That means that we are never too old to learn and for the brain to change – and learning to play an instrument or sing is a powerful way to stimulate the mind.

We can pick up just about any skill as an adult, and in doing so we can mould our brains. One of the most famous studies in this area was a study of London taxi drivers[2] which found that drivers who had a greater knowledge of London streets had a larger hippocampus; this part of the brain is associated with important functions for a London cabbie, such as memory, navigation and spatial awareness.

Even more convincing for the idea that adult learning influences brain structure are studies that teach adults a new skill from scratch and then watch to see if the brain changes over time and with practice. How about juggling? A study that scanned people's brains before and after just seven days of learning a new juggling trick found an increase in the density of a visual motor area of the brain.[3]

How much can music change the way that your brain looks and works? There is little evidence so far that just listening to lots of music causes any significant changes to brain structure or function. By contrast, there is a long history of exploring the changes that may occur as a result of musical training. In Chapter 2 we looked at how after only a short period of music training a child's brain starts to re-shape itself in response to its new musical input and skills.[4] In this chapter we will first look at the end result of all this practice – the brains of adult musicians – and see where and how they are different.

After looking at the brains of musicians we will explore how typical musical brain development can go awry, in a special population of adults who appear to be born 'tone deaf'. Hearing more about these people and their experiences will help set the musical skills that the rest of us have as adults, and may take for granted, into true perspective. Finally, we will look at the evidence that just about all of us can potentially change our brains by taking up music, at any age.

## Music learning and the brain

In the 19th century, scientists began to accept the notion that the primary causes of human behaviour lay in the brain. Previous to this, the soul and the heart were popular candidates. Towards the end of the 19th century, scientific interest arose in studying the brains of eminent people in order to determine what might have caused their abilities and expertise. Post-mortem brains of choice included those of mathematicians, poets and, of course, musicians.

Sigmund Auerbach (1860–1923) was a German surgeon who was fascinated by the structure of the brain. In his lifetime he contributed a great many works on the treatment of brain tumours, nerve damage and epilepsy. In the early 20th century he conducted a series of post-mortem brain dissections on five famous musicians of the time: the conductors Felix Mottl and Hans von Bülow, music teacher Naret Koning, the singer Julius Stockhausen and the cellist Bernhard Cossmann. Dr Auerbach wanted to see where and how their brains were different to the average one that he saw every day on his operating table.

Auerbach concluded that all five individuals had enlargements in the middle and back areas of the superior temporal gyrus. Let's break down that brain name. The brain is covered in folds of grey matter and a 'gyrus' is the upper part of a fold or bulge, as opposed to the crevice or gap (known as a 'sulcus'). The temporal lobe is behind your ears (on both sides) and is primarily interested in processing sound. 'Superior' means upper part (as opposed to 'inferior' which would be the lower part). So to recap, the superior temporal gyrus is a

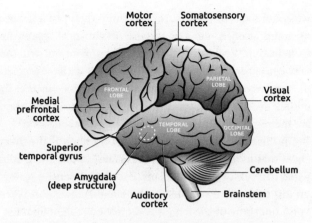

A representation of the human brain, showing the location of the superior temporal gyrus and selected other structures.

bulge in grey matter that lies in the upper part of the temporal lobe. In the five dead musicians Auerbach found a much bigger bulge than he was used to seeing.

He also noted other differences that happened in some individuals but not others, such as increases in grey matter in the posterior (back) part of the frontal lobe (behind your forehead). All in all, the brain differences he saw were not extensive, but remember we are talking about things that could be seen with the human eye and a magnifying glass.

Later studies backed up Auerbach's findings, including a study by Dorothée Beheim-Schwarzbach in 1974 on the postmortem brains of three musically talented individuals in the famous Vogt archives, a collection of brains amassed by the German neurologist Oskar Vogt, his wife Cécile, and their co-workers between 1928 and 1953.

Fortunately, the development of brain imaging techniques such as magnetic resonance imaging (MRI) in the 20th century made it possible to obtain three-dimensional, high-resolution images of the living brain instead of having to wait around for famous musicians to pass away. This development also meant we could look for the first time at more than just a handful of brains at once, allowing the use of statistical approaches to help objectively quantify differences in brain structure between experts and non-experts. Finally, as with the jugglers, these types of study make it easier to determine whether the unique anatomical features that we see in musicians' brains are the result, rather than the cause, of skill acquisition.

In this next section we'll look at a number of the differences that have been found in musicians' brains when compared to those of non-musicians. Excellent extensive reviews on this subject are available in the scientific literature;[5] here I pick out some of the largest and most consistent findings.

Two short but important points before we dive in. First, there is no consistent definition of a 'musician' in the literature – different studies tend to include people with different amounts of training and experience so there is no magic level that must be reached in order to be labelled as a musician. Typically, however, we are talking about people who have at least ten years' training and who are still actively playing on a regular basis.

The second point is that in most cases we can't say for sure whether musical training *caused* the changes that we see. It may be that any brain differences existed or were pre-programmed before the person started their training and this was one of the reasons that they went on to be a good musician.

The only long-term study at the time of writing that has scanned the brains of children before and after they started music lessons found evidence that the brain changes observed were not there at the start but instead were happening as a result of the training.[6] But the jury is still out on this issue so remember to take the following results with a pinch of salt – music may cause these brain differences in musicians, bring them out, or be a reaction to them. Whatever the truth, we can be sure that music training is involved.

## Brain structure

The brain has two hemispheres that are held together by a series of neural fibre connections in a structure called the corpus callosum. We need to be able to transmit information between the hemispheres quickly and effectively in order to coordinate activity in the left and right sides of the brain, including movements from the left and right sides of our bodies. The corpus callosum facilitates this connectivity.

One of the earliest (1995) brain imaging studies of musicians and non-musicians used in-vivo magnetic resonance morphometry. This method allows scientists to map the surface area of the corpus callosum using images from an MRI scanner. Gottfried Schlaug and colleagues[7] reported that the corpus callosum was significantly larger in 30 professional, right-handed keyboard and string musicians compared to 30 non-musically trained individuals that were matched for age and gender. Moreover, the difference was driven mostly by people who started their musical training before age seven. The conclusion was that the need for complex bimanual coordination when playing keyboard or string instruments necessitates growth in the brain area that facilitates communication between the hands.

Not only is the corpus callosum bigger in some professional musicians, it also has a different way of working. You get faster transfer of all kinds of information (including visual) between the hemispheres in musicians compared to non-musicians.[8]

As well as facilitating information transfer between the hemispheres, the corpus callosum has to maintain a certain level of inhibition or blocking. It is a delicate balance: too much information crosses the hemispheres and the messages from each side may get confused; too little and there is less effective coordination.

You might predict that musicians would have more corpus callosum inhibition because of the increased information from the two hands and the need to maintain independent control of movement. In fact, the inhibitory circuits in musicians have been shown to be *less* effective in this brain area, meaning that there is less blocking of signal transfer.[9] One theory to explain this situation is that professional pianists in particular have gained such high levels of independence between the messages from the two hands that they can afford to let down the floodgates and share information freely between the sides of the brain without fear of confusion and breakdown in performance.

The corpus callosum is not the only point of connectivity in the brain. The whole structure is covered in white matter pathways whose job it is to transfer signals between different parts of the brain. There is evidence that musical training has an impact on the structural integrity of some of these white matter pathways, perhaps making them stronger.[10]

A large study of professional pianists carried out at University College London found several areas of the brain where white matter fibres were denser (a greater number of them, better aligned and with more effective myelination*) and moreover this finding was associated with practice; the more someone practised, the denser the white matter. This finding hints at improved connectivity in a number of important brain regions outside the corpus callosum in musicians.

The enhanced connectivity effect is not limited to instrumental learning either. A study conducted by Gus Halwani and colleagues[11] tested the integrity of a particularly large white matter pathway (or 'tract') known as the arcuate fasciculus (AF). The AF connects the temporal and frontal lobes and is a very important pathway for carrying information about sound. We have two AF tracts, one in the right hemisphere

---

* The myelin sheath is a protective layer that coats the outside of a neuron. It is essential for the proper functioning of the nervous system.

and one in the left. Picture this structure as being like a hollow tube filled with rice noodles, which represent the flexible individual fibres within the tract.

Halwani and his team used a technique called tractography to measure the volume (the size of the tube) and the density of the fibres (noodles) in the AF tracts in both hemispheres in non-musicians, instrumental musicians and vocal musicians. The AF tract was larger and denser in musicians compared to non-musicians. Interestingly, in the left hemisphere, parts of the AF were bigger in singers compared to instrumentalists but were also less dense, meaning the fibres in the AF at these points were likely to be more criss-crossed or branching.

Why the difference in the left and right AF in the singers? One theory is that the right AF is more involved in understanding the relationship between sound and how we produce it, through our hands, feet or voices. In contrast, the left AF may be more responsive to how we use our vocal system to produce minute differences in sound. So the left side of the brain may be more focused on the demands of producing speech while the right side is more interested in all types of sound more generally.

The great point about this study is that it hints that you may get a boost effect in brain connectivity from singing, which is something that we can all attempt in our everyday lives without the need for an instrument. Of course, we now need research to establish whether this effect occurs in people who are new to musical training or if it is limited to highly trained musicians.

### Movement

If you play a musical instrument or sing then you need to develop complex and delicate motor control skills for optimal performance. The motor feats that top-level musicians can achieve are quite staggering. The best professional pianists can produce up to 1,800 notes per minute while compensating for tiny changes in volume and pressure, an amazing achievement for the fingers.[12] The presence of such incredible motor ability has consequences for the structure of the brain.

People who have developed advanced motor skills for musical performance tend to have measurable differences in the part of the brain that represents the body and its movement. This area sits roughly on the crown of the head, going down towards the brainstem, and comprises the somatosensory cortex and motor cortex. These two structures sit alongside each other and work together very closely.

The motor cortex is in charge of planning and making movements while the somatosensory cortex responds to information about our sensations of touch, including pain, as well as proprioception – our conception of where our body is located in space.

The somatosensory and motor cortices feature a logical, elongated map of the body. This map represents each part of the body to a different degree depending on the importance of fine control and regular use. Your body map would look strange if you were to see it represented visually, an image that has become known as the 'cortical homunculus' (see opposite); imagine a person with massive hands, feet, lips, and tongue but a tiny stomach, back, ears and neck.

The brain body map is not the same for everyone of course, as we use our bodies in different ways, and shifts in the map can occur during one person's lifetime in response to stroke or injury (to either the brain or body). Despite this variety, we can still see general differences between the brain body maps of musicians and non-musicians.

Keyboard musicians show increased tactile sensitivity in their hands[13] and perform better on tasks that require motor learning, especially when they have begun musical training early in life.[14] These traits are backed up by corresponding differences in their brain body map.

The cortical homunculus: a visual image that depicts the extent to which different body areas are represented in the motor and somatosensory cortices of the human brain.

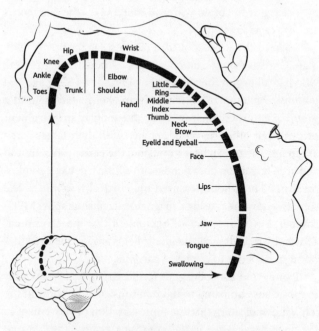

The relative location of different body area representations along the motor and somatosensory cortices.

Katrin Amunts and colleagues[15] used MRI to measure a part of the motor cortex where the hands are represented. The researchers found that non-musicians had a more asymmetrical structure, larger on the left compared to the right. This is the expected brain balance for right-handed people since the brain's representation of our body is crossed over (your right hand on the left side of the brain and vice versa). Keyboard players, by comparison, had a much more symmetrical structure, reflecting a much larger representation of both hands in the brain. This was especially true of people who had started their musical lessons early in life.

More recent studies have also found a more pronounced omega ('W' shaped) pattern in the motor cortex of musicians[16]. Amazingly, the effects in that study were identified just by looking at the brain with the naked eye – the differences are that clear to see.

Scientists have also looked at responses in the brain's body map. Christo Pantev and colleagues[17] studied string players who had all begun their musical training at a young age and who were still practising regularly and compared them to a group of control participants who did not play an instrument or carry out other rhythmic activity with their fingers such as typing. The researchers stimulated the participants' thumb and little fingers on both hands with a little harmless, painless pressure. They then measured the cortical response in the somatosenory areas using a magnetoencephalography (MEG) scanner, a sensitive piece of equipment that measures brain activity by recording the magnetic fields around the head that occur in response to electrical currents.

Pantev and his colleagues found larger brain responses in musicians compared to the non-musicians but only in the left hand, indicating that the representation of movement in the fingers was larger in the musicians' brains. The fact that this effect was larger in the left hand was probably driven by the large number of violin players in the study, who use their left hand for much finer movements than their right (bow) hand.[18]

These studies tell us that musicians' skills in fine motor control have consequences for the way that they perform on non-musical motor tasks in the lab, and that this difference shows up in the structure and activity of the brain body map that in some places you can actually see with the naked eye.

### Listening skills

In the previous chapter on music in childhood we saw that one of the first changes to the brain that occurs following music lessons is a boost in hearing skills – you may recall the phrase 'music for a smarter ear'. By adulthood we can clearly see the anatomical and functional differences in the brains of musicians who by the stage of adulthood are masters at perceiving and responding to small changes in sound, especially on their instrument/voice.

Activation levels in the primary auditory cortices of professional musicians in response to musical sound have been found to be 102 per cent larger than in non-musicians only 30 milliseconds after the onset of a tone. Furthermore, grey matter in parts of auditory cortex has been found to be 130 per cent larger.[19] Musicians also show enhanced perception of small music- and speech-like changes.[20] It is fair to say that musicians' brains are big, quick and powerful when it comes to analysing sounds.

One important point about musical experience is that it is not simply a 'volume knob effect'[21] where everything gets better. Neural responses to sound are balanced to leave more resources available for processing complex aspects of sound, which professional musicians can do better. The boost that occurs in auditory processing in musicians is in that sense an optimising process.

One of the consequences of this optimisation process is that you see the biggest boosts in processing familiar sounds – a musician's own instrument or voice – as compared to other sounds. Christo Pantev and his team demonstrated that musicians get an increased brain response (25 per cent larger) in the first milliseconds after hearing a musical tone.[22] No such boost occurred when musicians heard 'pure tones', artificial pitch sounds that a traditional instrument would never produce. (These tones are composed of all the basic elements of a sound wave – frequency, wave length and amplitude – so we hear pitch but without any of the overtones that arise from natural vibration of air caused by a piano string or a clarinet reed.)

In a second study Pantev compared the brain responses of violin and trumpet players to violin and trumpet tones.[23] The researchers measured the strength of the cortical response to the tones and found a clear pattern – a bigger boost for the more familiar instrument in both groups.

Most recently, Dana Strait and colleagues have demonstrated a similar pattern of results when looking at very early brainstem responses.[24] When exposed to sounds, the brainstem emits a wave signal in response, as a result of the electrical activity in the brain, which is called an auditory evoked potential. Think of it as being like the echo of your voice when you shout into a cave. The brainstem response can be measured to determine the extent to which it is similar to the original sound, in the same way that you could record an echo and compare it to your original shout.

Strait and her colleagues recorded auditory brainstem responses in pianists and non-pianists (all accomplished adult musicians) as they listened to three different musical sounds: 200 milliseconds of piano, bassoon or tuba. The pianists' auditory brainstem response to piano sound more closely resembled the characteristics of the sound wave compared to the brain responses of other musicians. In essence, the pianist's brains produced a more accurate looking brain 'echo' of their own instrument. In the paper the authors refer to this effect succinctly as the production of a more accurate 'neural snapshot' of piano sound in pianists.

All these findings suggest that the brain tunes its auditory system to a fine level, giving the musician a natural advantage when it comes to listening to music by their own instrument or voice. This likely occurs as a result of the stimulation of feedback and feedforward pathways in the brain as a musician strives to learn from their own sound and push the fine-tuning of their own performance for maximum effect.

This apparent blessing can also be a curse, however, as it puts trained musicians at a disadvantage if they are listening to their own instrument when it is slightly out of key. I have personal experience of this phenomenon, as very slight mis-tunings of the guitar used to drive me mad when I was judging competitions. This baffled me at the time as I knew that I was nowhere near as sensitive to the sound of other instruments, even though I was an avid music listener. Now I know why!

The enhancement in hearing skills that we see in musicians can get quite specific but you can also see general effects. One such effect is the processing of pitch in speech. Patrick Wong used the auditory brainstem recording technique to look at responses to Mandarin Chinese tones in musicians and non-musicians.[25] He found improved pitch tracking within the brain response in musicians who did not speak Chinese, even though they were listening to linguistic tones as opposed to musical ones. The musicians' tracking of the linguistic pitch was more robust and faithful. This finding may explain in part why musicians are often better at learning to speak a second language.[26]

Speech perception in our native language is a skill that

we have already seen to be enhanced in children who take music lessons compared to children who do not. In adults this relationship remains strong, and furthermore the amount of practice predicts the extent of the improvement in hearing speech in noise.[27] Adult musicians also show more finely tuned subcortical brain responses and improved discrimination ability when it comes to distinguishing similar speech syllables (such as 'ba' and 'da').[28] So if you need to follow a conversation at a noisy party then try calling on a musician in case you miss any words.

Finally, it appears that these differences in the early brain responses of adult musicians to speech sounds may also benefit them in later life, when the ability to track fast-changing speech often declines naturally. Evidence suggests that older people (average age 65) who have had a moderate amount (between four and fourteen years) of musical training early in life but who have not played for decades still have faster neural responses to speech sounds compared to matched individuals who had little or no musical training.[29] It may be that early musical training sharpens our sound systems in a lifelong manner.

### Motor response

Another interesting brain hearing effect that you can see in adult musicians is something that I like to call 'brain ghosting' in my classes. When musicians hear a piece of music that they know how to play or sing, their brain shows similar patterns of motor activation compared to that which we would see if they were actually playing or singing. Even when they are lying absolutely stone still in the scanner, their brain is 'ghosting' the music performance.[30]

This ghosting effect is recognised by musicians, who often report that they experience an automatic coupling between musical sounds and their associated motor actions. One interesting anecdote I heard in relation to this effect was that singers are often advised not to listen to recordings of music immediately before a performance. Even though they would not be singing out loud the fear is that they may strain the voice through automatic triggering of the brain's music motor ghosting system. Whether or not this could actually happen is not known, but this account suggests that the power of the brain's musical ghosting system is recognised by professional musicians.

### Memory and vision

Some musicians show advantages in mental abilities that have no clear brain basis or at least not one that we can currently narrow down to a single area or response. These types of ability are still worth a mention. They are most likely to be due to the combined effects of many of the areas that we have mentioned in previous sections or they could be caused by things we can't easily 'see' going on in the brain, like more effective use of cognitive strategies.

The primary mental skill of interest, and one I am particularly fascinated by, is memory. Unlike in taxi drivers, we don't see in musicians a big boost in the main memory brain area, the hippocampus. Despite this, there is little doubt that musicians have better memories in a variety of areas.[31] Obviously a musician will do better with a test of musical memory as they have more strategies to be able to remember the sounds: they can picture notes in their head or form a motor memory of what it feels like to play those notes. How about other types of everyday memory task?

One of the first large-scale studies of multiple memory tests across different domains (musical, verbal, visual) was conducted by two of my students Stefania Pileri and Cristina Di Bernardo. They tested matched groups of musicians and non-musicians on eight different memory tests and found that the musicians had enhanced verbal working memory, where you have to keep more than one thing in your mind at once. They did not find any boost to short-term speech memory (trying to keep a telephone number in mind for a few seconds), or visual or spatial memory.

This study shows clearly that musicians do not demonstrate a general memory enhancement from their training in the same way as working a muscle in the gym will make it bigger. Rather than simply gaining more 'capacity' in memory, my hunch is that musicians get better at using their memory, and this is especially marked when it comes to recalling and manipulating sounds, whether they are musical or not.

While we don't tend to see any effects of musicianship in memory for visual things (other than visual music), we do see some differences in musicians when it comes to visuo-motor skills: the types of skills where you need to co-ordinate your visual and motor systems in order to carry out an action. This is probably due to the fact that musicians who can read music spend so much of their time learning to associate a visual symbol (notes) with a motor response (playing or singing). This process likely sharpens up the systems that allow us to associate visual and motor representations.[32] The interesting next step will be to work out how wide-ranging this enhancement really is and whether it can help with other, more everyday skills that require visuo-motor skills such as driving or sports that require hand-eye coordination.

Over the years, many experiments have compared musicians and non-musicians in a variety of situations. In this last section I have outlined some of the most well-known areas of behaviour and ability that show promise for the future. What we need now are more studies that explore exactly *why* musicians perform better in these areas so we can understand better how musical training affects both the brain and behaviour in positive ways and the implications for future learning.[33]

So far we have managed to demonstrate that music making over a lifetime impacts on our minds – how exactly this happens is a mystery for the future.

## A music processing disorder

Now that I have outlined some of the differences you can see when comparing musicians and non-musicians, in both brain and behaviour, I am going to go right to the other end of the spectrum to think about people who struggle with musical sounds.

The aim of this section is to bring us all (especially the musicians) back down to earth and the reality that we are all musical. We are brought up with a stereotypical idea of 'musicians' and 'musicality' in Western society, one that really means 'expert'. Experts exist in all walks of life, but that does not alter the fact that we are all incredibly musical. I hope to convince you that the musical skills we possess as adults are, in fact, remarkable. One of the best ways that I can make my case is by putting those musical skills into sharp relief by looking at what happens when they don't develop in the typical way, as is the case in amusia.

The small population of individuals who have amusia experience genuine and specific music processing difficulties in the absence of a hearing problem or any other notable cognitive, emotional or social impairment.[34] I have been lucky enough to study this rare condition for five years and I am going tell you about what it is like to live without effortless human music processing abilities.

### The way you sing off-key

Amusia is often referred to as 'tone deafness', but let's be clear. We all know of a friend, colleague or family member who couldn't carry a tune in a bucket, whose singing causes genuine alarm, and who should be kept away from karaoke machines under public health legislation. The majority of these individuals do not have amusia. Most are just poor singers.

The best illustration of this point came from a study by Lola Cuddy.[35] She and her team went into Queen's University in Canada and asked how many of the students thought they were 'tone deaf' – around 17 per cent of just over 2000 people put their hands up. The researchers then tested 200 of these students for amusia (see below for how this is done). Only a handful of the apparently 'tone deaf' people had a genuine music processing difficulty. The vast majority who believed they were 'tone deaf' actually had a fine ear for music; most were just not that interested in music and felt that they could not sing well.

Nearly every self-confessed 'tone deaf' person that I know is haunted by the idea that they can't sing[36] – usually based on the harsh judgement of a schoolteacher, a choir leader or even close friends and relatives. Karen Wise and John Sloboda[37] studied self-confessed 'tone deaf' adults in the UK and found that while they did have some trouble singing, their biggest problem was that they were under-confident. They sang better with accompaniment, leading the authors to suggest that their difficulty was not insurmountable. They and most of the 'tone deaf' people you know would respond well to a few singing lessons. Singing training in amusics, by contrast, has led to comparatively fewer improvements and in most cases of severe amusia such training has little effect on the underlying music processing difficulty.[38]

In general, if a person says 'I sound terrible when I sing' then they are unlikely to be tone deaf, as in order to make this judgment a person must be able to recognise the mistakes they are making. An individual with amusia is more likely to say 'My family and friends think I am a terrible singer, but I'm not really sure either way'.

## Manifestations of amusia

It should be no surprise by now that musical understanding can break down in many different ways because so much of the brain is involved in processing music. Some people with amusia struggle with a sense of pitch and how it moves, a crucial skill for tracking how a melody unfolds over time. One of the main difficulties I see in amusics is a problem with the concepts of 'up' and 'down' in pitch.[39] Most of us take that skill completely for granted and can recognise if a sound is rising or falling without thinking, but this can be difficult for someone with amusia.

Other people with amusia may encounter difficulties with the quality of musical sounds, if their perception of timbre is impaired. Timbre is the quality of a sound that means we can tell whether a note is played on a flute or a cello, for example.

A classic case of a timbre problem was the man who went to his doctor with a unique complaint – Madonna was sounding funny all of a sudden. This man was a big Madonna fan but lately he had noticed that her voice was breaking up. He realised that there may be a problem with him (and not Madonna) when he noticed the same new tinny sounds when listening to her old records. This was not an obvious symptom of a medical difficulty to most, but it turned out that the man had suffered a very small stroke that had left him with a mild case of amusia.

## Diagnosis

Amusia is currently assessed and diagnosed using the Montreal Battery for the Evaluation of Amusia, a test developed by Isabelle Peretz and her colleagues.[40] During the test, a person listens to two short melodies and must say whether they think they are the same or different. For people without amusia, the occasional 'different' note in this test is pretty easy to spot. In fact, most of them stick out like a sore thumb. It is quite amazing to sit next to an intelligent person who listens to tunes with an obvious out-of-key note and says 'same'. But these people with amusia are absolutely genuine – they simply can't consciously recognise that the bad note does not belong; that it is not 'right'.

Amusia in the absence of a hearing problem can be either congenital or acquired: congenital means that an individual was probably born with the predisposition for their condition and it developed as they aged despite normal exposure to music. We can't say for sure that anyone is born amusic, as you can't measure for lack of a skill (music processing) that has not yet had the chance to fully develop. There are, however, a few documented cases of amusia in childhood, which suggests that the condition can develop early in life.[41]

Current estimates are that around 4 per cent of the population may have congenital amusia[42] though it is possible that this figure is an overestimate.[43] Acquired amusia, on the other hand, is the term given when an individual who has had no previous problems with music suddenly exhibits music processing difficulties, usually following a head injury, stroke or a coma.

Amusia is often defined as the inability to comprehend or respond to music; however, this is a misleading label. Individuals with amusia are capable of music appreciation. My much-missed colleague Diana Omigie[44] studied the types of music that individuals with congential amusia listen to in their everyday lives. She asked them to complete diary entries about their musical surroundings several times each day for one week when prompted by text message. People were asked about their level of choice in the music selection, their liking for it, the amount of attention paid to it and the effects of the music on their mood and emotions.

Many of the congenital amusics in this study tended to avoid music and preferred not to play it in their homes or cars.[45] But some did enjoy background radio and used music to modulate their level of energy. Interestingly, one of the most popular genres in the amusic group was jazz, a genre that does not rely so much on melody as pop, country or rock.

So the situation with amusia is not clear-cut; amusics don't hate all music and/or find it incomprehensible. This makes sense if you think about it: music is a complex sound with many different aspects that you might enjoy, such as the timbres, rhythms or lyrics. You might also gain pleasure from the social and cultural aspects, the benefits of music that go beyond the sound. You may associate a favourite tune with a first love, or the tune 'Happy Birthday' with the bright eyes of an excited child as they blow out their candles. The depth, power and reach of music in our lives means that we can gain appreciation through many routes, but those routes are likely to be different for a person who has an underlying problem processing the musical sound.

### Amusics in their own words

One lady, I will call her Pat, has been taking part in amusia trials for nearly a decade. She comes from a large family that lives in a stunning part of rural Ireland where there is a big community musical tradition. Pat's family run a local shop that sells traditional Irish instruments and she and her siblings were taught Irish music when they were children, as well as Irish dancing. Her brother is a skilled accordion player. She, on the other hand, could never seem to get the hang of playing, singing or dancing, although she did learn to read music. She tried her best, practising for hours, but she could never seem to move up grades and was never picked for local performances.

Nowadays she would never choose to listen to music, especially in her own car, where it is talk radio or nothing. However, she has always encouraged her children to be musical and delights in telling stories of their musical achievements. She also still enjoys visiting the traditional Irish session where music is played by friends and family in the local pub.

Pat has always been keen to understand why she is different. Why it is that, despite all her efforts over the years, musical performance and a true understanding of everyone's fascination with musical sound is beyond her.

Like many people in her situation she was happy to learn that there was a reason for her reaction. It was not that she was stupid, not trying hard enough, or, horror of horrors, had no taste – an accusation that many with amusia face. Thanks to the efforts of people like her, who kindly offer their time for testing, we now understand that she has amusia. Her brain is different in a way that means music processing is disrupted for her. It is not her fault and she can't help it. She is missing something that the majority of us take for granted.

One of the most common analogies that amusics use to describe their experiences is colour blindness. When I ask them, 'What is the difference between these two tones?' some amusics feel that the question makes about as much sense as asking a colour-blind person what is the difference between red and green. They understand that other people can probably perceive those colours in a different way to them but the clear distinction reported by everyone else is not something that is apparent to them.

One amusic told me that people often ask what her life was like without music. She said that this was the equivalent of asking a blind person what it is like to have never seen a sunrise: 'You are asking me about something I have never known … so why would I miss it?'

Other descriptions of amusia include having a 'Teflon mind' for music. Often a person will describe how the sound of music does not stick around in their head long enough for them to be able to fully process or understand it. It just slips away quickly and quietly. Alternatively, some describe it as like being handed an important piece of information and then having no idea how or where to file it away in order to be able to find it again.

During a recent conversation with an amusic lady, she described how fascinating she found it when someone played or sang music. She said that it must be like me watching another human fly around the room. Flying is not something I am personally capable of doing, so I do not associate it with the realm of possible human achievements. She feels the same way when she watches someone perform music.

Lastly I would like to relay the sentiments of another of my participants. This gentleman has always been clear with me that he does not want to be patronised or pitied for his condition; the thing that he finds difficult about amusia is other people's reactions. He is convinced that it is especially hard for children who find music difficult and he thinks that people in positions of authority, such as teachers, should be more aware that amusia exists.

### Differences in the amusic brain

The ability to make sense of musical sounds can be disrupted from the first points of perception through to musical memory,[46] and even the later, most complex stages of musical interpretation and integration. One of the consequences of this varied symptomology is that it has proved relatively difficult to track down consistent markers for congenital amusia in the brain.

There has been little indication that there is anything out of the ordinary in the temporal lobes, within the main auditory areas. Where structural differences are found they tend to be higher up the music brain system in both the left and right hemispheres, in particular in the inferior (lower) frontal cortex.

One possibility is that the white matter highways of the brain are more impacted than the grey matter centres in amusia. One white matter pathway of current interest is the arcuate fasciculus (AF); you may remember this pathway from earlier in this chapter, where I discussed how it was found to be denser in musicians. Scans have shown that the AF may also be less well developed in individuals with amusia.[47]

As well as difference in brain structure, there are differences in the way that amusics' brains react to musical sounds. Early brain responses, measured by EEG scans, can be 'muted' (smaller or delayed in time). Amusics' brains show expected responses to out-of-key notes or notes that violate expectation but the reaction seems somehow weaker.[48]

Interestingly, you can sometimes get a normal brain response to a musical oddity in amusia, in the absence of conscious awareness.[49] In these cases it seems like the brain spots the out-of-key note but the person remains unaware of this information. It may be that there is an abnormally high degree of disconnection between subconscious and conscious processing of music in amusia.[50]

This brief look at amusia shows us that so many of the musical skills that we possess, as simple as telling up from down, moving to the beat, or singing 'Happy Birthday', are all complex and impressive in reality. It has taken the whole of our childhood and adolescence to refine these musical skills and they are quite simply the best of any animal on the planet.

We take them for granted, just as we do the ability to read and speak. It is often only when these abilities break down or fail to develop that we see them for what they are – a truly remarkable achievement of the musician in all of us.

♪

We have now explored the extremes of musical experience in adulthood: expertise at one end of the scale, lifelong music difficulties at the other. That leaves the majority of us somewhere in the middle, with an interest in music and the ability to process it. The music of our lives has not impacted on our minds and bodies to the extent that it has in accomplished musicians but it has still had an effect on how we process the music around us.

## Biased by listening

I can prove that you have learned a lot just from listening to music, because it has biased your brain.

By adulthood most of us have had decades of experience of only one musical culture: in my case, Western tonal music. I have learned the structures and rules of that musical style in the same way that I have learned the structures and rules of my native language, to the extent that I don't need to think in order to understand and appreciate the sound. By comparison, when I listen to the music of another culture (for example, Javanese gamelan or Japanese hōgaku) that follows different rules and structures, I see the downside of my exclusive learning. On first hearing a new form of music you and I are as lost as if we were listening to a person speaking in a foreign tongue.

Scientists at the University of Washington have studied why we struggle when we first listen to music from other cultures. The situation is not hopeless, luckily, as people are capable of working out musical structures within unfamiliar music over time by just listening, in the same way that we can start to pick up the basics of new languages. This idea has been tried with a variety of cultures measured against the experience of traditional Western tonal music, including traditional Indian and Chinese music, as well as unfamiliar European styles such as Finnish folk songs.[51]

There are a few things that the majority of world musics seem to share. A recent study of music listening in adult

Congolese Pygmies found that both they and Western students reacted to the same simple emotional triggers in music like timbre and intensity. This result suggests there are some basic universals in world music communication that we can rely upon most of the time.[52] Apart from this however, there is a very strong bias in the way that we interpret cross-cultural music, which is based on our own understanding. The Pygmies in the above study showed fewer overall emotional responses to Western music compared to Western students. People are also less able to remember music from an unfamiliar culture.[53]

Finally, the brain shows an atypical response when listening to music from other cultures, reflecting the fact that we have to work harder to think about the sounds and are not so capable of understanding what might happen next.[54] All of this adds up to an 'enculturation effect' in adult music listeners. The fact that we can't instantly derive expectations for unfamiliar musical styles also means that typically we won't initially like what we hear.

## Bimusical brain

Enculturation may somewhat limit our first impressions of cross-cultural music as adults but we can learn about more than one culture at once while we grow up. Some of you out there may have a 'bimusical brain'.

People who are fairly equally exposed to different musical cultures during childhood and adolescence appear to develop different musical systems and patterns of brain activation compared to people who only really hear one kind of music. This is not like hearing half classical and half hip-hop – genres from within the same culture – as these will mostly use the same musical building blocks. To have a bimusical brain you need to be exposed to music that evolves from a different set of rules.

Patrick Wong and colleagues have been studying brain responses of people who were brought up listening to both Western and Indian music.[55] The researchers scanned the participants' brains while they listened to both types of music and compared the responses to those of mono-musical people, who had only heard Western music while growing up. The bimusical people showed more complex patterns of brain activation suggesting, in particular, that their emotional reactions to music are unique and have been shaped by their bimusical heritage.

Everything we see in the research about our cultural response to music tells us that we have become biased by what we learn as children. Plus, intuitively, we all think that it is easier to learn an instrument as a child than it is as an adult. This does not mean, however, that we can't learn music as an adult, either a new instrument or how to listen to the music of another culture. While there is some truth to the idea of critical periods in music listening where learning is easier, there is little truth in the idea that you must be young to pick up a new musical instrument or style.

## Music learning, extraordinary and ordinary

There are tales of musical brilliance achieved in adulthood in extraordinary circumstances, which give enticing clues about the power of music learning as adults. In his book *Musicophilia*, Oliver Sacks tells the story of a man who trained himself to be a concert-level pianist as an adult after a freak accident. This gentleman was hit by a lightning strike, a life-threatening accident which left him with remarkably few after-effects other than a sudden addiction to music where previously he had shown comparatively little interest. As well as upping his music consumption massively, he set about training himself to play the piano, and achieved concert-level standard in an incredibly short period of time. He became devoted to music and obsessed with music learning.

A similar tale was recently reported in the UK press: a 39-year-old man was left with serious concussion after diving into the shallow end of a swimming pool. Before the injury he had played in a few bands as a teenager but never really devoted much time to music. Now he has been diagnosed with acquired savant syndrome, meaning he has developed high levels of musical ability and technique (including composition) where there were no previous indications of such skills. He states, 'It's as if my knock on the head unlocked something latent, or enabled me to use some part of my brain I simply couldn't access before.'[56]

Our brains' party trick of plasticity means that we are born lifelong learners. We don't need a bolt of lightning or a blow to the head to be able to learn how to play music, sing or compose; we can do the unlocking ourselves. It will take longer and may be more hard work but I am pretty sure it is a lot less painful!

One of my favourite books on this matter is *Guitar Zero* by Gary Marcus, a psychologist who decided to take on the goal of teaching himself to play the guitar as an adult and analysed the experience from the viewpoint of a scientist.[57] It is an engaging and fundamentally hopeful story of how anyone can pick up musical skills at any age if they are prepared to put in the effort and consistently challenge themselves to reach new heights. Your plastic brain is there for the moulding.

As far as we can tell, learning of this kind at any age has the potential to alter the brain as well. The academic and author Steven Mithen[58] decided to take up singing lessons as an adult and was interested to see the effect this might have on his brain.[59] He contacted a colleague and neuroscientist, Larry Parsons, who agreed to scan Mithen before he started singing training and after a few months of lessons. The scans showed a significant difference in areas such as the auditory cortex and early parts of the frontal cortex. More recent studies of adult musical training have shown similar effects, with the most notable brain changes being to the structure and function of the auditory and motor cortices. These shifts look like the beginnings of the complex auditory-motor representations that we see in the brains of highly trained musicians.[60]

Music, it seems, has the potential to mould the brain in multiple ways at any age.[61]

♪

In this chapter we have explored the musical adult and revealed that the normal progression of musical learning through exposure, which goes on mostly behind the curtain of our consciousness, gives us an in-depth understanding of the music of our culture. In rare cases this typical development does not happen; adults with congenital amusia live with the everyday consequences of a music processing difficulty. If we choose to boost the typical path of musical development by taking on music education then our brain moulds itself in accordance with our new skills and this has consequences for the way that we think and behave in a variety of non-musical situations.

There are critical periods for learning about music but our flexible brains are still very much capable of learning in adulthood and music education at any age has many positive benefits both for expanding our minds and for our well-being, as we shall discuss in Chapter 8. Now that we have set the stage for our musical adulthood, let's take a look at how we react to music in the real world, starting with adults at work.

# Chapter 5
# **Music at work**

The majority of us will work for most of our lives in order
to earn a living, to provide for ourselves, our future and our
loved ones. Work is and always has been an inextricable part
of human life in every culture.

Sometimes, work is a pain. You may be one of the lucky
individuals who adores their job but even then there will be
days when the necessity of an occupation grates on your
nerves. On such occasions, we look for a way to dull any negative impact and make difficult work time pass more enjoyably.
One of the great escapes from work-related tedium and stress,
across the ages, has been music.

Music has been a feature of physical work for hundreds
if not thousands of years, serving a number of functions
including synchronising movement, creating social bonds,
relieving boredom and enabling communication. There are
traditions of work songs that span a multitude of cultures and
languages, including military marches, sea shanties, industrial
folk songs, cowboy cattle calls, and agricultural work songs.
Venezuelan work songs (such as Cantos de pilón) are an excellent example: these traditional folk melodies are often sung as
an accompaniment to activities such as milking cows, harvest-
ing coffee and producing cornflour.

Work music has the power to engage our mind, absorb our perception of time and lift our spirits. All of this makes music an ideal accompaniment to both physical and low attention demanding chores, which would otherwise be draining and tedious.

The history of the relationship between music and work in the modern age begins with studies of music in factories during the post-war period. These early psychological studies of the impact of music on worker responses, lead directly into the modern and ongoing controversy over whether we should have access to music at work: what are the benefits of being able to tap into music while at your desk, doing deliveries, or preparing food, and what kind of music should we be hearing? Is music actually good for productivity?

The use of music is not restricted to private work settings but is also prevalent in more public, commercial work environments: in our shops, bars, restaurants, garages, airports … in fact, nearly everywhere we spend our hard-earned money we are surrounded by music. Why is music played in the commercial working world? How does it affect the way that we behave in these places? Do we really spend more, walk faster, or eat greater amounts?

## History of music at work[1]

Some of the first psychological studies of music in the workplace took place around the time of the Second World War when the modern factory conveyor belt assembly line used so successfully by Henry Ford earlier in the century really came into its own on a worldwide basis, triggering an age of mass production. In this period before the widespread adoption of automated handling systems there were plenty of repetitive, tedious yet essential jobs along the production line that required a careful human eye and hand.

Unfortunately our minds are not designed to carry out the

same series of actions repeatedly for hours on end; boredom, lethargy and lapses in concentration are inevitable consequences of such work. Knowing this full well, factory managers began to investigate ways to enhance active productivity (increased speed and/or larger outputs) as well as minimise errors on production lines. One of the first ideas was to study the effects of piping music into the factory floor space.

The British government introduced music in armament factories in the later stages of the Second World War[2] and one of the first studies in this area was carried out in a fireworks factory.[3] These, as have several similar papers since, found a small (typically below 10 per cent) but significant increase in measures of productivity during repetitive jobs in the presence of music compared to silence.

As much as number crunchers would like to count every firework and relate this directly to 'productivity', it is also vital to consider indirect measures of productivity, such as worker well-being. Workers reported feeling less boredom and fatigue on days when music was played.[4] It may be more difficult to quantify the impact music has on productivity as it relates to well-being, but it seems clear that improving well-being can have an effect on outputs and profits as happier workers are more likely to support their team and less likely to be absent.

Why and how may hearing music influence productivity? We will go into this question in more depth soon when we dive into the psychology behind background music but the chief candidates for the increase in music-related productivity in these early studies were: 1) a boost in rhythmic synchronisation, which enhanced speed and hence regularity of output, and 2) physical responses to music such as singing and moving to the beat. These latter reactions were thought to contribute to increased energy levels, buoyed by positive impacts on physiological measures such as heart and breathing rate.

This is human science, however, so nothing is 100 per cent effective. It is important to stress that not everyone likes music at work. Up to 10 per cent of workers would much rather be left in silence and some studies have shown that quality of work can be adversely affected by music when people feel this way.[5] As we shall see later, the more complex the work is, the more likely it is that music will act as an unhelpful distraction and consequently will hinder rather than help productivity.[6] Overall however, the message from the early studies was that for simple repetitive jobs music is better than nothing.

The results from these factory studies began to reveal the effects of music on monotonous jobs and I certainly can agree, from my experience of cleaning windows as a young chambermaid, that music can be invaluable when it comes to engaging the mind during boring physical work. However, the kinds of roles that were put under the spotlight by these early factory studies are rapidly disappearing from the modern workplace thanks to mechanisation. We need to also look at environments where the majority of workers are engaged for at least part of their life – the office.

## Music in the modern office

Should you listen to music while you work in an office? This was the subject of a study by Greg Oldham[7] who looked at the use of stereo headphones in a multi-purpose office building in the US, where people were engaged in over 30 different jobs. Over four weeks he and his team tracked the progress of 75 individuals who typically brought in their own music and listened to it through headphones, and compared it to that of 181 people who did not tend to listen to music.

The music group had significant improvements in performance (rated by the employers), better opinions of work (less likely to be planning to leave), satisfaction with the work environment and better mood states, being more relaxed and enthusiastic.

An obvious problem with this study is its 'quasi experimental' nature – people were not *randomly* assigned to the two groups (music or no music), meaning it is hard to conclude that music listening was the thing that influenced their responses. All we can assume is that people who like to listen to music at work find it helps with their productivity and work satisfaction. So let's think about what happens if you take music away from these kinds of people.

Teresa Lesiuk asked what happens when you remove a music-lover's music in an office setting.[8] She followed the working lives of 56 software developers from four different companies across two different cities. The study itself was a time-based intervention whereby Lesiuk monitored reactions to music for two weeks, then removed the music for one week, and finally reintroduced it again for a final week.

During the music weeks the developers could choose from a wide range of tracks from a 65-CD library and could listen in the privacy of their booths. They had to avoid music completely in the middle 'no music' week.

In the weeks when the developers had access to music they measured significantly higher on mood. There was a noticeable dip in mood in the 'no music' week that then rebounded again when music was reintroduced in the final week. Quality of work was also rated as lower in the 'no music' week, and rebounded when the music came back.

One of the largest effects in the study was that of measured time-on-task: people took much longer to accomplish their jobs when their beloved music was taken away. Although this study lacks a proper control group, it seems clear that when people are used to being able to listen music in the workplace, removing it can trigger negative effects associated with psychological withdrawal.

Following on from this research, Anneli Beronius Haake conducted the first large-scale studies to chart the way that music is used in UK office settings and how it makes people feel. The conclusions from her research help to highlight how music has multiple pathways to increasing work satisfaction and productivity.

Firstly, Haake carried out a survey of the listening practices of 295 individuals who worked within computer-based UK offices.[9] Their occupations spanned administrative and management roles, as well as media and cultural services, medicine, science and technology, and teaching. She looked at how people chose to listen to music and what functions people felt music served. She also asked questions about what type of music people liked to listen to in the office and what reasons, if any, would put them off listening to music in this context.

The most popular workplace artists were Arctic Monkeys, The Beatles and James Blunt, a result which reflects the UK sample. The most popular work music genre was classical, with rock, pop and indie falling into a close second place. The least popular work music genres were soul and funk. Radio stations were also mentioned frequently as popular ways to listen to music in the office, with BBC stations taking most of the top spots.

Haake argued that the sheer variety of work-based music listening habits supports the idea that there is no typical best 'office music'. Therefore it is probably a bad idea to simply pipe music into a general office space containing many individuals who have different tastes, preferences and personalities.

People in this survey were listening to music for 36 per cent of their working lives, using headphones on 86 per cent of occasions. No one individual factor, including age, gender, stress levels or occupation, predicted music listening habits. One exception was that people who felt more stressed were more likely to report that music was relaxing. Music listening in the modern office environment is therefore a largely private pastime (hence the headphones) that each individual tailors in keeping with present demands and that can help manage stress.

Building on these results, Haake conducted interviews in order to understand how different situations and motivations influence music listening choices at work. One idea that came across strongly was that music creates an 'auditory cocoon' for people, isolating them from potential sources of stress and giving them a sense of escapism to a personal space within a public environment.

I often think of this cocoon idea when I see people charging around the London underground with headphones attached to their heads. Music in this case provides a welcome illusion of detachment; minimising the sounds of other commuters, tube trains flashing through tunnels and suitcases banging on escalators. Haake's office survey found that this self-created musical bubble can be especially useful in the workplace as it not only blocks stressful sounds but also replaces them with a source of inspiration and creativity. By these methods music can aid concentration, boost task performance and reduce the potential negative psychological impact of a long work day.

We must also consider the downside to music in offices. Some people in Haake's survey believed that music listening was viewed as unprofessional and avoided listening at times when they could be seen by senior colleagues or clients. This idea seems to underlie the misunderstanding that someone who is listening to music cannot possibly be working to their optimum. This is not true. In an open office situation it is important to be considerate to others and 'present' in the work space, but we should also accept that private music can be helpful. And as we have seen above, removing music as an option for someone who is used to its presence is probably going to do more harm than good.

There is a delicate balancing act to be achieved between the potential for music to distract or enhance performance. The key message is that music *can* help an individual in certain work situations. The important thing is to be consciously aware of the choices that we make. Since the effects of music are highly individual, each of us has to acknowledge when music is helping and when it is hindering – for optimal work success we must always employ 'smart music listening'.

## Is background music good for work?

Studies of music in the workplace draw heavily from literature on the general effects of background music, and it is here that we find answers to the questions of why and how music affects us in the workplace. Understanding these forces is an important step in developing 'smart music listening' techniques.

The types of study I will discuss in this section are not overly concerned with the work environment. They are relevant, however, as they tackle the question of whether music can aid cognitive or motor performance in all kinds of arenas such as studying, reading, problem solving and everyday tasks such as driving.[10] Most importantly, these studies are carried out in a controlled, scientific way so we can look carefully at the effects of music as we try to carry out other simultaneous tasks.

At the heart of all of these studies are a handful of mechanisms which hark back to the 'Mozart effect' (see Chapters 2 and 3): psycho-physiological arousal, cognitive engagement and mood effects.

### Psycho-physiological arousal

Arousal is an umbrella concept that describes your level of physical and mental alertness at any one moment. The most cited scientific model that relates everyday task performance to psycho-physiological arousal is the Yerkes–Dodson (Y–D) curve from 1908.[11]

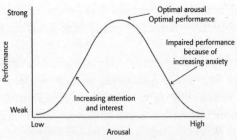

A Hebbian version of the Yerkes–Dodson curve.

This model and accompanying theory postulate that each person's 'base' level of psycho-physiological arousal is somewhere on this upside down U-shaped curve. Some people have a naturally high level and some people have a much lower level; the peak of the curve is the optimum where we are all able to achieve our best performance.

Music is an agent that can increase (push us towards an optimum) or lower (push us over the top) our position on the Y–D curve depending on the characteristics of the music, such as its complexity, volume and familiarity.

The effect of music on psycho-physiological arousal is one mechanism proposed to explain the so-called Mozart effect, whereby listening to music can temporarily improve performance on a spatial task. In studies of performance, the Y–D curve is often cited as an important factor that explains why, for example, fast and loud music can have a detrimental effect on reading comprehension compared to slow, quiet music:[12] the fast and loud music is more likely to push you over your optimum level of arousal and performance will consequently fall down into the area of weaker output.

### Cognitive engagement

Cognitive engagement describes the level of attention that we are able to devote to a task. An optimal state of cognitive engagement is a 'flow state' where motivation is focused on the job at hand and task performance is optimised.[13] One recognisable characteristic of such a state is that we tend to lose track of time.

Music has the potential to contribute to a flow state partly in relation to psycho-physiological arousal (which is tied to attention) but also by the nature of our limited attention system. In theory we have a certain amount of attention that we can devote to tasks; if we try to do too much then we experience anxiety and if we use too little then there is the danger that we drift off into boredom. In effect, music can soak up that extra unused attention during a simple task that may otherwise contribute to boredom and a subsequent sudden need to surf the net or call a friend.

### Mood

The effects of music on mood are well recognised (as seen in Chapter 3, and as we shall see again in Chapter 6). In relation to studies of task performance, music mood associations have also been called upon to explain findings such as the Mozart effect, as upbeat music that improves mood results in better task performance compared to slow, sad music that depresses mood.[14]

Mood and arousal are often seen to go together but it is possible for them to diverge; for example, you can be in a positive mood and either very relaxed or very alert. Therefore it is important to consider both arousal and mood as independent agents that can be influenced by background music.

These three agents, arousal, engagement and mood, all play a role in our response to background music individually and in combination. 'Smart music listening' is a balancing act that requires a person to gauge their own level on each of these factors and then to assess the demands of the task at hand. Smart music listening can then add a positive contribution to a task when it is used to adjust any or all of the factors towards an optimum for performance.

Even when we take into consideration general influences of arousal and mood, music does not impact in the same way on everyone. We need to consider the influences of personality, preference and choice.

## Personality

The last thing I did as part of my honours degree, back in 2003, was to design my very first experiment. I wanted to understand why we choose to listen to music in certain situations; the problem was that I had no idea where to start. One evening I came home from university to find my boyfriend of the time engrossed in a computer racing game. I slumped down on the sofa and watched his progress impassively for a while, glad of the distraction from my thesis dilemma.

Then an idea struck. Before each race, my other half was taking time to choose the music he wanted to hear. I asked him why. He said that the automatic music selection within the game software was 'rubbish' so he always had to select something more engaging. Was it because he didn't like some of the music? No, it was all pretty good, but some of it was more 'effective' than others. He believed that modulating the music level would improve his performance. I decided then and there – that was my thesis.

I think my professor was rather bemused the next day when I announced that I needed a room decked out with a sofa and a computer game console for my first experiment. Nevertheless we managed to obtain a TV from the home studies team and my other half kindly parted with his PS2 for four weeks.

The next step was to get some music. I decided to remain as true to the genre as possible and contacted computer game music composers. Many were kind enough to donate tracks for my experiment and I gathered in people to help me pre-rate the music for levels of excitement, complexity, engagement and variety. My aim was to select some low, medium and complex music in order to see if these different levels really had an effect on the way that people raced during a computer game.

On top of this I planned to have two upper levels where I added first the lyrics and then all of the game sound effects on to the most complex musical condition. Including the silence condition at the bottom, I now had six increasing levels of musical sound complexity in my computer game experiment.

During this design phase I came across an intriguing finding that changed one vital aspect of my experiment. Apparently, people with different personalities responded in a different way to background music. In particular I was struck by an experiment conducted by Adrian Furnham and Anna Bradley on the effects of background music.[15] They were interested in the influence of one personality trait: extraversion.

In 1967 Hans Eysenck[16] stated that extraverts and introverts differ in their level of cortical arousal, with extraverts having a lower baseline level than introverts. Think of this baseline as being like an internal source of stimulation or 'psychophysiological arousal', as I described in the last section.

You will remember that we all have an optimal level of arousal (the peak of the Y–D curve) where we function at our best, and because of this difference in baseline levels, introverts and extraverts differ in how much more they need to get to that optimum. Extraverts are naturally lower down on the left-hand side of the Y–D curve and introverts are comparatively higher up.

As a result of their higher level of internal arousal, introverts seek out less stimulation from the external world, preferring quieter and more familiar environments. They are already closer to their optimum point so do not need too much more before they are pushed over the edge into the area of poorer performance. Extraverts on the other hand, with their lower level of internal excitation, seek out stimulation, such as daredevil activities. They have a longer way to go to reach their optimum. Furnham and Bradley drew a clear prediction for their study of background music: extraverts should benefit from more musical stimulation whereas introverts probably won't.

The participants in the Furnham and Bradley study listened to three upbeat pop songs ('Sowing the Seeds of Love', Tears for Fears; 'New Sensation', INXS; and 'Strange Brew', Cream) while completing memory and reading tasks. As expected, the introverts had poorer memory for the things they had observed when music was playing compared to the extraverts. The introverts also had a lower score on the reading task when it was carried out in music compared to silence. Finally, the introverts reported that they were less likely to work with the radio on at home, listened to the radio less in general and found it more distracting during the experiment.

When I read this finding as an undergraduate I rethought one aspect to my computer game experiment. Maybe my partner was an extravert. It made sense on an intuitive level: he was certainly much more comfortable in a crowd or at a party compared to me, and to my horror he had recently begun to talk about skydiving. Maybe his desire to pump up the level of the music in his computer games at home was being driven partly by his personality. So I opted to test the impacts of game music on groups of introverts and extraverts.

My experimental findings replicated the Furnham and Bradley study result nicely: my introverts did worse in the most complex music conditions compared to the extraverts. Not only this but my extraverts showed a clear improvement as I pumped up the musical complexity. Introverts on the other hand got better up to about the middle level of complexity and then their performance started to go down as the level increased.

My experiment and that of Furnham and Bradley show clearly that background music complexity has a different effect on people's task performance depending on their personality.

There is, of course, another explanation. Because extra-verts tend to listen more to music in their everyday lives we can't rule out the possibility that all we did in these studies was create a more familiar environment for them.

Whether you buy the psycho-physiological response theory or another explanation, these studies and others conducted since[17] have shown that personality can influence task perfor-mance in the presence of background music.[18] Going back to our initial workplace question, the implication of these results is that unless you can guarantee that all the people in a work space have a similar personality then you are unlikely to be able to select music that has a positive effect on everyone.

## Preference and choice

In the early factory studies of workplace music there is often no description of the music heard other than a broad category such as 'dance hall'. And a fair few modern studies do not compare different kinds of music, preferring instead to simply compare the difference between music and silence. We know from discussions in earlier chapters that this type of research design is limited as it tells us nothing about music in particu-lar – it only informs us about the effect of doing something other than nothing. For all we know you may get a similar effect if you pipe in an audio book, the shipping forecast or animal noises.

If we are going to work out *how* music impacts on pro-ductivity and performance at work as opposed to other types of sounds then we need to explore what *kinds* of music have an influence on our psyche at work and why. In fact, personal preference and choice over music selection may be the most important influences of all.

A lack of choice and control over the music that we hear is frequently cited as one of the main reasons for a negative appraisal of that same music.[19] Simon Frith likened this adverse reaction to a social response to territory marking. In this sense, background music is an overt display that someone else has control of the space where you find yourself; this display can really irritate us.

Back in the lab, Joseph Parente found that people completed an attention-demanding test better in the presence of their preferred music than in the presence of their least preferred music.[20] Equally, more recent studies of music preferences and the effects of self-selected music have re-emphasised the importance of music preference and familiarity in everyday listening.[21]

So why don't scientists take more care with personal preferences when selecting music for experiments? Simply put, if researchers allowed people to bring in their own music to play during a test then people would likely bring in so many different varieties (slow, fast, loud, soft, all manner of genres) that it would be impossible to control the situation in the way that science demands.

The reality is that even if I did a huge study and found the most effective piece of background music for work then it would still have little positive influence on task performance if you hated it. So 'smart music listening' must take into account individual preferences and, ultimately, give an individual as much perceived control over the selection as possible.

## The bad news

The studies above make it clear that background music can help some people, some of the time, when we apply 'smart music listening'. We must not overlook the fact, however, that sometimes our performance does not benefit from music, whether the task is a driving game[22] or one that draws on vigilance,[23] memory[24] or writing.[25]

How do we reconcile these positive and negative results? In 2011 Juliane Kämpfe and colleagues carried out a large overview of studies into background music.[26] She found nearly 100 suitable studies that were classified into a positive or a negative effect of background music on performance. The studies were also classified based on the type of performance they measured: 'mundane behaviour' (eating, driving), 'cognition' (reading, maths), or 'emotion'.

Overall, Kämpfe reported that background music had no effect on cognition and only small effects on mundane behaviours. The strongest effect of music she found was on emotional responses, but this result was still rather small and unimpressive. Kämpfe was also able to look at the effect of music over different time periods, as far back as the 1970s – she noted no systematic change in effects that aligned with the increased exposure to music over recent decades.

This main set of findings is, of course, a bit general as it comes from combining together the results of many tasks. We are most interested here in effects that relate to work performance; and helpfully Kämpfe broke down the music effects for different tasks. Here the results are clearer.

The types of task that are most relevant to work relate to memory performance, reading and concentration. When it comes to jobs that tax our memory, overall there is a slight negative effect of music on performance. When it comes to reading, the result is the same, a minor negative impact. It seems that when a work task is complicated and requires a decent amount of concentration then most people (NB not *all* people) would perform better in silence compared to music.

♪

So after all that, is music helpful in the workplace?

I believe that music can help work productivity the most when we are engaged in simple, repetitive jobs, as it can counteract the negative side of such work on our physical and mental state, helping stimulate motor movements and boosting mood and arousal, without dragging significant attention away from the task at hand.

When considering whether music is helpful or not overall, it is important to remember that some people do not enjoy background music and certainly not the type of music that was originally designed to assist work. There was a backlash against the use of so-called functional or 'canned' music in the 1970s and 80s. Musicologists rightly objected to the use of music as a manipulative work tool and the development of mass-produced music – e.g. 'Muzak' – for this purpose.[27] There are many organisations who still believe that it is unfair to subject people to music en masse.[28] The right to auditory privacy is one that must be taken seriously, as not everyone reacts well to music, even in situations where research has shown overall positive effects on both productivity and work-related satisfaction.

When we are talking about your average working day in a modern office environment, there is little evidence that exposing people to music helps them to work significantly faster or better unless they are the type of person that already likes to listen to music while they work. In the case of such people, taking away or blocking music access will likely see a reduction in workplace satisfaction and decreased work output.

So the golden rule is choice. I hope we will never see an age where music is piped out in open offices, because the influences of personality, preference and choice mean that this action will likely impact negatively on as many people as it pleases. I am convinced, however, that providing access to music, for those who choose to listen to it in a private way, and encouraging 'smart music listening' (i.e. dependent on the cognitive demands of the task), makes for a better working environment than a strict 'no music' policy.

## Music in the commercial world

With a thorough understanding of the effects of music in the workplace, we can now take a different route and consider the effects of music upon the consumers of modern work environments. What about the diners, shoppers and customers? How does the music we play in this type of workplace affect consumer behaviours?

Most of you are probably aware of the pop psychology ideas that music makes us move faster, eat more, or buy more in shops and restaurants. And no doubt many people assume that this is why businesses must be interested in playing music. However, the real story is much more involved and interesting, and many businesses could learn a thing or two by glancing at the science.

Just before we delve into the impacts of music on the consumer, let's hold back for a minute and consider the people who work in these environments. Good businesses should and do consider the effect of music not only on the consumer but also on the staff. After all, we are talking about shops, restaurants, bars where people work every day. One excellent reason to consider playing music is for the benefit of the staff.

When I was sixteen I worked in a little gift shop in my home town of York. The shop always played background music and this was one of the main things I enjoyed about the atmosphere. In fact, this was the first place I was introduced to a haunting American vocalist and guitarist by the name of Eva Cassidy, whose music I have enjoyed ever since.

Quite apart from the potential influences of music in the workplace that we have already discussed, such as improving mood and boosting alertness, there is another magic trick that music performs in this type of environment for the benefit of hardworking staff: it can play with time.

## Music absorbs time

We are often left bemused by the passage of time because our internal clock can be easily influenced by how we feel (emotional, tired, and too hot[29]) and by things that draw our focus.[30] Music that we enjoy can also sway our sense of time, by altering our mood and acting as an attention-absorbing time shield that protects us from being overtly aware of the passage of time.

Sometimes music causes time to fly. Time used to drag when I worked in my little York gift shop on a Sunday. On this particular day I was usually alone, with no one to talk to apart from the passing trickle of Sunday shoppers. On these slow days the shop's enjoyable background music helped absorb the endless minutes as I dusted ornaments and refreshed pricing labels. I learned the words to the Eva Cassidy songs and sang along (in my head, to preserve the ears of any passing customer).

The new and interesting music captured much of my excess attention that was not demanded by the work tasks that I had performed over a hundred times before, attention that may otherwise have been focusing on time cues such as the ticking clock or the slow dimming of the light outside. As such, my concentration level continued on middle-ground optimum; the day did not whizz by but the music took away the drag.

Music for time absorption is equally important for consumers in shops and restaurants/bars. Waiting is a top annoyance – waiting at a changing cubicle, waiting for till service, waiting for your meal, waiting for the bill. The best businesses reduce the experience of waiting by adopting place filler techniques to break up your sense of time passage. An example is topping up your water to give the impression that although the thing you are waiting for (your meal) has not arrived, the level of service continues. Some businesses also use music to successfully warp the passage of time in their favour. In this case we tend to find higher perceptions of the level of service.

An important point however, is that the relationship between music and the passage of time is not always one-way or intuitive. Music may help time pass when we would otherwise be bored and/or waiting but what happens when we are busy shopping?

Richard Yalch and Eric Spangenberg[31] compared the effects of music familiarity on shoppers' estimates of the amount of time they spent shopping and the actual amount of time they spent shopping. In a replication of earlier studies,[32] people shopped for slightly longer when they were exposed to unfamiliar music compared to familiar music, though they actually felt that they had shopped for longer when they listened to familiar music.

How might we explain the feeling that more time has passed when the shoppers heard music that they knew? Surely this finding goes against the conventional wisdom that 'time flies when you're having fun'?

The researchers argued that when people listen to familiar music they get a boost in psycho-physiological arousal linked to enjoyment and that this effect can disrupt their perception of time. But because familiar music is more easily processed by our memory, we can take in more of the detail, thereby leading us to think we recall more time passing than when we try to process unfamiliar music. This process can lead us to overestimate the passage of general time.[33] Think of it as a magnifying effect of familiar music.

## Music and the consumer

Let us continue thinking about ourselves as consumers and the potential effects of music on how we behave in a shop or restaurant. Is there any truth to this idea that the presence of music influences how fast we move or how much money we spend?

There was a surge of music psychology studies in consumer environments in the mid- to late 1990s and there have been a handful of applied studies since. This number is still relatively small compared to other fields, largely due to the difficulty in carrying out scientific studies in real consumer environments. Although shop and restaurant owners are keen to understand how to get the best out of music, they are often reluctant to let a group of scientists loose with their space and, potentially, their profit margin. However, the work that has been done has benefitted our understanding of the impact of music in these environments.[34]

### Does music make us move faster?

Yes, it really does. One of the earliest studies in this area was conducted by Patricia Cain Smith and Ross Curnow in 1966.[35] They varied sound level (loud or soft) in supermarkets and found that people chose to spend significantly less time shopping during the louder music sessions. Interestingly, however, they found no significant difference in the sales between soft and loud sessions. It seems that people spent similar amounts of money whatever the volume but went about their business quicker when louder music was played in the background.

You could suppose many mechanisms for this effect; maybe people were annoyed by the loud music so got around the shop as quickly as they could. Not many people mention this possibility in the pop psychology consumer articles that cite this study but the fact that the loud music did not influence immediate sales that day does not mean that there are no negative effects of a loud music strategy in the long run. This study highlights the importance of not only looking at footfall or receipts – consumers can provide invaluable information about *why* they behaved the way that they did if only people would ask them.

This early supermarket study inspired one of the most discussed experiments in music consumer research, that of Ronald Milliman in 1982.[36] Milliman was interested in the influence of music speed on consumer behaviour, rather than volume. He trialled fast (94 beats per minute or more) and slow (72 beats per minute or fewer) instrumental music as well as a no music condition in a medium-sized supermarket in the nine weeks between New Year's Day and Easter. Importantly, the customers were asked whether they remembered music playing, although there is no record of personal reactions to the music.

Milliman recorded how long it took people to move between two pre-designated points in the store to give a measure of consumer pace. People moved slower with the slow music (128 seconds) and faster with the fast tempo music (109 seconds). When people heard no music their result was in the middle of these two figures (120 seconds). So the evidence suggests that music tempo was either slowing people down or speeding them up.

Of more interest to the supermarkets was the finding that people spent more when they heard slow tempo music ($16,740.23) compared to fast music ($12,112.85) – a 38 per cent increase in sales volume. An increase in spending in response to slower music has also been reported in restaurants in Scotland, where people dined for 13.56 minutes longer and spent 19 per cent more when the music was slow compared to fast.[37]

Were people aware of the presence of music in Milliman's study? In the 'no music' condition nearly 10 per cent of people thought they had heard music. In the slow and fast music conditions this figure increased to a measly 12 per cent and 13 per cent respectively. It seems therefore that when there was music, it went largely unnoticed. This result may be a function of the age of the study, conducted as it was at a time when music in stores was less prevalent than it is today. The important take-away point though is that awareness of the music did not increase significantly as the music speeded up, so the effect on consumer pace is not something that appears to rely on conscious awareness of music.

Many retailers base their music choice on reports of the Milliman study, and I can see why, as it is one of the best I have read in terms of being well controlled and executed. However it is dated and we need to look more now at the full range of modern retail outlets. Signs of a positive shift in this direction come from studies into alternative environments such as in craft markets[38] and telesales[39]; both have shown that the presence of music is associated with people choosing to linger for longer.

We even see an effect of music on movement when people are sitting at their computer. Chien-Jung Lai and colleagues[40] explored the effects of music tempo (fast or slow) and listening scenario (the same music continuously; the same music while browsing different web pages; and different music while browsing different web pages) on behaviour in an online store. Participants viewed more web pages and underestimated the passage of time more when they heard fast music. Playing different music was associated with more browsing, overestimating time passage and poorer memory for what had been seen. Continuous playing of the same music resulted in the best memory for the online store.

This last study asks new and important questions about the relationship between background music and our movement in commercial worlds. It is all very well measuring pace and time perception and showing that music can alter both, but studies need to focus on what people take away from their shopping and eating experiences if we are to understand how these visits may alter future consumer decisions. You may have moved faster in a store on one occasion because of the music but if that left you with a negative impression or no memory of the products then we must question the value of this strategy for the business.

### Does music make us spend more?

In the last section we saw a relationship between slow tempo music and spending more in a supermarket, probably as a consequence of how much more slowly we move around the aisles. Furthermore, people spent more money in a restaurant in Scotland when they heard slower music. But do these results replicate? And, importantly, do they hold for other consumer environments?

When it comes to money spend, research has had more luck manipulating genre rather than tempo or volume. That is not to say that these other factors are not potentially important contributors to how much we spend, but the strongest results have come from altering music at the level of genre.

Charles Areni and David Kim[41] looked at the influence of playing either Top 40 music (The Traveling Wilburys, Fleetwood Mac, Robert Plant, Rush) or classical music (Mozart, Mendelssohn, Chopin, Vivaldi) in the background while people shopped in a wine store. When people shopped during the classical music phases they spent more money (an average of $7.43 compared to $2.18) and purchased individual bottles that were more expensive.

This finding has been supported by a British study carried out in a restaurant. Here people chose a more expensive meal when classical music was playing as opposed to pop music,[42] though this effect was driven largely by people spending more on starters and desserts as opposed to main courses or drinks.

Why we choose to spend more in certain musical conditions is still a debated issue. One possibility is that people enjoy their time more in these environments. The classical music used in these kinds of studies tends to be instrumental only and it may be that people enjoy the chance to chat with a fellow diner or shopper in the absence of vocal music and as a consequence of this good experience they felt more inclined to spend. A simple preference for classical music in the people tested also remains a potential explanation for the effect.

Another possibility, and one that has captured more media attention, is that the music creates an environment which primes a context-appropriate response: in a more upmarket place we are subconsciously driven to spend more money because we feel it is what we are supposed to do. This may be the case. Alternative research, however, suggests a flipside to this theory whereby classical music can have a negative effect on purchases in some environments. In one study people were found to leave a restaurant earlier and consume less alcohol when background classical music was played as opposed to pop, jazz, easy listening or even no music[43].

There is a hidden factor in all of this that may help to clear up why the same genre can have positive effects on spending in one environment and not in another. There is not one simple formula for the effect of music on either movement or spending; it depends on 'fit'.

## Musical fit

One of the biggest influences on how we react to music in the commercial world is the level of fit with the environment. You can forget most of the effects highlighted in the last section to do with moving faster or spending more money if the music does not fit with the surroundings. In such cases, people are more than likely to take a quick scan and walk right back out again.

What is musical fit? I consider commercial musical fit to comprise two different ideas: how music aligns with an individual's perceptions of their immediate environment (the shop or restaurant) and how well it agrees with their subconscious ideas about the brand. The success of musical fit influences what we choose to buy and, more generally, how we feel about a brand and the likelihood that it will inspire loyalty in the future.

### Instant choices

Musical fit can prime our impulse buys. The most famous example is that of the supermarket where researchers played either German or French music. When French music was played, French wine outsold German wine by roughly 3:1. When German music was played, German wine outsold French wine 2:1. In an echo of the finding reported by Ronald Milliman, the wine shoppers were generally unaware of why they had chosen a particular bottle.[44]

Another nice example for you romantics out there is the study in a flower shop. Céline Jacob and her colleagues played either romantic music, pop music, or no music in this environment. The mean amount of money spent on flowers was significantly higher in the romantic music condition compared with the other two. The pop music condition did not lead to an increase in the amount of money spent compared with the no music condition.[45]

These two studies together demonstrate the effect of musical congruence in priming consumer behaviour. The music in these cases fit with the environment as well as with a certain instant reaction (indulging in romance) or selection (wine from a particular country). There is a strong argument that the music inspired these choices.

In general, consumers are more likely to purchase products when the music associated with them is well matched. This is because, cognitively speaking, we love a situation where nothing is clashing or competing for our limited attention and where, consequently, the drain on our processing resources is minimised. Well-matched music can create this kind of easy-to-process environment and act as a seamless 'cue to execution'.[46] These effects, matching associations and positive reactions, also work for brands.[47]

Michael Beverland and his team revealed the importance of musical fit on customers' idea of a brand through a series of twenty in-depth interviews.[48] Music was found to be an important initial signal as to the brand's position, image and quality. Another clear result was that when a person perceived well-matched music and store/brand image they experienced delight that then fostered brand loyalty. One of the most telling quotes was provided by a person identified as 'Melissa', talking about a furniture store:

> 'It's South American music and it's got that whole ethnic feel. I love it. The music fits in perfectly and it almost made the environment more jovial... It's like it could be in South America, because of the music... You just feel welcomed there, you feel at ease'.

## The secret messages in music

Our impression of a brand is not only influenced by how well the music fits but also the ideas or messages the music communicates on top of this congruence. Mark Zander asked 132 people to listen to 30-second radio commercials for a fictitious brand of mineral water and then rate the endorser's personality, their brand impression and their future buying intentions.[49] They heard three different musical backgrounds to the same advert: lively swing music, a slow piano ballad or no music at all.

All the music was rated as congruent with the brand but the two musics created different impressions of the spokesperson and the brand, and provoked different reactions. The endorser was seen to have the most self-control when he spoke over the lively music. With the quiet music the brand itself was rated as more 'soft, reserved, devoted and gentle' as opposed to those who heard the swing music, who rated it as more 'agitated and animated'. Moreover, Zander reported that these brand associations were quickly learned and hard to undo, as participants had made a connection between music and advert, preferring always the first versions they heard, after only a couple of exposures.

All this research highlights the multiple levels on which music can operate and why it is so important to go beyond simple 'fit' and think about what the music alone may contribute to consumer messages. Music is capable of being a player in a brand concept but you must be careful to understand its impact on top of this supportive role.

♪

In this chapter we have taken a tour round the world of work from many different angles and explored how and why background music can influence the way we behave, think, react and feel in work environments. The next step in music psychology research will be to move away from searching for largely fruitless generalised effects (there is no one 'best' music for work) and strive towards effective assessment of critical variables, such as feelings of control and consumer reactions, in the many individual varied and complex situations that make up our modern working world.

In the next chapter we will take a breather from all this thinking about work and indulge in some relaxation. We use music for our play even more than we use it for work; it is inherent to many of our fun rituals surrounding sport, dance, romance and TV/films. How and why has music become interwoven within our play activities and how does it affect our precious downtime?

# Chapter 6
# Music at play

*'There's people making babies to my music.*
*That's nice.'*
BARRY WHITE

The last chapter examined how music has woven its way into the many different manifestations of our working world. This chapter will expose how music is also an important part of our downtime, our leisure – our 'play'.

It is not surprising that music has become such a central part of our leisure time, as it's clearly something that we enjoy. However, music consumption by itself is not something most of us tend to do much anymore. By that I mean it is rare for people to just sit quietly and listen to music for pleasure. In my case the last time I did anything like that was well over a month ago when I decided it was time I sat down and listened to the 45s I had been given by my dad. I had a great time reminiscing and dancing around (yes, I do that) and thought to myself, 'I should do this more often'; naturally, I have not done it since.

Some of you will be regular concert goers or festival attendees. This is probably as close as most of us get to a music-focused, relatively high-investment activity in the modern world. On average I go to the opera, a show or a gig two to three times a year and I always have a wonderful time but it is a treat rather than a regular pursuit. Most of us could, if we wanted, just sit and listen to music any day of the week, as I did that one rainy afternoon with my dad's 45s. But the fact is that we don't.

Music psychologists exposed our lack of interest in focused music listening by conducting Experience Sampling Method (ESM) studies, where participants are prompted at regular intervals during their everyday life (typically by text message) to report on their music listening behaviours and reactions. Using this method in 2004, Adrian North and colleagues[1] confirmed that music was far more likely to be heard during leisure as opposed to work time but also that this music exposure was mostly heard as a backdrop rather than being the primary focus of attention.

A recent follow-up study by Amanda Krause[2] confirmed that, thanks to modern technologies, music has moved into nearly every aspect of our leisure world. Moreover, Krause made the important point that this evolution of music listening has been an active decision on our parts rather than a passive reaction to the boom in music access. We put music in our play time because we want it there.

Instead of listening in a focused way we have brought the music that we love into the background of our leisure time, in much the same way as we have invented ways to bring it into our working lives. When it comes to play, however, we have been more inventive than we have been at work; we use music for numerous rituals and pastimes including dance, romance, cinema and exercise/sport. In this chapter I will explore all of these activities, uncovering the role of music and exposing how important it is when it comes to maximising our enjoyment.

## Music and dance

Dance is rhythmic movement. The origins of dance stretch far back in human history and, as far as we can tell, dance and music have always been intricately linked. There are languages that make little differentiation between the words for dance and those for music.[3] Music and dance also have many overlapping purposes. Performance of either makes extensive use of movement and sound, allowing an individual to demonstrate skill and stamina as well as empathy. They are mediums by which we can make expressive gestures, with the aim of both communicating and triggering emotion in an audience.[4] Music and dance may also have both evolved as part of a human coalition signalling system, allowing us to form and strengthen social group bonds, and signal group membership.[5]

Having said this much, music psychologists pay relatively little attention to dance in their research, preferring instead to study music in isolation without its long-standing cultural partner. To a certain extent this is justified as there are many forms of music that were never intended to be paired with dance. And some forms of dance can be beautiful in the absence of music. The fact remains, however, that music and dance go together naturally for humans, indicating that they must, at some point, have been combined to communicate something unique and special. What exactly does music add to dance, other than a simple auditory signal to bring us together?

### Animals move to the beat

We gain interesting insights into the reasons why music and dance may have come together by looking at animals and their ability to move to the beat, which is an important component of dance.

There are numerous examples of animals that use coordinated vocalisations or movement displays as signals. On the vocal side, gibbons and cuckoos duet to defend their territory, while whales, mice and skylarks sing to attract a mate. On the movement side, Jamaican lizards bob their heads and perform vigorous push-ups to attract a mate while mute swans rotate in synchronised circles to regulate their borders. Finding an animal that both vocalises and synchronises beat-like movements however, is another matter.

One reason for a lack of dance-like behaviour in animals may be that the majority are not able (or willing) to move to the beat in music. I am not talking about clever synchronised movements here; I am talking about the equivalent of tapping your foot to the beat. For most humans this is easy. For most animals this is seemingly impossible.

Humans may be born with the understanding necessary to move to a beat. The beat, the thing we tap along to in a great track – the pulse of music – is not something that necessarily needs to be explicitly audible in music. Musicians do not need to emphasise the beat of music constantly in order for us to sense the pulse. We are capable of extracting the beat from music and, in most cases, a good beat will entice us to bob our head, move our foot, or snap our fingers.

Beat that is not audible is often referred to as 'implied'; it is something we perceive out of the sound, like the way we extract a sense of depth in a flat picture. A great example of the use of implied beat exists in groove-based music where the beat often emerges from a complex, multilayered and syncopated pattern of rhythms and instrumentation. Groove music is present across a range of genres including funk, soul, hip-hop, drum and bass, jazz and world music.[6]

You don't have to be a trained musician or even an adult listener to get 'beat'. Henkjan Honing and colleagues demonstrated that newborn babies, even when they are asleep, exhibit an identifiable brain wave signature in response to a violation of a basic beat.[7] In Chapter 1 we saw that Honing made use of implied beat, using simple drum patterns, and measured the responses of newborns to a dropped beat. The significant change in their brain wave signature in response to the dropped beat indicated that these infants were sensing the beat, as they reacted when it went away.

Honing conducted a follow-up study with adult rhesus monkeys to determine if their brains showed a similar beat detection response. It turns out that those monkeys were sensitive to the basic temporal structure of the music, such that they noticed when important notes were removed. But their brains did not respond to a dropped beat.[8] It appears that some of our closest ancestors hear music at only a surface level, without the cognitive skill of extracting the hidden groove.

It is not only our closest animal relatives that apparently lack the ability or inclination to move to the beat. There is little evidence that animals like dogs or cats, which have lived in domesticated situations with humans for thousands of years, spontaneously respond to the pulse in music without being cued or pre-trained.

Oddly enough, though, this lack of interest in moving to the beat is not true of all animals. So far scientists have identified a rather strange-sounding collection of animals that may be able to move to a beat. These include some species of parrot, songbirds, dolphins, bats, seals and elephants. What do we have in common with this motley assortment of creatures, and what does this tell us about the nature of music and dance?

'Snowball' is the name of probably the most famous animal in music psychology. If you have not heard of him then he is easy to find by typing 'snowball dancing' into your preferred search engine. Snowball is a male Eleonora or Sulphur-crested cockatoo (*Cacatua galerita*) who first came to the attention of science in 2007 when he arrived at the Birdlovers Only Rescue Service in Indiana (USA). He was dropped off at this shelter with an accompanying CD of his favourite dance songs. Aniruddh Patel and his colleagues have spent many hours since observing Snowball and putting his 'dancing' to the scientific test.

The researchers took Snowball's 'favourite song' ('Everybody' by the Backstreet Boys) and altered the original recording speed to make versions that were both slower and faster by up to 20 per cent. They then filmed his dance-like movements, paying particular attention to the synchronisation of his head bobs to the beat of the music.[9]

Snowball did not move much to the very slowest versions of the song but he did bob along frequently to many of the faster versions. In all cases his head bobs were fairly well aligned with the beat, certainly above chance levels. This result represents a remarkable feat considering Snowball is highly unlikely to have ever heard his favourite song at these fast tempi.

The discovery of dance-like musical synchronisation[10] in a non-human animal gives us clues as to why music is so important for our dance rituals. Animals that are capable of synchronised beat movements, like Snowball, rely heavily on links between the auditory and motor parts of the brain, as these facilitate the ability to vocalise and imitate other animals' cries. These facts lead people to speculate that the ability to vocally imitate may have driven the evolution of musical synchronisation.[11] This theory relied on there being no evidence for spontaneous beat synchronisation in animals who are not natural vocal mimics; and no such evidence was found for quite a few years until just recently when somewhat reasonable tapping to the beat was found in a female chimpanzee called Ai and a female California sea lion (*Zalophus californianus*) called Ronan.[12]

We definitely need more evidence of flexible rhythmic movements in true non-vocal mimics before we dismiss the vocal imitation theory of musical beat development. And even if vocal mimicry can't explain the development of musical synchronisation by itself then maybe a combination of ancient drives is responsible.

Animals such as Snowball rely (as ancient humans relied) on vocal mimicry as a crucial element for social bonding and display rituals, which also frequently includes the use of coordinated displays of movement. At present, the idea I find most compelling as an explanation of why Snowball and I both like to move to music is that the past survival of our species relied on the coordination of sound and movement for important signals.

This theory leads to the intriguing idea that music and dance co-evolved together in humans, since both social vocalisations and movement displays were useful to us, at some point in our history. Dance and music could send a more powerful message in close proximity than either could accomplish in isolation; important messages like 'we are a couple', 'we are a group', 'we are together' and 'we are strong – so watch out!'

These animal studies give us hints about the origins of the pairing of music and dance but we need to look at our own behaviour today to understand how we currently use both art forms and what they may usefully communicate in the modern world.

Of the two main animal reasons to combine sound and movement, defence or mating, modern humans tend to go for the latter. There are examples of ritual human defence-motivated displays still in existence, one being the New Zealand rugby team's use of the Māori Haka war dance and cry (most typically one called *Ka Mate*) before international matches. The nature of modern conflict has minimised the demand for such demonstrations in general, but music and dance for romance has never gone out of fashion.

### Sexy dancing

When we move our bodies we give away all kinds of information about ourselves: age and sex, the state of our health and fitness, and more subtle inferences such as our emotional well-being, truthfulness and confidence levels. All of these cues are useful for someone with romance on their mind. Music provides a way to facilitate these communications as it allows us to show off our ability to synchronise and respond to the beat and emotionality in music.

Geoff Luck and his colleagues from the University of Jyväskylä in Finland conducted an experiment to determine exactly how much information we gather from dance signals.[13] The researchers made use of point-light display technology, where an individual wears a set of sensors at key points along their body that can then be illuminated against a dark background. What you see from the point-light display is identifiable as human movement but is really just a group of moving dots. This means the viewer's judgements are unaffected by any other attractiveness cues that might draw their attention.

Luck used this technology to ask the question, what type of musical dance moves are most appealing to a potential mate?

In this experiment 62 heterosexual adults watched a series of 30-second point-light animation clips of both men and women dancing to music from the techno, pop and Latin genres. Luck and the team had previously rated each video on seven different body-movement-related criteria: 1) body symmetry, 2) hip-body ratio, 3) shoulder-hip ratio, 4) hip-knee phase angle, 5) shoulder-hip angle, 6) hip wiggle and 7) downforce. The video watchers were asked to rate the dancers for femininity/masculinity, sensuality, sexiness, mood, and interestingness.

For women watching men, 'downforce' was most strongly related to ratings of sensuality. Men who danced with a lighter touch, making more use of bounce, for example, were perceived as more sensual. In their final conclusions, the researchers considered this aspect of the male physical display to be the best indicator of attractiveness in dance.

In contrast, men watching women found 'hip-body ratio' to be more indicative of sensuality, sexiness and positive mood. 'Hip-knee phase angle' (the degree of synchrony between the movement of the hip and knee) was positively related to perceived mood and interestingness of the dancer.

This study shows that the way men and women respond to music by dancing leads to a number of impressions in potential romantic partners. In fact, movement to music was found to be a more helpful cue to attractiveness in this study than many of the more static measures of body symmetry or ratios. Music therefore provides an important medium by which we can display visual attractiveness cues through the synchronised movement of our bodies. Speaking from personal experience, this all seems very convincing. I met my partner through a salsa event a few years ago and to this day he captivates me when he dances.

## Music for romance

Now that this chapter is firmly placed in a romantic frame of mind I will move on to look at the use of music in other courtship behaviours and the potential importance of music for the success or failure of such endeavours. In this section we will see how music can attract a mate before you even meet them and can influence their reactions to a subsequent romantic approach.

### Match making

Your musical likes and dislikes speak volumes to a potential mate. That is one reason why dating agencies all over the world ask about musical preferences before attempting to pair people up. In Chapter 3 I discussed the importance of music as a social signal for teenagers. As an adult your musical preference remains an important part of your social identity.

Differences in musical taste are unlikely to be a deal breaker for people choosing who to date but similarities in tastes are a key variable in early attraction. A study at a midwestern United States university carried out by Dolf Zillmann and Azra Bhatia[14] looked at 239 heterosexual undergraduates' evaluations of a potential date based on a videotaped presentation. Everything was kept the same about the videos except that the potential suitor talked about her or his love of classical, country, soft rock, or heavy metal music.

A love for country music was associated with a slight lowering of ratings given by both men and women. A love of heavy metal music made men more attractive to women but a similar musical fascination made women less attractive to men. The reverse interaction was true for classical music, which lowered the attraction of men but increased ratings for women.

What I find more interesting than the general trend in genre reactions in this study (which is naturally biased by the location and age range of the participants) is the perceived importance of having matched tastes, which varied by gender. Women appeared to care less about whether a man shared their musical tastes but this same factor had a big influence on men who, whatever the genre, were more likely to give high ratings to a woman if she shared their musical tastes.

This is one area of research where we would benefit from new studies to track how our responses to and levels of attraction towards potential dates based on musical preferences may have changed as music has become more a part of everyday life. No doubt reactions to different musical genres depend on time and place in the world. The most important finding here is that when we are seeking a mate many of us place a heavy weighting on avoiding a music mismatch.

### Pick up line

Music not only acts as an attractor based on preferences, it can also impact more directly on the success of our courtship attempts.

Imagine the following scenario: you are a single, available woman (sorry gentlemen, but there is a reason for this request as you will find out below) and you are taking part in a survey about organic products. Your role in this research is to eat some organic and non-organic cookies and then to chat about your opinions of the two products with another person who is also taking part in the study. Could background music affect your responsiveness to a potential advance from this fellow participant? According to sneaky psychologists, it can.

The above scenario was part of an experiment conducted by Nicolas Guéguen and colleagues in 2010.[15] Unknown to the female volunteers in this study, their discussion partner for this organic cookie experiment was an actor who was in league with the researchers. The actor (or 'confederate') was a male who had been chosen specifically as someone that the female volunteer would be likely to find attractive, although not too attractive or people might be suspicious – about a '5' on a rating scale of 0–9.

This confederate had a script to follow during the experiment to ensure that he gave the same responses to every woman when discussing cookies. Before entering the main discussion room, the female participant was told that her discussion partner was late, and asked to wait in a separate room. In this waiting room background music was playing, music that had been pre-chosen by other people as either romantic or not romantic (neutral). She spent three minutes in the room before being summoned for the experiment.

The two strangers were then introduced by the experimenter in the main discussion room and had their five-minute chat about cookies. The experimenter came back into the room and announced that the study was over but that she needed two to three minutes to finalise the data. The experimenter then left the room.

During this period of time the confederate launched into the key phase of the whole experiment. According to the paper, 'he was instructed to smile and to say to the participant: "My name is Antoine, as you know. I think you are very nice and I was wondering if you would give me your phone number. I'll phone you later and we can have a drink together somewhere next week."'

The whole point of the study was to determine whether the female volunteer was more likely to give out her phone number if there had been romantic music playing in the waiting room before the fake cookie survey. It turned out that in the romantic music condition the man's success rate was 52 per cent; he got 23 out of 44 phone numbers. In the non-romantic, neutral music condition he got only twelve numbers.

In a recent follow-up study the same researcher group took their paradigm out on the streets.[16] In this case the male confederate (again he was called 'Antoine', but it is unclear if it was the same actor) approached ladies on the street to ask for a date when he was carrying a guitar case, a gym bag or nothing at all. Again there was a script for his approach to the unsuspecting members of the public and the researchers noted his success in getting phone numbers.

When he was accessory-free, Antoine's success rate was 14 per cent. When he was holding a sports bag this rate went down, though not significantly, to 9 per cent. When he carried a guitar case he was significantly more successful, with a 31 per cent phone number conversion rate.

The presence of music or a musical instrument does not, of course, guarantee that any eventual dates will be successful or that a person will even turn up to a date once they have had a chance to go away and think about the situation, but it does apparently help to create a mindset where individuals are more accepting of an on-the-spot romantic overture.

The scientists argue that these two studies demonstrate the effect of music and musicianship on immediate prosocial thoughts, choices and behavioural responses. Admittedly this is rather gender-biased work given that the research has only been done on a male approach to a female, but this general argument is supported by previous UK research where 'positive music' (that is, uptempo pop music that was perceived as 'uplifting') was associated with an increase in prosocial behaviours such as agreeing to distribute leaflets for a charity.[17]

How does the effect work? In the case of the cookie study it could be that the romantic music puts people in a better mood and this in turn makes them more likely to accept the charming confederate's advances. Or it could be a more direct effect whereby the romantic music primes congruent responsive behaviours. For example, the act of recalling past romantic actions and/or events from life is known to result in more chivalrous behaviour in males.[18] In the 'on the street' case it may be that in a young attractive man the appearance of being a musician is associated with additional physical and intellectual abilities. These intriguing possibilities still need to be picked apart, and looked at properly across genders, if we are to fully understand the effect of music and musicians on our heartstrings.

## Music and films

Cinema has used music longer than voices. The world of the silent film was far from silent, being filled with dramatic orchestral, piano and organ scores including some of the best film music ever made. You only have to watch the recent Oscar-winning silent film *The Artist* to experience the cinematic power of music in the absence of the human voice.

Music is undoubtedly intertwined with film thanks to its ability to trigger emotive responses in the listener. But how does this happen? And do films really *need* music? We have been talking romance for a while now so let's examine two of the other key functions of cinema: to trigger fear or joy, and to make us cry.

### Emotions

Have you ever watched a really scary film without the music? Most people that I know (I have been observing them slyly since I started to write this book) tend to do one of two things when a film reaches a really scary moment: they cover their eyes or stick their fingers in their ears. I am an ears person, every time.

This anecdotal evidence suggests that a great film soundtrack has a big influence on our emotional reactions; in the case of a scary film, silencing the expertly crafted fright music can be sufficient to render an otherwise unbearably scary moment watchable again.

Does film music really have the power to scare us? Our subjective feeling of fear is associated with the activity of several brain areas but in particular one small structure called the amygdala (from the Greek word for almond, as it is shaped like one), which sits more or less in the centre of your brain (see diagram on *page 83*). The amygdala is a relatively primitive brain structure that has reportedly changed very little throughout mammalian evolution.[19] It is part of the limbic system, which is associated with the regulation of emotional responses.

The amygdala sends out messages that trigger activity in our sympathetic nervous system, which regulates many aspects of body function including the famous 'fight or flight response' whereby our body prepares for action when faced with a threat: our breathing quickens, our pulse races as blood floods into our muscles, and we begin to sweat.

Numerous studies have shown that emotional music can trigger activity in the amygdala.[20] One patient who suffered amygdala damage reported that he could no longer experience the peak emotional responses to music that were common for him before his brain damage.[21] Another study of patients with amygdala damage found that they could no longer experience fear when listening to scary soundtracks such as the theme tune to *Jaws*.[22]

All this evidence suggests that scary music directly activates our brain fear centre; however, it is also likely that activation of the amygdala is linked to the context of the music, since the amygdala has an additional role in memory formation. Is it really the music that we find scary, or is there something magic going on between music and film?

Eran Eldar and colleagues[23] explored whether context is important to how much we feel moved by film music. Volunteers in their study rated novel 'scary', 'joyful' or 'neutral' music alone for arousal (low to high) and valence (negative to positive emotions). The volunteers then made a similar rating when each of the music clips was combined with twelve seconds of neutral, no-dialogue film, such as a scene where a car drives across a desert.

Sure enough the neutral music added no emotion to the neutral film clips, whereas the negative music made the same clips seem more scary (high arousal and negative emotion) and the positive music made things more joyful (high arousal and positive emotion). This result supports our suspicions that music can inject emotion into an otherwise bland and meaningless film scene.

Importantly, the people in this study also rated the films, the music and then the combination of music and film for their 'concrete content'. Concrete in this sense means that something is tangible or real as opposed to feeling abstract. The music in isolation was all rated as very low in concrete content, reflecting the fact that music on its own in this case means very little. The film clips with and without music, by contrast, were rated as significantly higher in concrete content.

One final key finding was that the addition of music significantly increased the concrete nature of the film. Therefore this study shows how music can give film its emotional overtones and film in return gives music a tangible meaning.[24]

What is happening in the brain when all this is going on, and more specifically in the amygdala? In a second phase of Eldar's experiment, new volunteers lay in an fMRI scanner and watched the film clips while they were paired with the positive (joyful), negative (scary) or neutral music. When people heard the negative music combined with the film there was greater activation in the amygdala compared to when they heard only the music or saw only the film clip. A similar pattern was identified for the positive music/film combination but this was less consistent, which makes sense since amygdala activation is more strongly associated with fear than happiness.[25]

The combination of fearful music and a neutral but concrete film clip therefore triggered a greater matched emotional reaction than either the music or the film alone, as rated by hand in the first study and as evidenced by brain activity in the second.

Overall, film music by itself can be mildly scary but when embedded in cinematic concrete context it has the power to enhance our sensory experience and to really frighten us; this film/music combination makes something more emotionally engaging than either watching or listening in isolation. The presence of film permits the meaning of the music to be directly interpreted in a similar way by everyone, something that is more variable if we just hear music on its own.[26] For example, we can easily confuse a film soundtrack as being romantic instead of dramatic when we are missing the film context.[27] In return, an otherwise neutral visual film scene gets enhanced emotional attention and engagement thanks to the music-related activation of our brain's limbic system.[28]

### Tears

Film music can be designed to do more than just scare us. It allows us to experience an enhanced wealth of emotions. I tried a recent experiment with this book in mind, where I watched the two films that are guaranteed to make me cry: *The Notebook* and *The Bridges of Madison County*. Both of the key scenes where I tend to break down (if you have seen these films then you know what I am talking about) have no language content, just beautiful music and heart-wrenching visual scenes. So I tried watching them without the music. Nothing: dry eyes. And I tell you something, I am never doing that again. It did not ruin the whole film – just the best part.

This personal experiment and my reaction raise an interesting related question. Why would I want to make myself cry with music? I was not in a particularly low mood on the days that I watched these films and in general I am not a fan of making myself miserable. This question is relevant to the larger question of why we choose to listen to sad music at all.

According to David Huron[29] the science behind sad music can be traced back to our brain's response to sad events in real life, such as heartbreak or the loss of a loved one. When genuine sad events befall us, our brain reacts to tears by releasing neurotransmitters into the brain that will alleviate the gut-wrenching emotion. That is why many people report feeling better, or at least numbed from their pain, after a good cry. When we listen to sad music in the absence of a sad trigger event we are creating a kind of 'pseudo-sadness' situation within ourselves, effectively tricking our minds into thinking we are terribly sad when in fact nothing is really wrong.

One particular neurotransmitter that may be a target for our 'pseudo-sadness' music listening behaviours is prolactin, a brain chemical that is naturally released in response to genuine grief. In the case of music listening, in the words of Huron himself, 'now you have the prolactin release without the psychic pain. So at the end of the day, you're actually feeling quite good.' Sad music in a film has the potential to raise the emotional stakes, stimulating a brain response that has an effect on how we feel when the titles roll.

This theory may explain why I did not enjoy my favourite sad films when I turned the sound down. No music = fewer tears = less cathartic release and not so much of a mental hug. So, I say three cheers for film music writers and their ability to take the emotional impact of the best stories to a higher level.

### Meaning

The final role of music in film is to help guide us towards an evaluation of meaning. This goes beyond the emotional meaning as described in the last few sections as music can also inject meaning regarding characterisation, including responses, reactions and intentions of actors.[30] These techniques and effects are inherited and adapted from earlier art forms such as opera.

The simplest form of musical meaning in film is the identification of genre, series and characters. Film music is full of 'leitmotifs', short repeating musical phrases that reoccur at various times throughout the film. Leitmotifs were famously used by Richard Wagner in his cycle of four operas, *Der Ring des Nibelungen*, with a similar aim of relating the audience to specific characters and situations. Most films nowadays have their own leitmotif, one that is related to the main theme tune, and that reoccurs throughout the action in order to reinforce the character of the individual film or film series (such as in the James Bond or Indiana Jones films, for example).

Film characters can also have their own personal leitmotifs to mark their presence in the story, either physically or in the minds of other characters on the screen. This is sometimes referred to as the musical indicator or 'mark'. The *Superman* films provide a prime example of this technique. For the audience, the sound of that classical triad-based motif signals to us that the man of steel is on his way and that the chaotic destruction unfolding on the screen will soon be fixed. Similarly, thanks to the use of a simple two-note motif in the *Jaws* films, you don't need to see a fin in the water to know that trouble is close by.

A film soundtrack can also lead us to understand far more subtle aspects of characterisation. For example, consider *The Artist*, the excellent Oscar-winning silent film starring the talented Jean Dujardin and Bérénice Bejo as George Valentin and Peppy Miller. The vast majority of this film contains no clue as to the feelings or plans of the two main characters other than their facial and body reactions and the incidental music that accompanies the entire film.

In this style of film, the music is an integral part of the action description for the audience, which guides evaluation and predictions for what might happen next. Aspects of these soundtracks help us to understand what is happening and whether we should regard this change of events in a positive or negative way. This is often referred to as the use of *idée fixe*, a technique that probably predates leitmotifs in cinema and which was arguably far more important in the silent film genre. It represents the use of music to reveal hidden or invisible connections between characters (such as hidden passion or antagonism) or to indicate links between different elements in a plot.[31]

In conclusion, a film soundtrack, something many of us probably hardly notice until it is taken away, has the power to lead us gracefully and gently through the many layers of narrative, characterisation and plot twists within a film. It can take us to the heights of emotional reaction and reveal the hidden depths of a great story. You know where you are in a film thanks to the music.

## Music and sport

For the few, sport and exercise is a career choice but for the majority of us it is a leisure activity that we engage in for fun and/or health benefits. Many of us also choose to watch sport in our free time and can devote our lifelong loyalty to a particular team or sportsperson. Whether as a participant or as a spectator, music plays an important role in sport and exercise in terms of motivation, performance and team spirit.

### Get moving!

In the previous chapter I gave examples of how music at different tempi and volumes can change the way we move around commercial spaces such as supermarkets. It should not come as a huge surprise then that music can help us move while we engage in sport. In the case of sport, however, it is usually the individual themselves that seeks out the music to try to help them keep moving.

Most of us expect to hear a certain type of music in the gym, a type of music that we assume is going to somehow assist us with our workout.[32] People also spend time designing and updating their own music playlists for workouts. Is all this music really helping?

It is now widely accepted that music can aid exercise effectiveness, which is defined in different ways depending on the exercise but can include measures such as how long someone continues to work out (endurance) or the amount of effort that they exert (strength and power).[33] The term used for music in this context is *ergogenic*, which means that it is an external agent that has a measurable impact on performance.

So caffeine is also ergogenic, as are performance-enhancing drugs. How does music have these kinds of effects?

Music works well as a blocker for the signals of mental tiredness and physical exhaustion that your brain receives during exercise. Listening to complex music (as opposed to simpler music) is thought to occupy a significant amount of our limited attention system and may therefore reduce the number of these tiredness messages that get through, or may reduce their effect on our reactions.[34] One of the results of this is that we lose track of how hard we have worked or how long we have been exercising. The typical reaction to this situation is to work out for longer; music 'colours' our impression of fatigue.[35]

If the only mechanism at play here is that of blocking out the world and thereby tricking us into working out for longer, then we might ask why music should be any more effective than audio books or podcasts. These options are popular with some people but their usage cannot compare to the vast majority who would prefer music. What is it within music that encourages us to exercise harder, for longer?

In two review articles published in 2012, Costas Karageorghis and David-Lee Priest summarised the research into music and exercise over the last decade, since the introduction of good controls and the use of standardised protocols recognised by sports bodies.[36] They identified a multitude of positive music effects on exercise other than a simple draw on our attention: triggering or regulating emotions, altering moods, evoking memories, psycho-physiological arousal, reducing inhibitions, and encouraging rhythmic movement. Music is doing a lot more for your workout than simply occupying your mind.

Pre-exercise music can be a useful way to stimulate arousal levels up to those which are needed for effective exercise. In one memorable experiment, researchers played either the theme from *Rocky* or silence before sending volunteers out on a 60m dash; the music condition led to faster times and physiological reactions that were consistent with a pre-stimulating agent, including increases in breathing rate and muscle tension.[37] Enjoyable music can also boost our confidence before going into an exercise routine, which may then have knock-on positive effects on success.[38]

During exercise, music can aid movement by acting as a synchronisation partner that in one study lengthened a treadmill-based routine by 15 per cent on average.[39] The overall average expected enhancement effect of music on people's (perceived) effort expenditure in low to moderate exercise is estimated at a reasonable 10 per cent.[40] The use of music before and during exercise has also been found to increase strength output as measured by the amount of time people are able to hold a weight out in front of them at arm's length and shoulder height.

The newest music contributions to the exercise world are programs that adapt themselves to the pace and pattern of the user, using changing rhythms to encourage optimum movement and to 'reward' people when they keep up with the pace.[41] So far these music programs have found some success with reported motivation and focus but the jury is still out as to whether the music really helps people move to a certain pace or significantly reduces how exhausted they feel.[42] One factor that needs to be considered is whether people like the music, since preference for music has been shown to have a measurable effect on important exercise outcomes such as the (perceived) rate of exertion.[43]

The tempo of music is one of the most crucial aspects that may alter exercise outcomes; this varies little from individual to individual. When it comes to motivation, the music that makes me feel good during exercise relates to my individual preferences and previous associations with the music.[44]

When it comes to tempo, however, the current advice is that younger adults should be listening to music within the high tempo band of 125–140 beats per minute when engaged in repetitive, aerobic-type activity.[45] At the time of writing there is not enough research on older adults to be able to draw a comparable figure.

Conversely, medium tempo music apparently has enhanced effects on our perception of flow and motivation during exercise compared to fast or mixed-up tempos.[46] Interestingly, tempo may be less effective when removed from a musical context. When scientists have tried using just drumbeats, they have often found poorer outcomes compared to when those same tempo rhythms are embedded in normal music.[47]

Gender plays a role in responses to music in exercise as well. There is some evidence that women respond better than men to 'motivational' music in exercises such as circuit training, whereas men outperformed women in a condition where they listened to a simple metronome. In fact, the men did as well with the metronome as they did with the motivational music, which suggests a greater reliance on beat within music for pacing, whereas women get an extra boost from music content.[48]

One notable point about the music and exercise literature is that there are a number of published studies that report insubstantial or null impacts of music on performance. In some areas the number of such publications is significant enough for us to question whether music really has a reliable effect on everyone when it comes to all forms of exercise. However, the potential power of music in well-controlled studies to reduce fatigue and extend/enhance aerobic and strength performance is such that, overall, the findings advocate trying music if you are interested in upping exercise performance.

## Athletes

Trained athletes are often seen using music while training and before competing. During the London Olympic Games I watched swimmer after swimmer approach the pool in headphones, only removing them at the last minute before diving into the water. Ethiopia's Haile Gebrselassie famously requested that Scatman John's 'Scatman' be played before a world record attempt[49] while Olympic gold medal-winning shooter Suzy Balogh from Australia is partial to a wide range of music including Jamiroquai's 'Canned Heat' and the *Star Wars* theme before a competition.[50]

Athletes report using music as a motivational tool and some claim that it really makes them work harder.[51] I have no doubt that in a packed arena full of screaming and chanting people it is very useful to be able to block out distractions and focus on the all-important mental preparation before a race, bout, match or performance. But is there any truth in the belief that music can actually aid top athletic achievements?

A recent study of the effects of music on high-intensity short-term exercise in trained athletes was carried out by a research group in Tunisia.[52] The authors selected high tempo music (120–140 beats per minute) and had twelve male athletes either listen to the music or silence during a ten-minute warm-up before they performed the Wingate test, a measure of peak anaerobic power in the legs. The athletes then did the test again after a 48-hour recovery period. Heart rate and measures of fatigue were not affected by the presence or absence of music but power output during the test was significantly higher after the music-based warm-up compared to silence.

Another recent study suggests that music may be good for team sports as well as individual performance.[53] Researchers at the Institute for Sports Science at the University of Hannover in Germany presented findings that suggested synchronised rhythmic music is associated with better performance of a football team. Compared to hearing nothing or asynchronous music (through wireless headphones), players who heard synchronised fast music performed better on measures of teamwork, including frequency and accuracy of passes.

Unfortunately the results of both these studies, while convincing, do not allow us to better understand *why* the researchers found better individual or team performance, as they reported no effect of the music on any direct physiological or psychological measures – only performance output. It could be the case that athletes perform better in those conditions because they simply believe music is good for them.

Two studies have actually suggested that music may be more beneficial for untrained people when compared to trained athletes.[54] The music in these studies had a better effect on positive outlook following an exercise session in untrained people, a finding which suggests that music may be most beneficial to those starting out in a new sport as opposed to those who already have their own routines and habits. The authors also speculated that trained athletes benefit more from intense mental concentration during their sport and music that they are not used to could provide an unwelcome drain on their precious mental resources.

One promising area in the linking of music to athletic prowess is the effect of music on synchronised movements. One study tested the performance of elite triathletes on a treadmill where they had to run hard until they could run no more. In the presence of synchronous music the athletes were able to endure the run for longer and reported better mood and physical reactions after the run compared to when they heard neutral music or nothing at all. The authors argued that the synchronised music helped to encourage exercise that was more oxygen-efficient by stimulating the athletes into a more rhythmic and regular pattern of movement; their running was effectively made more economical.[55]

Athletes who are used to music as part of their rigorous and extensive training regime would not go without it in a major competition. Luckily modern music technology means that they can now bring their musical sports world into the international arena for us all to see. This display of sporting headphone use does not mean, however, that music is necessary or even beneficial for elite athletes. Attempts to understand exactly why music can mentally influence athletes have often struggled to pin down really convincing patterns that are true for one person as much as the next.[56] This difficulty at least partly stems from the fact that the effects of musical listening in elite sportsmen and women are highly influenced by the individual's sport of choice, their personal habits during a lifetime of training and, crucially, their preferences for techniques that help reduce anxiety and get them 'in the zone'.[57]

♪

In this chapter we have seen that music has once again crept into our daily life, this time during activities that we enjoy for relaxation, for energy, for health and for escapism. Music is frequently an essential partner to our precious free time, whether we prefer to spend it dancing the night away in a club, curled up on the sofa watching a good film, or jogging around the local park. The music in these activities is an enhancing agent, moving us to a higher level in every sense: physical, psychological and emotional.

Throughout the book so far we have seen evidence that our reaction to music depends very much on our own life experience with music and our own preferences. In the next section of the book we will move from looking at general adult life (work and play) to viewing the broader context of our whole lives. It is time to look at how we develop these musical personalities and how they can influence our life journeys.

In the next chapter we will move on to a subject that I find uniquely fascinating within the field of music psychology: memory. I will break down the different components and influences of music on our minds to answer the question of why musical memory is so powerful. Why does hearing a tune take you right back to that special event or person? Why is it that musical memory seems to survive in many cases when other memory systems are beginning to fail or are damaged by trauma? And why do musical memories regularly pop into our head and then repeat themselves, stuck on a loop, driving us mad? The stories of musical memory portray the development and power of your life soundtrack.

# PART III

# Music across
# the lifespan

## Chapter 7
# Music and memory

*'What I like my music to do to me is awaken*
*the ghosts inside of me. Not the demons,*
*you understand, but the ghosts'*
DAVID BOWIE

I have always been fascinated by memory. I have explored many different aspects of human psychology with relation to our musical lives, but whichever way I turn, the subject of memory appears. When I am examining the abilities of amusics, I end up looking at memory function. When I am researching how music can aid language learning,[1] I find myself talking about the important role of memory in the process. Even when I am looking at the positive effects of music in cancer care the importance of each person's musical memory begins to take centre stage.

What is memory? To most people memory is the part of the mind that helps us remember a shopping list or a pin number while also seeming to delight in hiding the last known location of our keys. To me, memory is the key to understanding our experience of consciousness, learning and sense of identity; it is the glue that holds us in the present moment, allowing us to reflect on the past and plan for the future. We'll see later in this chapter how the destruction of memory can have a devastating impact.

The term memory encompasses many different processes that enable us to hold on to and manipulate information and life events.[2] There are two main memory systems discussed in this chapter that I will elaborate on before we begin: episodic and semantic memory.

Episodic memory is memory for events in time while semantic memory is static knowledge. Consider an orange (I just happen to be eating one as I write): an episodic memory for an orange could be the memory of a shopping trip the last time you bought one or the memory of a fantastic meal that featured orange; a semantic memory by comparison would be the knowledge of how to eat an orange or how you might cook with one.

Episodic memories have a temporal element to them, meaning they can be replayed in your mind's eye. They can be autobiographical too, if they are your memories for events that have happened to you. With these kinds of memories people can often re-imagine themselves in that situation, relying on the ability to indulge in what the psychologist Endel Tulving referred to as 'mental time travel'.

But there is also another, secret memory system. Implicit memories are the kinds of knowledge that we find hard to describe to another person, typically our skills and abilities such as playing a musical instrument, riding a bike, driving, swimming or walking. It is impossible to verbally describe all the knowledge necessary to ride a bike – you can guide a person, but ultimately the new learner will just have to get on a bike and have a go. They need to establish their own implicit memories for the various muscle movements, balance challenges and visual skills necessary to accomplish this complex activity. Implicit memories are built subconsciously and quietly support our activities as we go about daily life.

These different memory systems may be partly distinct but they also overlap and interact. The majority of semantic memories require the initial input of an episodic memory.

Implicit memories can also begin life as a series of facts and events that are very fresh in our minds and that then gradually melt away into implicit memories as they no longer require conscious access or attention. Anyone who has learned a skill will recognise this process of going from laborious, focused thought to much more effortless and automatic skill. The memory systems that I have described are therefore not separate 'storage boxes' in our minds but intertwined processes that play different roles depending on the task we are trying to accomplish or the problem we are trying to solve. They are part of a larger network that functions together to allow us to understand and learn about the world around us.

In this chapter I will take you on a journey through musical memory, and in particular through the more extreme manifestations of our tendency to remember, forget, and be chased around by our musical past. By looking at the unusual and often less understood features of musical memory, the exceptional cases of skill and loss, we gain a unique perspective and understanding of the more everyday interactions that we all experience with our musical minds.

In three tales we will now explore musical memory: I call these tales 'the star', 'the survivor' and 'the miscreant'.

## 'The star' – expert musicians

Musicians face a unique challenge if they want to make it as a world-class performer. For the last 200 years or so, the fashion has been to play from memory in concert. This is not true of all kinds of music performances but it is typified most strongly in the virtuoso style, where 'the star' musician aims to display their skill on the stage. You will even see performance from memory featured in competitions for young musicians nowadays, and I recall from my teaching days that there were more points available to exam candidates who could play their pieces from memory.

I will confess now: as a performer, my musical memory is pretty terrible. I never encouraged my students to play from memory, preferring them to have the score available just in case they suddenly went blank. This preference no doubt sprang from my own experience; I never performed from memory. Quite apart from my stage fright, which meant my public performances were few and far between, I was always a visual musician. When I think of music or attempt to play from memory I see the notes, the score, rolling in front of my eyes. Over time I convinced myself that some people were naturally good at playing from memory and that I was simply not one of them.

My assumption seemed to be supported when later in life I went to judge music competitions and saw candidates playing from memory. It all looked so effortless ... and completely impossible. Then there are the tales of music memory experts. In particular there is the often-told story of the early 20th-century conductor Arturo Toscanini, which goes something like this:

Just before the start of a big concert, an agitated musician from the orchestra hurried up to Toscanini, who was waiting for his cue to go on stage. The desperate musician reported to his conductor that the key for the lowest note on his bassoon was broken beyond repair and at such short notice, nothing could be done – surely he could not play in the concert? Toscanini sighed, shaded his eyes with his hand, thought for a moment, and replied: 'It's all right – that note does not occur in tonight's concert.'

Not only did Toscanini apparently know every note for every orchestral instrument in that concert (probably around 70 musicians and at least two hours of music), but it has been estimated that he knew by heart every note for every instrument of about 250 symphonies, the words and music for 100 operas, plus volumes of chamber music, piano, cello and violin music, and songs. How on earth is a memory feat like that possible?

I only learned later in life, once I began my PhD, that musical memory is a skill, not a gift, one that develops with practice and that relies on the types of techniques that just about any memory expert will use, adapted for musical purposes.

Memory experts exist in all walks of life and the World Memory Championship is the largest gathering of such individuals. The World Memory Championships contain many different disciplines revolving around tasks such as remembering images, numbers, poems, dates, or packs of cards.[3]

In order to attain grand master status a person must: 1) memorise the order of 520 randomly shuffled cards (ten complete packs) in one hour; 2) memorise 1,000 random numbers in one hour; 3) remember the order of a randomly shuffled single deck of 52 cards in two minutes or less. Sounds utterly impossible. However, as of September 2013 there were 133 memory grand masters from eighteen countries.[4]

What all these grand masters of memory and expert musicians have in common is a great deal of hard work in developing strategies – mnemonics – to help them expand the basic performance ability of their memory, which is really no different to yours or mine. Memory is not a muscle, you can't just work it and it will get bigger. Memory is more like a bag of tools, and you can accomplish just about anything if you put in the time and effort to learn how to use your tools well.

### Learning

The first group of important mnemonic techniques is based on learning to manipulate the information as it is being learned, at the point of encoding. Good memory is as much about how the information goes in as how you attempt to get it out again.

The first important encoding strategy for any memory

expert is to reduce apparently large bits of information to smaller bite-size chunks. The task of breaking information down is called chunking (no, really) and memory experts achieve this by creating links between smaller bits of information, packing them together, and then attempting to remember these more meaningful chunks as opposed to their component parts.

A memory expert who wants to remember a shuffled pack of cards might represent each of the cards as a meaningful character, an object or a location, as opposed to an abstract card. They will then create stories or journeys involving these characters, objects and so on, thereby linking them together in their mind. Eventually all they have to know in order to recall the whole pack of cards is one story, as opposed to all the items from which the story was created.

A musical memory expert, by the same token, will not try to remember every note. Before they even play or sing a note they will study the musical score and identify points where larger melodies or movements in the music fuse into meaningful chunks. They then focus on remembering these large sections of the music as one.[5]

An expert musician will use their long-term knowledge of music, of scales, arpeggios, cadences and harmonic relations, to give meaningful forms to large sections of the music[6]. This process of analysis has been found to benefit final performance[7] and has been studied in both classical[8] and jazz performers[9] to date.

Musicians see meaning and structure in music naturally, without any instruction to do so. Even I recognise the consequences of subconsciously structuring music in this way. An example would be when my guitar teacher would point to my music and say, 'Can you please begin here?' I would often wince and reply, 'Well, I can start about two bars earlier if you like – that would be much easier.' It is easier to start in some places compared to others because these places mark the subconscious boundaries that we create as a consequence of the learning process.

My musical memory would be a lot better than it is today if I had got into the habit of using these meaningful musical structures, creating sections and playing each section from memory, making each one bigger over time; and then slowly linking them together so they eventually became one piece, one memory. Studies have closely observed such processes when professional musicians learn a new piece of music and have noted their importance for performance success.[10]

### Retrieving memories

Structures in musical memory are also important when it comes to the other end of the process, retrieving the information we want. I think of this as a process akin to fishing: somewhere in that deep, dark lake of your mind is a memory that you want to get at and the best way to bring in that fish is to use a good rod. For our purposes, this means that we stand the best chance of retrieving information from memory if we use a good retrieval structure.

Structural bars, the bars where musicians prefer to start and stop, are a key to the retrieval of music. Musicians practice their structural bars more, on average, compared to non-structural bars, reflecting their importance in retrieval.[11] Aaron Williamon[12] from the Royal College of Music (UK) was the first to show that you can see the consequences of using retrieval structures in music, by looking at the way that a musician's brain reacts to viewing music.

Williamon asked six musicians to learn the Prelude in A Minor from J.S. Bach's *Well Tempered Clavier II (BWV 889)*. Once they had learned the piece, they were asked to identify bars in the music that they considered to be structural. The following task was visual recognition: the musicians were shown several bars and asked to say if they were from the prelude or not. During the task, the researchers measured brain responses using an electroencephalogram or EEG.

Overall, the musicians were faster at correctly identifying structural bars compared to non-structural bars, indicating that these more important parts of the music were easier to spot. Not only this, but the identification of structural bars was associated with a unique pattern of brain activity, an exaggerated negative peak in the electrical signal at around 300–400 milliseconds after the bar was shown, emerging from the right-central area of the brain. This type of pattern is associated with the retrieval of complex, meaningful structures. This result may therefore be the first indicator of a retrieval structure in the musical mind.

Once a performer has chunked their music into meaningful units and created reliable retrieval structures, the next and final step is simple: practice, practice and more practice.

The aim of practice once a piece is learned is to speed up recall; to automatise the memory. By this method a musician will activate the implicit memory system, as we do in many other everyday activities such as learning to ride a bike or drive a car. Over time and with practice, a once-complex conscious activity no longer requires quite so much thought. This transformation from high- to low-attention memory processing is especially important for musical expertise because of the high level of demand made on skilled motor coordination during performance.

Eventually, recalling a large piece of music should feel relatively effortless, and it is at this point that a performer really becomes flexible and skilled with the demands of performance itself. Once the notes can be retrieved, in the right order, then the musician can focus almost entirely on the fine art of musical communication, the nuances of an emotional performance.

## 'The star' – all of us

Amazing musical memory is not just the preserve of world-class performers. My musical memory as a performer may be poor but there is nothing wrong with my memory for 1960s Motown, the Beatles' back catalogue, or Beethoven's symphonies. I can play them all in my head anytime, anywhere.

When I tell people that I study musical memory they often ask me why they have such a great memory for music and lyrics but can't remember important dates or all the items on their shopping list. What makes musical memory so powerful by comparison?

Let's start by blowing this illusion apart. Our memory for music on first hearing it is pretty terrible. Andrea Halpern and Daniel Müllensiefen[13] presented 63 undergraduate students with 40 unfamiliar short tunes. They then tested memory for these new tunes when they were buried among 80 test tunes. Memory performance across the undergraduates was only barely above chance; this was a difficult task.

Changing the instrument during the test made memory judgements even worse, indicating how fragile and shaky our first memories for new music can be. This result also suggests that when we first hear music we are particularly attracted to the 'surface' features, the nature of the actual sound or speed, and pay less attention to the deeper structures, harmonies and/or rhythms that are present.

To give you an idea of how poor this level of memory performance really is, we can compare it to our memory for photos. In 1973 Lionel Standing[14] presented volunteers with a collection of up to 10,000 novel photographs. He was hoping to demonstrate the limits of the long-term memory system and you would assume that with a maximum of 10,000 images he had gone rather overboard. In fact, he found an amazing level of performance and demonstrated that our memory for images is far superior compared to memory for words. People who were shown all 10,000 new images were estimated to have retained 6,600 when tested only two days later.

How do we reconcile our poor initial memory for new music against the impression that we all have large and accurate musical libraries in our heads, filed with thousands of tunes, songs and instrumental pieces?

Research carried out on our long-term musical memories says we are right to have faith in our mental musical store. When we test recall of familiar and favourite music we see evidence for the amazing speed and accuracy of musical memory, even in individuals who have not had a single day of musical training.

Daniel Levitin[15] asked volunteers to select a favourite piece of music from a large collection of CDs that he had in his lab. Once the volunteers had selected their favourite track they were asked to have a go at singing it. Levitin recorded their performance and measured it for accuracy against the original CD. The majority of people demonstrated 'absolute memory' for their favourite recording, meaning that they were able to reproduce the first pitch of the track within a very small margin of error.

What is more, this finding has recently been well replicated across six different European labs.[16] On average singers produced their favourite tracks a little flat, but the majority were able to either hit the exact right note of a favourite pop song or at least get within a semitone. Overall, it appears that our memory for our favourite music is very good.

So how do we go from a shaky impression of new music to an almost accurate blueprint of our favourite pieces in memory? The keys are time and exposure. To go back to the comparison of memory for new music with that for photographs, the difference is that music is complex, multi-layered and evolves over time. There is just so much more to absorb on the first listen than there is to see in a photograph.

When we first hear a piece of music we are attracted to the surface features of the sound, the qualities of the singer's voice and the timbres of all the different instruments. We are easily distracted by musical 'surprises', such as changes in key or tempo. It is the equivalent of being a kid in a large and exciting sweet shop – so much to enjoy but where to begin and what to try first?

Studies by Jay Dowling and colleagues[17] have shown how our memory for music develops over time after this first rush of listening excitement. Imagine this process as similar to that which happens when a house is built. Over the first few exposures to new music we put in the foundations of our house and create the skeleton structure: we build an idea of key (major or minor, and how these fluctuate) and the contour, the ups and downs of the tune. Over time, and with more exposure, we begin to add the bricks and windows to our house: we add in musical details such as the exact pitches, the different instruments. Finally we add the furnishings: the micro-variations in performance such as the accent of the singer or minute changes to tempo and volume.

It takes a lot of time and exposure to build a good musical memory but once it is built, like any well-built house, it is strong and long lasting. And unlike building a house, there is almost no effort required on the part of the listener. Your mind does the work for you; all you need to do is to listen.

### Boosting musical memory

We remember the music that we hear in different ways. Some pieces of music take longer (i.e. more exposures) to learn well whereas some appear to bury themselves in our memory relatively quickly. One factor that influences the speed and accuracy with which we remember new music is personal preference.

It makes sense that we might better remember what we

perceive to be 'good music' compared to 'bad music', because memory and emotion have strong links in our minds. The music we like is more arousing, meaning that we experience greater attention capture and engagement, which is then associated with better memory. Positive mood is also associated with better memory for novel music compared to negative mood.

Stephanie Stalinski and Glenn Schellenberg[18] demonstrated the power of the relationship between musical memory and liking. Fifty-five volunteers rated how much they liked 24 novel musical extracts that each lasted around fifteen seconds. There was then a ten-minute break wherein they filled out questionnaires, followed by a memory test where each person heard 48 pieces of music, 24 from the first phase of the experiment and 24 which were new but similar to the first set. Each person decided whether a musical clip was completely new or something that they had heard before.

The results were clear. Despite our pretty poor memory for novel music, the people in this study could remember enough of the short tunes for the researchers to be able to assess the impact of liking. Musical clips that were liked were remembered significantly better than tunes that were rated as neutral or disliked.

The researchers went further. They wondered what would happen if they tried a longer delay, which is more like what would happen in the real world. They tried a 24-hour delay and found the same result: liked music was remembered better. The effect also held when they tried different listening situations, and even when they told people of the upcoming memory test and asked them to try to remember the music by creating visual memories while listening.

Over time it makes sense that we remember music that we like, as we will clearly choose to listen to this music more often. This research, however, demonstrates that the impact of our initial reaction to music has a measurable effect on how well we remember what we hear after only one listen.

We also remember vocal music better than non-vocal music. Michael Weiss and colleagues reasoned that we may be more attuned to remember vocal music as compared to instrumental sounds as vocalisations are more biologically significant to us as humans.[19] They tested people's memory for melodies that were either sung or played on various instruments, both familiar (piano) and less familiar (marimba, banjo).

The researchers chose 32 unfamiliar folk tunes from the UK and Ireland for their study, which took place in Canada. The short melodies were sung by a female vocalist, who performed all the notes on the syllable 'la'. The researchers then generated instrumental versions of the vocal version that were perfectly matched in pitch, duration and amplitude. Each participant listened to sixteen of the melodies, four in each type of sound, followed by a questionnaire break and finally a memory test.

Memory was better for the vocal melodies compared to any of the other instruments, which did not differ from each other. Piano sounds were no better remembered than the marimba so we can rule out a simple effect of sound familiarity. The authors reasoned that, similar to liking, vocal music may stimulate higher arousal and attention engagement in listeners, an effect that may be driven by a biological propensity to be attracted to the human voice over musical instruments.

All the experiments in the last section demonstrate that multiple factors influence how well we remember new music, and no doubt there are many influences yet to be discovered and documented. All the factors, including our liking response and apparent attraction to vocal music, contribute to the eventual laying down of strong and long-lasting musical memories.

### Name that tune – in 400 milliseconds or less

I keep saying that musical memories are super strong but where is the evidence?

One indicator of the power of musical memory is the 'plink study'. Carol Krumhansl[20] investigated the processes underlying musical memory by presenting people with the smallest examples of music that you can imagine; 300 and 400 millisecond 'plinks'. If you go to your favourite music player and play a piece for just one second then you will appreciate how little you really hear in a plink of around a third of that time.

Krumhansl played people plinks of music from the 1960s through to the 2000s and asked them to name the artist and the title as well as the decade of release, style (a broader and more reliable category than genre), and the emotional content. Sounds impossible, right?

The volunteers in Krumhansl's study had a good amount of musical training (around ten years) and were reasonably avid music listeners (an average of around 20 hours a week), but they were young adults and certainly not experienced musicians or music writers / critics. They listened to 28 musical plinks in total, chosen from top songs in lists by *Rolling Stone*, *Billboard* and *Blender*. Nearly 30 per cent of the participants claimed to be able to recognise the songs after hearing only a 400-millisecond plink, and of this group 95 per cent correctly identified the title and artist.

The best recognised plinks were Britney Spears' 'Baby One More Time' and Aretha Franklin's 'Respect'. Also high in the recognition ratings were The Police's 'Every Breath You Take' and John Lennon's 'Imagine'. At the lower end were Louis Armstrong's 'Wonderful World', Coldplay's 'Viva La Vida' and U2's 'Beautiful Day'.

The volunteers who spotted the plinks were also good at identifying the release decade, suggesting that this information is recalled or inferred quickly along with the title and artist. Even when people were not able to spot the songs they were often able to identify emotional content and style. Krumhansl then tried a similar experiment with 300-millisecond plinks. As expected, accuracy went down but remained above 10 per cent.

Overall, the plink study shows that memory for well-known music is incredibly detailed and reliable; a miniscule extract can trigger recall of the whole song to the extent that people can identify the artist and title, and decade of release. The fact that emotional judgements and style were not always so tightly linked to correct identification tells us that these aspects of musical memory may be stored differently in our minds.

Interestingly, there was also a preference for older songs in the study, from the 1960s and 1970s, even though the participants were young adults. This result could be interpreted as an impact of more distinctive styles and recording techniques on memory; a 'uniqueness effect'. Or maybe songs from that era were associated with more iconic representations of history that were stronger in general episodic and semantic memory. Possibly there was an increase of exposure effect on memory, with the young adults having heard the music of their parents for longer than their own.

Or perhaps, as Krumhansl puts it, 'it may be better music': an interesting and, to my mind, not entirely fruitless argument.

Finally, Krumhansl used her study as a basis for estimating the capacity of musical memory. If you listen to twenty hours of music a week (like her volunteers) then you will hear an average of 22,000 songs every year (based on about three minutes' length each). Although that includes many repetitions it is still reasonable to assume that an average memory for a listener of this frequency would extend to hundreds of thousands, if not millions, of identifiable memorised pieces of music over a lifetime.

### It's a musical life

Another indicator of the power in musical memory is its longevity. David Rubin wrote about oral traditions[21]; how many folk, children's and tribal songs have remained in human culture for hundreds if not thousands of years without ever being written down. It appears that music can survive perfectly well relying only on human memory over countless generations.

Musical memory also survives well over the course of a single human lifetime. My grandma is an example of someone with an excellent and longstanding musical memory. She loves to sing and will very often come out with a tune just because you utter a phrase that reminds her of a song. She has a particularly good memory for songs she heard as a child or young woman, a feature of general memory called *the reminiscence bump*.

Studies have shown, in fact, that older listeners retain many important music memory skills such as the ability to recognise alterations to melodies, even though performance is slowed slightly in line with theories of cognitive ageing.[22] And as we shall see more in the next chapter, the music that provides comfort and stimulates memory most effectively in older people is most commonly the music that has been in their memory for the longest time, from their reminiscence bump.[23]

The fact that music memory lasts well for a lifetime is the basis for the popular radio format where a well-known individual tells the story of their life through their favourite music, for example the BBC Radio 4 programme, *Desert Island Discs*. Listening to an individual's memories told partly through their musical choices provides a unique insight into a person's experiences but also their personality and outlook.

Over our lifetimes, music becomes a part of who we are because it interweaves so well with our episodic memories for events and people.

In this section we have seen some of the true capabilities of musical memory. It may not be the most reliable memory system when it first hears a piece of music but, given time, it can build durable and long-lasting musical memories that easily mix with our life experiences to become a central part of who we are as people. In the next section I will look at the power of musical memory from a related angle: its ability to survive.

## 'The Survivor'

To anyone who has cared for an elderly individual it will come as no surprise that musical memory can often survive when other aspects of memory begin to fade. I have heard many heartwarming stories of individuals with dementia-related illnesses or Alzheimer's who find comfort in music and who may even manage to retrieve memories in its presence that otherwise appear to be lost.

A favourite anecdote that has stayed with me for a while (such that I cannot recall the source, I am afraid) was of a gentleman in a care home who had become largely immobile and very quiet. Most of the time he sat in his chair or lay in bed simply staring: it had been a while since any of the staff could remember him engaging in conversation. The man valued his privacy and preferred the door to his room to be closed during the day. The nurses were happy to oblige his wishes; they would always knock before entering and wait for his permission to enter.

One day the staff nurse became worried as the man did not respond when she knocked on his door. She tried once, twice, three times. No luck. At this point she decided to go in and make sure he was okay. She was greeted by the sight of him dancing round the room and singing to 'Rock Around the Clock' by Bill Haley and His Comets. Apparently a cleaner had left their radio in his room by accident during morning rounds.

From then onwards the nurses made sure that the man had access to music that he liked. He was still a quiet man but the music often put a smile on his face and encouraged him to chat more with residents and staff. A small difference perhaps, but a positive effect nonetheless.

At this point I would like to make it clear that music is no 'magic bullet' or cure for memory loss. Some individuals will never respond to music and others may prefer silence. The point rather is that musical memory can often survive even in extreme cases and can therefore be a method by which to reach someone who has suffered memory loss.

Perhaps the most compelling case of musical memory survival is that of Clive Wearing. In the early to mid-1980s Clive was reaching a high point in his career as a musicologist, keyboardist, singer and conductor. He was the choirmaster of the London Sinfonietta and director of the London Lassus Ensemble. He was a well-respected researcher and expert in early/Renaissance music and was given the prestigious role of managing the music for BBC Radio 3, a UK classical station, on the day Prince Charles wed Princess Diana. Clive was himself newly married to his second wife Deborah.

According to reports, sometime in March 1985 Clive fell ill with a headache and flu-like symptoms. His doctor prescribed painkillers and advised him to rest. His symptoms rapidly worsened and he was found wandering the streets in a confused state. He was taken to hospital where he began to experience seizures and fell into a coma. A brain scan revealed the terrible truth: Clive had contracted herpes simplex encephalitis, a rare but severe virus that attacks the central nervous system from within the brain.

While in a coma, Clive's brain swelled with infection and was crushed against his skull. For most people this condition is fatal, so doctors were pleasantly surprised when Clive awoke from his coma. However, it quickly became apparent that all was not well. Clive remained confused and did not seem to remember anything about his life. Such confusion is not unusual after a prolonged period of unconsciousness but Clive did not show any signs of recovery as the weeks and months went by. His wife Deborah has said since that 'the virus caused a hole in his brain and all the memories fell out'.

The swelling in Clive's brain had deprived several vital neural structures of oxygen and the cells had subsequently died. The most severe damage was within the frontal lobe and the brain areas that support memory function. Like many with frontal lobe damage, Clive's personality changed and he experiences waves of emotion and anxiety that he is unable to control. Unlike most people, however, Clive has a deep and dense amnesia, or memory loss; arguably the worst case in medical history.

As a result of his illness Clive has lost the majority of his life's memories and is unable to make any new ones. These conditions are known as retrograde and anterograde amnesia, respectively. In reality this means Clive has little to no idea of his past or conception of the future. He is stuck in a time window of a few seconds – the present moment. You can ask him a question but by the time he gets a few sentences into his answer he will have forgotten what you said. That is the length of his memory span.

Two things seem to have survived this dreadful destruction, nearly 30 years on: Clive's love for his wife Deborah, and his music. There have been a few documentaries of Clive over the years and if you watch one you will see that he greets Deborah with joy and rapture whenever she walks into a room, as if he has not seen her for years, even if she has just stepped out to make tea. And Clive still enjoys playing the piano.

The videos I have seen show Clive playing from a musical score, so even though he may not be able to play from memory any more (no one has ever confirmed to me that he can) he retains the memory of how to sight read music. He also plays with emotional inflection, showing that some of the techniques he once learned about the art of musical performance remain with him: all this despite having no episodic memories of his musical training or his illustrious and successful musical career.

Clive may be an extreme case of memory loss but he is not alone. In 2012 Carsten Finke and collagues[24] reported the case of an amnesic cellist. The German patient, known only as 'PM', suffered from the same rare illness as Clive and also had severe damage to his memory. His doctors had no idea that he could still remember music until he was spotted playing his cello at home by neighbours. PM had not wanted to play for anyone since his recovery: he felt he was no longer very good. This fact alone suggests that PM had some memory, deep down, for his previous musical abilities.

Spurred on by this discovery, the doctors carried out tests on PM's musical memory to see which elements may have survived. They played him two pieces of music at a time and asked him which he recognised. One of the two pieces was always a well-known concerto or sonata that he would have heard before his illness, such as the first movement from Mendelssohn's Violin Concerto in E minor (1843). The other was a more recent piece, similar in style and instrumentals but composed after his illness, such as the Andante/Reflection piece from Max Richter's *Waltz with Bashir* soundtrack (2008). PM successfully identified 93 per cent of the older pieces of music.

The doctors then played PM the new pieces later that same day. Even though he had no episodic memory of having heard them before, he was able to identify 77 per cent. This result suggests that not only has PM retained memories of music from his past but he is also capable of learning new music. This latter ability has been described as 'astonishing' by his doctors.

Finally, just to show that tales of music memory survival are not limited to cases of herpes encephalitis patients, Séverine Samson and her colleagues have reported relatively spared memory for music in two different brain disorders, medically intractable epilepsy and Alzheimer's, despite both populations having severe verbal memory impairments.[25]

The burning question is: how and why does musical memory survive in these and other cases of memory loss. Is musical memory special?[26]

There are a number of reasons to suspect that the answer to this question is 'yes'. Some of these reasons have to do with the memorable structure of music, which I have already outlined in the section on musical memory as 'The Star' (page 171). I also believe that musical memories survive because of the way they are processed in our minds.

Firstly, for many people music is a motor skill (as for Clive and PM), like riding a bike. Not a great deal is known about what happens to memories when a skill moves from requiring great demands on our attention and focus (when we first learn to walk or drive a car) to being more automatic; from being conscious to non-conscious. But we do know that memories move from the systems that demand heavy resources, episodic and semantic memory, into the more low-demand implicit memory system.[27] This means that when music becomes a skill, when it becomes a habit, it gains a great deal of power in the mind in terms of longevity and resistance to decay.

For someone who has had a degree of musical training, musical memory also becomes partly procedural – a term used to refer to the motor- or movement-based aspect of memory. Amnesia and other memory disorders are characterised by the loss of conscious memory processes while the implicit procedural memory systems are, by comparison, spared.[28]

Clive and PM may have lost access to the episodic memories of their music lessons and careers but they do not need to access these conscious memories in order to be able to play their instruments. The rest of us do not need to remember our childhood cycle lessons in order to be able to ride a bike.

Another reason why musical memories survive is again linked to the implicit memory system but has to do with emotional reactions. Our emotional responses to music are often formed through conditioned responses; for example, I am more likely to have a positive emotional reaction to music in a major key as my memories of happy music, as a Western tonal music listener, have been mostly linked to music in the major key. Conditioned emotional responses such as this also tend to survive in memory disorders.

There are some physical clues in the brain as to why the implicit memory system survives well in extreme cases of memory loss. Emotional reactions are at least partly driven by the activity of central brain systems such as the amygdala. In previous chapters we discussed how amygdala activation has frequently been measured in response to hearing emotional music.

The amygdala, with its central location, has a higher likelihood of surviving brain damage as compared to an area such as the frontal cortex when it comes to brain swelling or a blow to the head. Therefore an individual may lose the conscious memories of why a piece of music causes them to feel a certain way (thanks to the destruction of areas around the frontal cortex) but still experience the core feeling (thanks to the activity of the amygdala).

So, to sum up, apart from the nature of music itself, musical memories survive at least in part because music activates brain systems that 1) are more likely to survive the more common types of brain damage, and 2) drive non-conscious and conditioned implicit responses to stimuli, such as motor and emotional behaviours. Musical memories really do, in every sense, become part of our inner being.

## 'The Miscreant'

So far in this chapter I have talked about the great and good of musical memory; the natural learner and the strong survivor. In the interests of fairness and giving a balanced view, it is only right that I finish this chapter with a discussion of the naughty side of musical memory.

Ever had a tune stuck in your head? A little ditty or perhaps even a longer song or musical piece that goes round and round in your mind's ear? If the statistics are right then over 90 per cent of you should be nodding 'yes' at this stage.[29] If you have never experienced a tune stuck in your head then you are in rare company. Some people experience repeating music in their minds so frequently that they claim to have an almost constant musical soundtrack to their daily lives.[30]

We currently refer to this phenomenon as involuntary musical imagery, but in everyday lingo it is most commonly known as an 'earworm', a translation of the German term *Ohrwurm*. This experience has had many labels in the past, including 'brain worm', 'sticky music',[31] 'cognitive itch'[32] and 'stuck song syndrome'.[33] In my lab, day in and day out, we call these stuck tunes earworms, so I will use that term from now on. Let's blow a few false assumptions out of the water first.

*Fact 1:* Earworms are not always annoying. When you first ask people about their earworms they will often tell you about the experiences or episodes that get on their nerves. However, if you look at large population surveys or take diary studies of people's reactions at the time of each episode, you find that the majority of earworms are actually not bothersome (rated as 'neutral') or are even enjoyable.[34]

In my own research I ask people how they control or try to cure their earworms. I have a sizeable number of responses that say something akin to 'Why would I want to control my earworms? They don't bother me and sometimes they keep me company.'

*Fact 2:* Earworms are not always pop songs or jingles. As much as the advertising industry would like to believe that we only get short, catchy tunes stuck in our heads, I can give you hundreds of examples of people who get complex music stuck in their heads, including classical works, modern jazz and new age music. It is true to say that the majority of earworms that I have been told about to date are melodic, vocal and simple, but to deny the existence of other kinds of earworms would be to ignore important information about the possible causes of the experience.

*Fact 3:* Musicians do not get them more often. This is not a closed issue but present research suggests that it is not those with the most musical training who experience the most frequent and/or longest episodes of earworms. In fact musicians with the highest levels of training (more than fifteen years) often report fewer earworms than people with less training.[35]

Our research has found that people who enjoy music every day, in particular those who like to sing along, report the most habitual and recurring earworms.[36] A nice side effect of this pattern in the data is that those people who like a good singsong are also more likely to enjoy their earworms.

A number of studies have tried to identify traits that predict higher risk of frequent or more disturbing earworm experiences. An interesting concept in this area is 'transliminality'. If

you are the kind of person who measures high on transliminality then you are more sensitive to recognising thoughts and
feelings that originate in the non-conscious mind. Another
way to put it is to imagine that a layer or barrier exists between
our conscious and non-conscious mental life. This barrier is
more permeable in people who have high transliminality.

Mike Wammes and Imants Baruss reported that individuals who were high in transliminality were more likely to
report persistent and distracting earworms compared to those
who scored low on the same dimension.[37]

Other studies have reported a link between earworms
and neuroticism,[38] and between earworms and nonclinical
obsessive-compulsive traits.[39] No doubt other individual factors will emerge over time but it is interesting that at present
most of the traits identified are marked by a tendency towards
rumination, being more likely to focus on and worry about
past or present events.

Studying the type of people who get earworms is one way
of trying to get at the question of why they happen. Another
way is to explore the circumstances under which they appear
in daily life. That was the aim of a study of mine in which I
analysed hundreds of earworm stories about why tunes got
stuck in people's heads.[40] To be clear, only about a quarter of
people in the study claimed to have any idea why a tune was
stuck in their head, which leaves us a lot of unaccounted for
earworm episodes.

### What triggers earworms?

When people were able to describe the circumstances of their
earworm they most often described recent and repeated exposure to the tune that was stuck in their head. This finding
aligns with Oliver Sacks' idea that the preponderance of easily accessible music in the modern world is at least partly to
blame for the frequency of earworms.

But the prevalence of modern music can't be the whole story; we know that earworms were a well-known phenomenon long before the modern age of ubiquitous recorded music. In 1876 Mark Twain wrote a short story entitled 'A Literary Nightmare', in which he describes a jingle getting stuck in his head and disrupting his concentration level so much that he is forced to pass it on to someone else in order to get rid of the experience.

Another common trigger of earworms, one that has nothing to do with hearing music, is the activity of involuntary memory. To give an example, one of the people in my study described seeing a licence plate that reminded her of the title of a Michael Jackson song ('PYT'), and for the rest of the day that tune was stuck in her head, even though she had not heard it for a long time.

We are a long way from understanding why memory 'pops' in this way between thoughts[41] – between things we see and hear in the world and related images or sounds in our minds.[42] From findings like the Michael Jackson story above, however, we can see that mind popping is a strong trigger for earworms. Short of sitting in a dark room with nothing to see or hear, there is little we can do to control this type of mental activity. Mind popping appears to be a natural consequence of the way our memories operate, and as long as music is held in our memory then there is a chance that it will be triggered by a random encounter with something that reminds us of its contents.

It is also possible that emotional conditioned responses may be behind some of our earworm experiences. In my survey, some respondents reported that they always experienced the same earworm in response to certain moods or circumstances. In my case, when I am happy I often have Doris Day singing a lively rendition of 'The Deadwood Stage' in my head. It always makes me smile.

Future research will help us untangle other possible causes

of earworms, including the prospect that some earworms may help to modify our state of attention or mood for the task at hand. It is a nice thought that the mind may be selecting tunes from our mental jukebox in order to support our activities in the same way that we ourselves might select a tune to boost our confidence before a night out or calm us down after an argument.

One thing we have little idea about as yet is the repeating, looping component of earworms. Why do they get stuck? Again, earworms are not the only type of thought to loop in the mind. Worries or rumination can also be cyclic, especially in times of stress. I have often heard people speak about other types of repeating sounds, such as words from poems, prayers or even jokes. The great thing about earworms is that because they are so regular and common compared to these other kinds of mental activity, they are a useful research tool that may help us better understand other types of repeating thoughts in the future.

♪

Memory is so much more than a collection of stories, skills and ideas. As we have seen in this chapter, memory is vital to learning, whether we are training as a musician or simply learning about the music of our culture through everyday listening. It is an essential component of our experience of consciousness that keeps us connected to our past and future on the thin sliver of time that we think of as the present moment. Memory can also be involuntary, it can 'pop' and repeat on us for reasons we do not yet fully understand.

In all these three guises, 'the star', 'the survivor' and 'the miscreant', musical memory has shown itself to be crucial to our understanding of our musical world and also to our understanding of what we believe, what we have been through in our life, and how we came to be who we are today.

In the next chapter we will see how musical memory is also an important ingredient in the potential of music to provide comfort and to support healing in times of illness and injury. In the final part of our musical life journey I will discuss the various ways in which music has been found to have a positive impact on our health and state of well-being.

## Chapter 8
# Music and lifelong well-being

*'One good thing about music; when it hits you,*
*you feel no pain.'*
BOB MARLEY

Throughout this book there have been countless points where I could have discussed how music can help to alleviate or remediate mental and physical conditions. Music has the potential to provide valuable and powerful support for well-being across the whole of the lifespan, from infancy right through to end-of-life care. In the end I decided not to bury these interesting ideas among the chapters but to bring them into a light of their own.

Before beginning down the road of exploring music for lifelong well-being, I want to make a few things clear. Firstly, and most importantly, music is not a cure-all for everything that ails us in life. If it was then someone would have noticed by now.

In 2005 John Sloboda[1] wrote a wise cautionary note warning against the 'vitamin' model of music. This refers to the danger we evoke when expecting that certain music will have the same impact on everyone; the idea that music might be prescribed in tones, rhythms and timbres depending on the way you want to feel or for a particular health-related outcome. 'This is the best music for heart disease'; 'this is best for depression'; 'this is better for sleeping', and so on. To go down this road, given the individualistic nature of our musical skills, preferences and memories, is foolhardy.

You may see echoes of this kind of 'pharmaceutical' approach to music and well-being in some of the studies in this chapter. This is not a terrible thing, as demonstrating the potential power of music for well-being was an important early step for supporting future work and interest in this area. What is important now is where we go from here.

Similarly, I do not believe that music should be treated as a whole, something we use under one generic label. Music is the most wonderfully diverse human activity, full of different styles, instruments, voices and performance traditions. We need to honour this variety. We are only at the very beginning of understanding how music relates to health and well-being outside Western cultures, although efforts are being made to highlight this gap in our knowledge particularly by the fields of medical ethnomusicology and cultural anthropology.[2]

Finally, I make one pre-emptive observation that will become clear to you as I describe studies of music and well-being. As yet, we have only rough ideas of *how* music contributes to positive health outcomes. Much of what you will read or hear on this subject is speculation. Many researchers are still operating largely on intuition when engaging with the therapeutic impacts of music. It is early days for science in this area and we are finding our way. Once again, a hope for the future is that we can move towards isolating some of the mechanisms behind positive outcomes so that we can move from intuitive to more informed engagement with music for well-being.

In this chapter I am first going to talk about ways in which music can bring about positive impacts for lifelong well-being, and outline the kind of mechanisms that are currently the hot contenders for explaining positive effects. Then we will look at the different ways that people are engaging with music for well-being and the important differences between music therapy and music medicine.

Once all these concepts are settled in place I will move on to the research itself, spanning as it does the whole of the human lifespan: a selection of some of the most interesting studies to date, showing how music can support growth in babies and children, boost communication and support language development, aid movement, calm distress, and play a role in how the brain repairs itself after illness or injury.

As humans we have spent thousands of years developing, expanding and refining this amazing tool and ability that we call music, without any real drive or purpose other than the pleasure and passion that we feel as a result. That same music is now beginning to reveal its power to help us along our life's journey.

♪

I have thought carefully about the term to use when talking about the ways in which we engage with music for non-music related benefits. After a few false starts I decided that 'well-being' suited best.

Well-being does not have one single definition since the word is used across multiple disciplines including but not limited to medicine, economics, politics, social studies and psychology; it is no wonder that we can't all agree. My preferred shorthand description though comes from an economic background: 'doing well – feeling good'.[3]

The 'doing well' part of well-being refers to objective standard of living. It may seem like this refers only to economic prosperity but you can think of it more widely as what a person can or can't do well in their everyday life: for example, whether a person is mobile enough to work and take care of themselves or whether they can communicate well enough to take part in activities with family and friends.

The 'feeling good' part of well-being refers to our subjective level of life satisfaction, given our personal circumstances.

Feeling good is also about our sense of social identity, as personal reflection on how we may feel is compared to values and expectations, given our society and background, and to our perception of the people around us.

When we talk about music and well-being, therefore, we must think beyond the instant 'feel good factor' that we encounter when we play a bit of music to cheer us up after a long day and instead consider the widest possible well-being outreach of any music-related intervention.

Having set my net so wide, I now have to admit that there is no way that I could discuss all the well-being-related studies of music that exist. There are excellent texts devoted to this subject alone that far exceed the size of this book.[4] My aim in using such a wide definition of well-being is to give myself enough wiggle room to touch on as many different studies of lifelong well-being as possible, to give you a broad flavour of the areas in which we are starting to see potential for music.

## Music therapy and music medicine

I attended a very inspiring conference a few years ago in Austria, entitled 'Mozart and Science'. These were my first steps into the world of music and well-being research, and marked my first interactions with music therapists. Apart from a head full of ideas and motivation, this conference left me with one overriding impression: that music therapy and music medicine were two different things that should not be confused. I still think this is an important concept to emphasise.

We all use music in ways we may think of as 'therapeutic' when we need cheering up, consolation, support or comfort. What we do in these circumstances, however, would not be classed as music therapy in a strict sense. Definitions of music therapy vary but they all come down to a situation where 'the therapist helps the client to promote health, using music experiences and the relationships developing through them'.[5] Music listening can be a part of music therapy but they are not the same thing. Music therapy needs the presence of a qualified therapist.[6]

I have had the privilege to observe a handful of music therapy sessions over the years in various situations, from a nursing home to neurological care and at a school for severely disabled children. I can say from this small experience that the presence of the therapist, as a guide, a focus and a source of connection for the client, was absolutely essential.

There are aspects of the human interaction in music therapy that we will probably never be able to quantify with scientific studies and I can therefore fully sympathise with practitioners who may be reluctant to engage with research on therapy. However, I believe that we should at least try to understand some of the mechanisms behind the effects of music therapy: by doing so we can learn more about the kinds of techniques and activities that are effective for different patients. Certainly at the conference I was attending there were plenty of therapists who were keen to explore the physiological and psychological mechanisms that may underpin their important work in order to make sure their approaches were as informed and as effective as possible for their clients.

Having defined music therapy, we are left with a large body of research without a name: studies where music was used with the aim of improving a condition or situation but where no therapist was present. If a researcher uses music for health-related outcomes in the absence of a therapist then we can use the term 'music medicine'.

There are many advantages to considering music therapy and music medicine as options in care plans. At safe hearing levels there are no reported negative side effects to music. Music interventions can be planned in combination with just about any other form of therapy or medication without fear of negative interaction effects. In addition, many music interventions do not require verbal communication, which makes them ideal for patients whose speech is impaired or absent. Music therapy and music medicine can also be viewed as overall cost effective: with their use, patients can often be discharged sooner, use less medication, and require less intensive staff care.[7]

## How does it work?

Setting aside the differences between music medicine and music therapy, how might listening to music impact on our state of well-being?

Music has a varied list of measurable effects on our physical and psychological state that we have touched on throughout the book, relating to our emotions, moods, memories, attentional focus, and mental and physical arousal. One or two of these mechanisms deserve an additional special mention here.

Perhaps the most cited reaction to music that is associated with improved well-being is the relaxation response of the autonomic nervous system, which includes a variety of body markers such as the lowering of heart rate, breathing rate, blood pressure, muscular tension and oxygen consumption.

There are many beneficial secondary effects to this autonomic relaxation response, including the reduction of pain,[8] anxiety and stress. These combined outcomes can lead to positive effects in medical situations: for example, studies at Yale found that spinal surgery patients who could control their own pain medication used up to 43 per cent less when they had access to their favourite music.[9]

A second mechanism of effect for music and well-being are brain responses to our favourite music, in particular the release of neurotransmitters (for example, dopamine) that are associated with psychological experiences like motivation and pleasure. Hearing favourite music is associated with the activity of neurotransmitters in the brain's reward circuitry: deep connections between the limbic emotion centres of the brain and the higher pre-frontal decision-making and evaluation areas.[10] The latest research indicates that even brand new music can stimulate aspects of this brain reward circuitry, if that new music comes from a style or genre that we already enjoy.[11]

The autonomic relaxation response, combined with the activity of the brain reward system, impacts on our hormone and immune response. The body produces natural opiates in response to our listening to enjoyable music and often we can see a marked reduction in levels of cortisol, a marker of a stress response in the body.[12] Even a single music therapy session has been associated with a significant increase in measurable salivary immunoglobulin A, a natural antibody in our immune system.[13]

Finally, when we consider the effects of music *therapy* on well-being we must not forget about the less tangible but very real influences of increased human contact, communication and empathy, guided reflection and emotional support.

As a result of the sheer number of possible explanations for music's effects on well-being it is not uncommon for researchers in this area to ascribe a positive impact of music to a collection of these mechanisms. The problem is that most studies have no idea how music leads to a positive effect.

I am no different. I have run these kinds of music and well-being studies and as a researcher you get really excited about the fact that music appears to be helping people, but then realise that, apart from a few intriguing leads, there is no clear reason why.

Another problem is that many music and well-being studies are correlational in nature; this means that researchers introduce music into an environment (for example, a hospital, a care home) and then look for changes in behaviour and/or feelings of the patients/clients/participants. Any changes that the researchers observe could have come from any number of underlying causes, and probably emerge from a complex, unique combination of the brain and body mechanisms I have listed above.

The most comprehensive studies that I will tell you about in the next section take as many brain and body measures as they can to try to narrow down likely mechanisms in the effects observed.

Having laid down definitions and cautionary notes, we can now proceed into the research itself. I will touch on general well-being in several places in the next section, which moves in life stages from infancy right the way through to end-of-life care, but I will focus on music medicine and music therapy for brain, body and behaviour syndromes and developmental issues.

## Music and well-being in infants
### Premature babies
In Chapter 1 I talked about the development of human hearing in the womb. Sometime between the fourth and sixth month of pregnancy a foetus will develop the physiological structures in the ear and brain that are necessary to perceive sound. When a full-term baby is born it has had months of experience of hearing the muffled rhythms and melodies of sound that pass into its fluid-filled environment. You might think of this as the 'music of the womb'.

Sadly, not all babies reach full term. Happily, medical science has made remarkable steps when it comes to caring for babies born as young as 22–23 weeks, such that many go on to survive. The priority for these premature babies is to take care of their underdeveloped organs and support their growth to maturity as far as possible.

At a conference called 'Music and Neurosciences' in 2011 I first heard about the work of Amir Lahav, director of the Neonatal Research Lab at Brigham and Women's Hospital in Boston, Massachusetts. Lahav had just completed a series of studies in which he simulated a neonatal hearing environment for premature babies. Why would he do this? Surely there are more important matters than worrying about hearing in a premature baby?

Consider for a minute the auditory environment inside a neonatal intensive care unit (NICU): quiet but with occasional loud machines bleeping and buzzing, intermittent piercing alarms, medics shouting important, emergency instructions. All that noise constitutes massive overexposure if your tiny ears have only just begun to process sound.

Lahav and his research team reasoned that babies who reach term in the womb get a much gentler and information-rich introduction to sound over several months that helps to develop the fine structures in the ear and the auditory cortices in the brain. Through this early, muffled, music-like exposure, their brain develops invaluable pattern-recognition and memory skills which will be important for later development of speech and language comprehension. Before they are even born, babies come to know important rhythms and melodies like their mother's voice, heartbeat and breathing patterns.

Lahav decided to try and replace some of this lost opportunity for brain and ear sound experience in premature babies by simulating a neonatal sound environment in their NICU cots. He speculated that recreating, in particular, the maternal speech that the babies would hear in the womb may also have benefits for the development of their tiny bodies, by minimising heart and breathing stress responses.

The researchers introduced recordings of mothers' voices and heartbeats into the NICU environment of fourteen premature babies (born between 26 and 32 weeks) by way of a specially created mini-audio system.[14] The babies served as their own control group, as they heard normal hospital sounds as well as maternal sounds. The researchers monitored the number of times babies experienced adverse breathing and heart responses and found that these were significantly lower when the babies were listening to their mother's voice and heartbeat.

This study does not use 'music' in the traditional sense, but remember that infants at six months' gestation would never hear music in the way that we can. They would hear muffled pitch patterns (melodies) and rhythms filtered by the womb.

Exposing premature babies to real music in an NICU also leads to promising outcomes according to a two-and-a-half-year study of eleven different hospital sites, led by Joanne Loewy. She showed that live music therapy in NICUs (by a qualified therapist, making use of singing and instruments) had measurable beneficial impacts on babies' vital signs and sleep patterns.[15]

Music therapy was a crucial choice in the above study, as a therapist can react flexibly to changes in a baby's breathing, heart rate or movement patterns. Positive effects of music have also been seen in the way that premature babies respond to necessary but often painful and stressful procedures.[16]

There is a tendency for clinicians to be concerned – rightly – about the negative impact of noise in an NICU, including music.[17] But given the presence of predictable structures like melody and rhythm, it is reasonable to hypothesise that soft, simple music that reduces the possibility for over-stimulation would be supportive for developing ears as well as minds and bodies in premature babies, especially when combined with the sounds of maternal speech and heartbeats.[18] Guidelines for music use in NICUs have been created with this in mind.[19]

Another problem for premature babies is feeding. Weight gain is one of the most important factors in healthy premature development but babies born before 34 weeks often have pronounced difficulties coordinating sucking, breathing and swallowing. They can be tube fed, though this increases the risk of stress responses and can stall development of musculature in the gastrointestinal system. In short, it is important to encourage a premature baby to learn how to feed as soon as possible.

Work by Jayne Standley[20] established that music can be a valuable tool in helping to encourage premature infants to adapt their sucking reflex to feeding. Standley developed a pacifier that plays recordings of pleasant female singing when babies suck correctly, which can apparently help to speed up a baby's ability to feed independently. The impact of lullabies on feeding, in combination with more traditional pacifiers, has also been supported by recent studies,[21] though it has yet to be established whether music helps infants learn how to coordinate their sucking through rhythm or simply encourages them when they happen upon the right technique.

The challenges facing a premature infant are great as they fight to survive and grow outside of the protection of their mother's womb. This period is a stressful time for all and well-chosen music, especially in the hands of a trained therapist, can help foster relaxation that has positive impacts on body and brain mechanisms. These effects have secondary benefits for processes such as sleep and feeding, which all contribute to development.

## Music and well-being in children

I only have the space to touch on a few of the areas where music medicine and music therapy can help to support well-being in children who have been diagnosed with conditions that impact on their physical and/or mental development. All of these conditions also exist in adults but I talk about them here as the majority of the research has looked at children. In theory there is no reason why this work could not be extended to adults in the future: as we know, the brain is capable of lifelong learning and change (see Chapter 3).

### Autism spectrum

My beloved nephew Eneko has fragile X syndrome, a genetic syndrome that leads to a number of unique physical and mental characteristics, the latter of which resemble autistic traits. Eneko is a happy ten-year-old boy who I adore. Although he can barely speak, he is very ticklish, curious, and we laugh all the time when we play games. Because of his syndrome he can be quickly distressed by changes to the environment, loud noises or disruptions to his routine. He is crazy about music, in particular Vivaldi. I once got him a baton so he could conduct orchestras that he hears on CD or sees on the TV.

Music can be an invaluable way to communicate with children like Eneko who show autistic traits and who also may have very limited verbal output. Children on the autism spectrum can show unique sensitivity to musical sounds[22] and at least 12 per cent of autism clinical interventions currently feature music-based activities.[23]

Music therapy, when compared to play therapy, can result in significant improvements in non-verbal and gestural communication, including eye contact and turn-taking behaviours.[24] Adding in musical elements to vocal training has also been found to have beneficial impacts on low-functioning autistic children who are learning to speak.[25]

A related developmental challenge associated with severe autism is limited or absent verbal communication. One exciting breakthrough in this area has been the development of a music-based therapeutic technique that supports verbal learning. Catherine Wan is a researcher in the Music and

Neuroimaging Laboratory in Boston where she developed Auditory-Motor Mapping Training (AMMT), an intervention to help non-verbal autistic children.

AMMT purports to encourage auditory-motor mappings in the brain by teaching children to speak at different pitches while playing tuned drums. While this kind of therapy is still in the early stages of development, it appears that AMMT sessions are associated with significant improvements in speech production even in children who have uttered hardly a word their whole lives.[26]

Children on the autistic spectrum may also benefit from movement therapy to help them learn coordination and control behaviours. Eneko has equestrian therapy and his motor coordination seems to have benefited from his riding lessons. Combining music and movement therapy can have positive effects in helping children with autism to improve in restlessness, tantrum and inattentive behaviours. The rhythmic aspects of music in particular can help promote fine and gross motor skills.[27] Meanwhile, I can report that Eneko's conducting is going from strength to strength.

The latest review on the subject of music therapy on the autistic spectrum[28] has laid down several useful guidelines for clinicians, including the use of better measures of movement skills and placing a higher priority on interactive musical therapies that feature singing, music making and synchronised rhythmic activities. All signs point towards these kind of group-based social therapies being more effective than passive music listening.

### ADHD

Attention Deficit Hyperactivity Disorder (ADHD) is a multi-symptomatic condition that is marked by impulsivity, hyperactivity and a difficulty in focusing attention. These behaviours are associated with maladaptive outcomes including poor educational attainment and fractured peer/family relationships. The condition is most frequently diagnosed in childhood and currently affects somewhere between 6 and 8 per cent of children in the UK.

Given the controversy surrounding medication for ADHD, there is a growing pressure to investigate alternative therapies. Interest in music therapy for ADHD stems from a desire to provide structured and focused activities that capture attention and allow for personal expression while requiring a degree of cooperation with others.

Interactive music therapy can also help children with ADHD to tap into their emotional reactions in a safe and supportive environment and to learn how to recognise and respond to shifts in mood.

To date, studies have reported generally favourable outcomes,[29] although there are individual differences meaning that some children benefit from music compared to other visual therapies whereas others can be adversely responsive.[30] A review of music therapy trials in ADHD that met excellent clinical standards[31] is being conducted at the time of writing and conclusions should be available in the near future.

### Dyslexia

Dyslexia is a broad term that encompasses learning difficulties centred on reading and spelling. Severity of dyslexia varies widely and difficulties can extend into verbal memory and verbal processing speed. The NHS's current estimate is that between 4 and 8 per cent of school children in England have some form of dyslexia.[32]

Music has been thought of as a therapy for dyslexia thanks partly to the similarities between music and language, including the fact that both use structured sounds that unfold rapidly over time. Music is not a language but there are many overlaps in the way that we process and integrate these two forms of sound communication,[33] and as such there may be scope for supporting language learning by boosting musical skills.

Studies of auditory brainstem response (see Chapter 2) have shown that children with dyslexia have less stable encoding of sound, further supporting the idea that musical training may aid the development and function of neurological systems that support reading (*see page 42*). One hope for future research is that musical training may be able to help steady these unstable representations in the brain.[34]

It has long been known that there is a small but significant relationship between reading and music-learning skills.[35] Marie Forgeard and colleagues conducted an extensive study with normal-reading and dyslexic children to test the patterns in the relationship between music and reading.[36] Their findings suggested a tight coupling between the types of sound skills that can be boosted by musical training and the types of sound skills that help support the development of reading skills, in all of the children.

One additional interesting avenue of music and dyslexia research is concerned with the influence of rhythm. In 2003 Katie Overy[37] investigated whether musical support could help the timing issues that many children with dyslexia encounter.[38] She found that dyslexic children often scored higher on musical aptitude tests compared to their control group counterparts, except in the area of timing skills. She suggested that supporting rhythmic training with music could help tune reading skills such as the ability to segment syllables in language, leading to easier comprehension and improved spelling.[39]

All this research suggests that a music intervention which strengthens the basic auditory skills of children with dyslexia and other reading difficulties, especially one that incorporates rhythm, may help support their language learning.[40] At present there are no clinically accepted trials from which to draw firm conclusions about how music education may help reading,[41] but hopefully such studies will emerge in the future, with useful guidelines for best implementation.

### The future
There has been a small but significant explosion in music therapy and music medicine to support children's development and care over the last decade, and I have just touched on some of the areas here.

In practical terms there are proving to be lots of opportunities for musicians, psychologists, doctors, carers and engineers to come together and build useful technology to support these efforts. A project that acts as an example of this is the Virtual Musical Instrument (VMI).[42] The VMI is a visual computer interface that allows people with varying levels of mobility to create nice musical sounds in response to body movements. Eneko would love that. Such new music rehabilitation tools hold great promise for therapists, families and children.

## Music and physical well-being in adults
In this section I will talk about conditions that are more likely to strike in adulthood, such as serious brain injury, stroke, conditions like Parkinson's, and mental illness. Here we will see how music can help with recovery, re-learning and rehabilitation. I will refer often to the Cochrane reports, systematic reviews of research in health care that are internationally recognised as the gold standard in evidence-based health care.[43]

We begin with brain injury. Our brain is a wonderfully complex thing, which of course means that it can break down in a myriad of diverse ways. Misfortune can visit in the form of traumatic accidents, stroke, illnesses, infection and toxic exposure (for example, to carbon monoxide). More people than ever survive such life events thanks to the advances of modern medicine.

Let's be clear. Music is unlikely to help you survive a brain injury. But it could have a useful role in recovery.

Let's assume the worst first: that a brain injury or illness causes a spell in a coma or similarly altered state of consciousness, and a stay within intensive care, probably on a ventilator. How can music help in these circumstances?

### Coma and ventilation

Even in the deepest states of unconsciousness a person may continue to hear the world around them.[44] This means that music therapy is possible when someone is in a coma. Therapists can improvise singing or playing instruments to the rhythms of a pulse or breathing pattern.[45] These kinds of techniques can set up a channel of communication, an outside link for a patient in a coma.

Measurements taken during such music therapy sessions indicate that coma patients often show signs of relaxation (for example, their breathing settles on a steady, slow rate). EEG recordings of brain activity have also shown that the types of brain waves that are prominent during therapy are associated with a relaxed state. Importantly, a coma patient can respond to quiet and gentle singing, even in a noisy hospital environment.[46]

The Cochrane reviews noted many cases where music therapy and music medicine (listening to calming music) can reduce heart and breathing rate, and help keep coma patients stable over a period of time. Other physiology measures, such as blood pressure, respond less reliably to music interventions in ventilated patients, a result which offers a welcome cautionary note about expecting too much of music interventions in patients who are critically ill and heavily medicated.

To date, however, because of the positive indicators and since music listening is an easy intervention to implement, the Cochrane review has concluded that music listening should be offered as a stress management intervention to coma and ventilated patients.[47]

### Stroke

A stroke happens when blood flow in the brain is disrupted by a leakage or a blockage. Cases of stroke are on the rise, partly due to the increase in our life expectancies. Worldwide, fifteen million people suffer a stroke every year. The World Health Organization (WHO) predicts that the disability-adjusted life years lost to stroke will rise from 38 million in 1990 to 61 million in 2020.[48]

Teppo Särkämö has studied music in the recovering brain at the Cognitive Brain Research Unit in Finland.[49] In his thesis Särkämö explored the impact of music listening on stroke patients against listening to audio books or no listening activity. All the patients had a thorough neurological examination six months post-stroke to check on their progress. Both the music listening and the audio book patients showed improvements to their auditory processing, but only the music listening group showed a benefit to their verbal memory and focused attention. Music listening was also found to be better for tackling feelings of depression and confusion. This research strongly supported the inclusion of music as a 'rehabilitative leisure activity after a stroke'.

Music therapy has been found to be helpful in cases of unilateral neglect after stroke. Neglect happens when a stroke patient seems to be unaware of part of their environment despite no problems with their vision. Patients with neglect may only eat part of the food on a plate or shave only part of their face. Listening to classical music has been associated with improvements to attention in patients' otherwise neglected field.[50] Music therapy, in particular the use of playing scales on chime bars, has also been found to help patients reorient to their neglected field.[51]

## Movement

Around 80 per cent of stroke patients experience a loss of mobility. Mobility is also a primary issue in conditions such as Parkinson's, where damage to the dopamine regulatory processes and basal ganglia in the brain leads to disrupted physical movements. Stroke and Parkinson's patients face different challenges to recovery and remediation of their condition but music therapy can support movement for both populations, and potentially for other groups where motion is an issue.

A simple metrical rhythm can help guide patients to walk with less rigid motion and at a steadier pace.[52] This kind of music therapy has become known as rhythmic auditory stimulation (RAS) and has been developed greatly in the last ten years. RAS typically consists of metronome-pulse patterns embedded into rhythmically accentuated instrumental music. Some patients can have measurable improvements in their walking within 24 hours of a first RAS training session.

Although the biological mechanism by which rhythmic music can help support walking and other movements is not yet certain, it is thought that having an 'external timekeeper' helps patients to synchronise their motor movements as opposed to relying on the disrupted internal timing signals from compromised areas of the brain.[53]

The Cochrane reports found several studies where RAS was associated with better walking in stroke patients, including improved speed, stride length and symmetry, all of which makes for a steadier and safer pedestrian.[54] These studies took place in the presence of a music therapist but I have heard many anecdotal reports of patients listening to and even composing music on their own to help with their movements.

One of the latest developments in this field is called 'Walk-Mate'. While steady RAS rhythms may be helpful, they are not very adaptable if a person starts to struggle or speed up their pace. Walk-Mate is a project that features interactive and real-time responsive rhythmic sound to support move-ment.[55] It is still early days for this technology but results have shown even more advanced therapeutic benefits compared to fixed RAS.

### Speaking

Disrupted motor movements may also impact on speech. Aphasia, a word which originates from the Greek for 'speech-less', is another common symptom post brain injury or stroke. Aphasia can relate to the understanding or comprehension of language as well as the production or expression of speech. There are a huge variety of aphasic conditions but music ther-apy offers new hope for those who struggle to speak after brain injury.

Many of you will be familiar with the case of Gabrielle Giffords, a Member of the United States House of Representa-tives who was the victim of an assassination attempt in early 2011. Gabby, as she is known, was left fighting for her life with severe brain injuries after being shot in the left temple. Despite such a devastating injury, after much hard work in recovery, Gabby was able to address the US Congress just over one year later. She credits music therapy for its part in helping her incredible progress in regaining her speech.

I have already discussed how a form of music therapy, AMMT, can help speech production in autistic children who struggle with verbal development. AMMT grew out of an earlier development in music therapy that has helped speech recovery in many adults post brain injury: melodic intonation therapy (MIT).[56] The reports and images of Gabby Giffords' music therapy seem to suggest it followed a similar protocol to MIT.

During MIT a therapist will use sung patterns of exagger-ated speech, beginning with just two different pitches (one high and one low) and eventually accompanied by well-known melodies like lullabies. The therapist will also tap the rhythm of the singing with the patient's left hand.

MIT is most successful in people who have had left hemisphere strokes[57] or brain damage, like Gabby; such an injury would typically damage language ability. It is important that the right hemisphere is relatively spared as MIT helps to retrain that part of the brain to support speech.[58] Specifically, MIT has been associated with the increased recruitment of parallel circuits in the right hemisphere that would normally support language in the left hemisphere, such as premotor areas (for speech planning) and the superior temporal lobe (sound analysis), as well as crucial white matter pathways that connect these areas.

The mechanism behind MIT is not yet certain and there is an ongoing debate about which aspects of MIT are actually having an effect. Some claim that singing is not necessary, that the rhythmic content is most helpful for regaining speech.[59] One important point that such studies overlook is that real music may work well as it is engaging and fun. At the time of writing, this debate rumbles on. What is undeniable is that music therapy has played a crucial role in the speech recovery of many people such as Gabby Giffords.

♪

To end this section on physical health I want to touch on two of the biggest killers in modern society: cancer and heart disease. Music will never cure either of these life-threatening conditions but thanks to many of the effects of music medicine and music therapy that we have already discussed (increased relaxation, reduced pain), as well as secondary effects (better sleep,[60] faster response to treatment, better perceived quality of life), music can help to support recovery from cancer and heart disease, and aid in the experience of what can be painful and distressing (although necessary) treatments.

Several trials of music therapy and music medicine in cancer patients have shown measurable effects on the autonomic relaxation response. Listening to music can reduce heart rate by an average of 4 beats per minute (bpm) and respiratory rate by an average of two breaths per minute,[61] with some comparable reduction in blood pressure. Similar results have been reported in patients with heart disease.[62] Those changes may seem small but each average 10 bpm reduction in heart rate may reduce the risk of cardiac death by up to 30 per cent.[63]

Having a tool that can trigger real physiological relaxation in this way over time also has far reaching effects for how people feel from day to day. The Cochrane reports suggest that music therapy and music medicine interventions have a beneficial effect on anxiety, mood and quality of life measures in people with cancer. The results of some trials suggested that music also has a moderate pain-reducing effect. Finally, the autonomic relaxation response reportedly reduces muscular tension and vessel constriction – thereby increasing the success rate of painful procedures.[64]

## Music and mental well-being in adults

Given the positive impacts of music therapy and music medicine on the body it should come as no surprise that there is also potential for the treatment of mental health and well-being.

A recent review of the past twenty years of research in this area[65] reported that music therapy, in particular active music making, can be used as a complementary therapy in the treatment of depression,[66] schizophrenia,[67] and dementia,[68] as well as problems of agitation, anxiety, sleeplessness and substance misuse. Just a few sessions can be enough to see small measurable effects in symptoms, though larger numbers of sessions (16–51) achieve better results; this finding suggests that it might be a case of the more treatment sessions, the better.[69] I will touch on three specific areas of music and mental well-being here to bring our journey through music and well-being to a close.

### Post Traumatic Stress Disorder

Some of the earliest recorded use of music therapy dates from the 1940s when musical interaction and listening was used to help veterans suffering from 'shell shock' after the Second World War. This kind of therapy was thought to help relieve the high state of anxiety in what is now recognised as Post Traumatic Stress Disorder (PTSD) and to encourage a sense of community out of the isolation that often results from leaving the armed forces.

Today we know that music can help trigger autonomic relaxation responses that can help lower the heightened states of anxiety and vigilance that people with PTSD often experience, even if only temporarily. Being able to escape from negative mind and body states plus the increase in personal sense of control over mental activity can all have measurable effects on quality of life. Music interventions can be incorporated as part of therapies designed to help with tension regulation and complex thinking, to assist the client with mental challenges like planning, assessing outcomes, and controlling impulsive behaviours.[70]

### Depression

Music therapy is effective in depressive patients because active music making within a therapeutic framework offers a person the unique opportunity for new 'aesthetic, physical and relational experiences'.[71]

Practically, this means that music therapy provides an enjoyable way for people who are depressed to increase their level of basic physical activity in a social context with other people who may or may not be facing similar difficulties to themselves. Building on communication and interaction in this way is seen as a primary goal of therapy for an individual in a serious state of depression where inward, negative-biased reflection can be distressingly dominant.

Another benefit of music therapy and music medicine for people with depression is that it gets a high degree of treatment compliance in a population that can often be resistant to interventions, especially in the initial stages of treatment.[72] The fact that music listening is enjoyable and can be tailored to each individual to access pleasant life memories (see Chapter 7) also allows for a personal approach to interaction with a therapist and a flexible, portable form of mood regulation that a patient can learn to use by themselves.

### Dementia and Alzheimer's

Dementia is a wide-ranging term that encompasses a number of conditions that are characterised by a decline in a person's mental faculties. Dementia-related illnesses, including Alzheimer's, are associated with multiple cognitive, emotional and behavioural problems that are underwritten by a state of confusion and loss of connection with the social world. Music therapy and music medicine can provide not only a valuable source of cognitive stimulation but also a conduit through which carers, families and friends can re-learn how to communicate and interact with their loved one.

In Chapter 7 we talked about how music is strongly linked to our memories and how musical memories can often survive in cases where other forms of life memory seem inaccessible, including after brain injury and in dementia.[73] This strong link to music in our memory can provide an invaluable link to a person's sense of personal history and identity.

Music also provides a useful way for Alzheimer's patients to learn new information.[74] This finding may in time provide a basis for music-based practical memory training that would allow an individual to maintain their independence for longer.[75]

Music can be used to help patients in the later stages of dementia to re-engage with the people around them, after the point where verbal contact has been lost. Activities such as moving and singing to music encourage physical and mental engagement with loved ones and carers that can be beneficial for the patient's state and bring about changes in quality-of-life measures for family and friends. Music therapy has been associated with significant reductions in both long-term anxiety and depression levels in these patients.[76]

Another issue with later-stage dementia is that the person can become distressed by changes to their environment or activities. These changes can be as simple as getting ready for bed after dinner or meeting a new doctor. In these cases music can be introduced as a cue for transition, in order to reduce associated stress reactions.[77] Over time, music comes to act as a relaxed 'primer' for activities that the patient can come to recognise, meaning times of transition will be less of a stressful burden for them. When such stress reactions are minimised a person can have better access to their implicit, procedural memories for old habits (such as dressing and washing), allowing for a calmer and more successful, independent everyday routine.

Back in 2003 the Cochrane report found no strong evidence either in support of or against the use of music therapy and music medicine for individuals with dementia; the accumulation of evidence I have described in this section indicates how far research can come in a decade. Although no formal update of this 2003 report presently exists I am more convinced than ever about the benefits of music in this group of patients.

## What kind of music?

As with many of the effects we have seen attributed to music throughout this book, when considering the best type of music for well-being, personalisation is crucial; there is no one perfect genre or style of music for everyone. This point brings us right back to the 'vitamin' model of music that John Sloboda so wisely warned against at the start of this chapter. A good reaction and positive outcomes from music therapy or music medicine for any one person depends on the kind of music that they like.

Just to make this point even stronger, we see the consequences of not taking a personal approach when researchers choose a particular generic type of music, with all good intentions, believing it to have good effects, only to find that this blanket introduction of music makes a situation worse.

In one case, classical music was played in the communal area of a home for people with dementia.[78] Behavioural disturbances were found to be significantly worse during these musical periods, and many patients demanded that the music be removed. However good the intentions of such research, it goes to show that the most important person in any situation where music is introduced for well-being is the patient or client – their needs, likes and desires must drive the selection of music.

There are some general rules that can guide music selection beyond simply making sure it is enjoyed by the client. Where possible, patients should be encouraged to select music characterised by a slow tempo and that lacks abrupt harmonic changes and sharp timbres, in order to have the best chances of promoting autonomic relaxation. In addition, music that evokes strong emotional reactions, which may be caused by memories associated with the music, should be avoided when used for stress and anxiety-reduction purposes.

There is another caveat to the general conclusion that patient-selected music is best. In some cases unfamiliar music may be more helpful; emotional associations with music can disrupt and distract from a person's attention to aspects of the music which may be critical for their therapy. For example, a therapist or a patient may wish to focus on the rhythm of music in order to help movement but emotional music may distract focus from this part of the sound.

Finally, we must consider how we introduce music to medical and therapeutic environments. Listening to music through headphones may not be wise during painful procedures because it prevents the patient from hearing instructions or comments by the medical staff. This interference and lack of contact with staff who are administering treatment may increase patients' anxiety and, consequently, their perceived pain. In the case of such procedures, it is probably better to listen to music without headphones.[79]

In our final chapter we have taken a tour through the various ways in which both music therapy and music medicine have been trialled as adjunctive treatments to support well-being through the whole of the human lifespan. The music of your life may one day have the power to support you through difficult and traumatic times, though I very much hope that these are few.

Music psychology research allows us to better understand how the brain and body react to music in clinical and care situations, and permits therapists and medical staff to optimise the use of music in these situations, always putting each individual at the forefront of planning.

Music is not a pill, a solution or a cure when it comes to times of trouble but it can be an important and flexible source of personal support, consolation, connection and inspiration.

Through the course of your life journey you have developed a wealth of musical skills, understandings and memories that are completely unique to you – a musical being that will never be recreated no matter how long the human race lasts.

Music will be your lifelong friend and personal companion, your reflection and your shadow. You really are the music.

# Notes

## Introduction

1 Mayle, P. (1978), *Baby Taming*. New York: Crown.

2 Changizi, M. (2011), *Harnessed: how language and music mimicked nature and transformed ape to man*. Dallas: Benbella Books.

## Chapter 1: First musical steps

1 Ruthsatz, J., Ruthsatz, K., and Stephens, K.R. (2013), 'Putting practice into perspective: Child prodigies as evidence of innate talent', *Intelligence*, http://dx.doi.org/10.1016/j.intell.2013.08.003

2 Pujol, R., Laville-Rebillard, M., and Lenoir, M. (1998), 'Development of sensory neural structures in the Mammalian cochlea', in: E.W. Rubel, A.N. Popper and R.R. Fay (eds), *Development of the auditory system. New York: Springer Handbook of Auditory Research* (pp. 146–193). Springer-Verlag.

3 Abrams, R.M., et al. (1998), 'Fetal music perception: The role of sound transmission', *Music Perception*, 15, 307–317.

4 Smith, S.L., et al. (2003), 'Intelligibility of sentences recorded from the uterus of a pregnant ewe and from the fetal inner ear', *Audiology and Neuro-Otology*, 8, 347–353.

5 Draganova, R., et al. (2007), 'Serial magnetoencephalographic study of fetal newborn auditory discriminative evoked responses', *Early Human Development*, 83(3), 199–207.

6 Richards, D.S., et al. (1992), 'Sound levels in the human uterus', *Obstetrics & Gynecology*, 80(2), 186–90.

7 Ando, Y., and Hattori, H. (1977), 'Effects of noise on sleep of babies', *Journal of the Acoustical Society of America*, 62, 199–204.

8 Granier-Deferre, C., et al. (2011), 'A Melodic Contour Repeatedly Experienced by Human Near-Term Fetuses Elicits a Profound Cardiac Reaction One Month after Birth', *PLOS ONE*, 6(2): e17304.

9 James, W. (1890), *The Principles of Psychology*. Cambridge, MA: Harvard University Press (1981).

10  Winkler, I., et al. (2009), 'Newborn infants detect the beat in music',
    *Proceedings of the National Academy of Sciences USA*, 106(7):2468–2471; info
    and stimuli available at http://www.mcg.uva.nl/newborns/

11  Bull, D., Eilers, R.E., and Oller, D.K. (1985), 'Infants' discrimination of
    final syllable fundamental frequency in multisyllabic stimuli', *Journal of the
    Acoustical Society of America*, 77(1), 289–295.

12  Nazzi, T., Floccia, C., and Bertoncini, J. (1998), 'Discrimination of pitch
    contours by neonates', *Infant Behavior and Development*, 21(4), 779–784.

13  Mampe, B., Friederici, A., Christophe, A., and Wermke, K. (2009),
    'Newborns' Cry Melody Is Shaped by Their Native Language', *Current
    Biology*, 19(23), 1994–1997.

14  Falk, D. (2004), 'Prelinguistic evolution in early hominins: Whence
    motherese?', *Behavioral and Brain Sciences*, 27, 491–541.

15  Cooper, R.P., and Aslin, R.N. (1990), 'Preference for infant-directed speech
    in the first month after birth', *Child Development*, 61(5), 1584–1595.

16  Werker, J.F., and McLeod, P.J. (1989), 'Infant preference for both male and
    female infant-directed talk: A developmental study of attentional affective
    responsiveness', *Canadian Journal of Psychology*, 43(2), 230–246.

17  Masataka, N. (2003), *The onset of language*. Cambridge: Cambridge
    University Press.

18  Boukydis, C.F., and Burgess, R.L. (1982), 'Adult Physiological Response
    to Infant Cries: Effects of Temperament of Infant, Parental Status, and
    Gender', *Child Development*, 53(5), 1291–1298. Swain, J.E., Lorberbaum,
    J.P., Kose, S., and Strathearn, L. (2007), 'Brain basis of early parent–infant
    interactions: psychology, physiology, and in vivo functional neuroimaging
    studies', *Journal of Child Psychology and Psychiatry*, 48(3–4), 262–287.

19  Werker, J.F., and McLeod, P.J. (1989), 'Infant preference for both male and
    female infant-directed talk: A developmental study of attentional affective
    responsiveness', *Canadian Journal of Psychology*, 43(2), 230–246.

20  Trainor, L.J., Austin, C.M., and Desjardins, R.N. (2000), 'Is infant directed
    speech prosody a result of the vocal expression of emotion?', *Psychological
    Science*, 11(3), 188–195.

21  Kuhl, P.K., et al. (1997), 'Cross-language analysis of phonetic units in
    language addressed to infants', *Science*, 277(5326), 684–686.

22  Burnham, D.K., Vollmer-Conna, U., and Kitamura, C. (2000), 'Talking to
    infants, pets, and adults: What's the difference?', paper presented at the
    XIIth Biennial International Conference on Infant Studies, Brighton, UK.

23  Trainor, L.J., and Desjardins, R.N. (2002), 'Pitch characteristics of infant-directed speech affect infants' ability to discriminate vowels', *Psychonomic Bulletin and Review*, 9, 335–340.

24  Kitamura, C., and Lam, C. (2009), 'Age-specific preferences for affective intent', *Infancy*, 14, 77–100.

25  Sakkalou, E., and Gattis, M. (2012), 'Infants infer intentions from prosody', *Cognitive Development*, 27(1), 1–16.

26  Pinker, S. (1994), *The Language Instinct: How the Mind Creates Language*. New York: HarperCollins.

## Chapter 2: Music in childhood

1  This phrase refers to the use of the term in the academic literature and does not intend to refer to the copyright term 'The Mozart Effect®', copyright Don Campbell.

2  Rauscher, F.H., Shaw, G.L., and Ky, K.N. (1993), 'Music and spatial task performance', *Nature*, 365, 611.

3  Rauscher, F.H., Shaw, G.L., and Ky, K.N. (1995), 'Listening to Mozart enhances spatial-temporal reasoning: Towards a neurophysiological basis', *Neuroscience Letters*, 185(1), 44–47.

4  Rauscher, F.H., and Shaw, G.L. (1998), 'Key components of the Mozart Effect', *Perceptual and Motor Skills*, 86(3), 835–841.

5  Nantais, K.M., and Schellenberg, E.G. (1999), 'The Mozart Effect: An Artifact of Preference', *Psychological Science*, 10(4), 370–373.

6  Schellenberg, E.G. (2012), 'Cognitive performance after music listening: A review of the Mozart effect', in R.A.R. MacDonald, G. Kreutz and L. Mitchell (eds.), *Music, Health and Wellbeing* (pp. 324–338). Oxford: Oxford University Press.

7  Husain, G., Thompson, W.F., and Schellenberg, E.G. (2002), 'Effects of Musical Tempo and Mode on Arousal, Mood and Spatial Abilities', *Music Perception*, 20(2), 151–171.

8  Steele, K.M., Bass, K.E., and Crook, M.D. (1999), 'The Mystery of the Mozart Effect: Failure to Replicate', *Psychological Science*, 10(4), 366–369.

9  Chabris, C.F. (1999), 'Prelude or requiem for the "Mozart effect"?', *Nature*, 400, 826–827.

10  Schellenberg, E.G. (2012), 'Cognitive performance after music listening: A review of the Mozart effect', in R.A.R. MacDonald, G. Kreutz, and L. Mitchell (eds), *Music, health and wellbeing* (pp. 324–338). Oxford: Oxford University Press.

11  Brandler, S., and Rammsayer, T.H. (2003), 'Differences in Mental Abilities between Musicians and Non-musicians', *Psychology of Music*, 31(2), 123–138.

12  Schellenberg, E.G. (2004), 'Music lessons enhance IQ', *Psychological Science*, 15(8), 511–514.

13  Schellenberg, E.G. (2006), 'Long-term positive associations between music lessons and IQ', *Journal of Educational Psychology*, 98, 457–468.

14  Weiss, M.W., and Schellenberg, E.G. (2011), 'Augmenting cognition with music', in I. Segev and H. Markram (eds.), *Augmenting cognition* (pp. 103–125). Lausanne, Switzerland: EPFL Press.

15  Trainor, L.J., Shahin, A., and Roberts, L.E. (2003), 'Effects of musical training on the auditory cortex in children', *Annals of the New York Academy of Sciences*, 999, 506–513. Shahin, A., et al. (2008), 'Music training leads to the development of timbre-specific gamma band activity', *NeuroImage*, 41(1), 113–122.

16  Krumhansl, C.L. (1990), *Cognitive foundations of musical pitch*. New York: Oxford University Press.

17  Strait, D., and Kraus, N. (2011), 'Playing music for a smarter ear: Cognitive, perceptual and neurobiological evidence', *Music Perception*, 29(2), 133–146.

18  Strait, D.L., Parbery-Clark, A., Hittner, E., and Kraus, N. (2012), 'Musical training during early childhood enhances the neural encoding of speech in noise', *Brain & Language*, 123, 191–201.

19  Kraus, N., and Chandrasekaran, B. (2010), 'Music training for the development of auditory skills', *Nature Reviews Neuroscience* 11, 599–605.

20  http://www.soc.northwestern.edu/brainvolts/projects/music/music_video.html

21  Parbery-Clark, A., et al. (2011), 'Musical Experience and the Aging Auditory System: Implications for Cognitive Abilities and Hearing Speech in Noise', *PLOS ONE* 6(5): e18082. Kraus, N., Strait, D.L., and Parbery-Clark, A. (2012), 'Cognitive factors shape brain networks for auditory skills: Spotlight on auditory working memory', *Annals of the New York Academy of Sciences*, 1252, 100–107.

22  Moreno, S., and Besson, M. (2006), 'Musical training and language-related brain electrical activity in children', *Psychophysiology*, 43(3), 287–291.

23  Moreno, S., et al. (2009), 'Musical training influences linguistic abilities in 8-year-old children: More evidence for brain plasticity', *Cerebral Cortex*, 19(3), 712–723.

24  *Ibid.*: 'Music training was based on the following aspects: Rhythm— children were trained to produce and improvise rhythms in different tempi and meters; Melody—exercises comprised the production and improvisation of melodies as well as inner audition. Children were taught

to classify pitch contour and intervals [e.g., going up and down; low, middle and high tones; relative music reading]; Harmony—children listened to harmonic progressions like I--IV--V--I, I--V--IV--I, or I--IV--V--VI, which they were trained to recognize, discriminate and produce; Timbre—recognition of timbres from different instruments and voices; Form—children listened to classical music and to children's melodies.'

25  Anvari, S.H., Trainor, L.J., Woodside, J., and Levy, B.A. (2002), 'Relations among musical skills, phonological processing, and early reading ability in preschool children', *Journal of Experimental Child Psychology*, 83(2), 111–130.

26  Strait D.L., Hornickel. J., Kraus. N,. (2011), 'Subcortical processing of speech regularities predicts reading and music aptitude in children'. *Behavioral and Brain Functions*, 7, 44.

27  Hallam, S. (2010), 'The power of music: Its impact on the intellectual, social and personal development of children and young people', *International Journal of Music Education*, 28(3), 269–289.

28  Sloboda, J.A., and Howe, M.J.A. (1992), 'Transitions in the early musical careers of able young musicians: choosing instruments and teachers', *Journal of Research in Music Education*, 40(4), 283–294.

29  Sosniak, L.A. (1985), 'Learning to be a concert pianist', in B.S. Bloom (ed.), *Developing talent in young people* (pp. 19–67). New York: Ballantine.

30  Sloboda, J.A., and Howe, M.J.A. (1991), 'Biographical precursors of musical excellence: An interview study', *Psychology of Music*, 19(1), 3–21.

31  Davidson, J.W., et al. (1998), 'Characteristics of Music Teachers and the Progress of Young Instrumentalists', *Journal of Research in Music Education*, 46(1) 141–160.

32  *Ibid.*

33  Austin, J., Renwick, J., and McPherson, G.E. (2006), 'Developing motivation', in G.E. McPherson (ed.), *The child as musician: A handbook of musical development* (pp. 213–238). Oxford: Oxford University Press.

34  Hallam, S. (1998), *Instrumental Teaching: a practical guide to better teaching and learning*. Oxford: Heinemann.

35  Ericsson, K.A., Krampe, R.T., and Tesch-Römer, C. (1993), 'The Role of Deliberate Practice in the Acquisition of Expert Performance', *Psychological Review*, 100(3), 363–406.

36  Marcus, G. (2012), *Guitar Zero: The New Musicians and the Science of Learning*. London: Penguin Press.

37  McPherson, G.E., and Renwick, J. (2011), 'Self-regulation and mastery of musical skills', in B. Zimmerman and D. Schunk (eds), *Handbook of self-regulation of learning and performance*. New York: Routledge.

38  McPherson, G.E. (2005), 'From child to musician: Skill development during the beginning stages of learning an instrument', *Psychology of Music*, 33(1), 5–35.

39  Sloboda, J.A., and Davidson, J.W. (1996), 'The young performing musician', in I. Deliège and J.A. Sloboda (eds.), *Musical Beginnings: Origins and development of musical competence* (pp. 171–190). Oxford: Oxford University Press.

40  Pitts, S., and Davidson, J. (2000), 'Developing effective practise strategies: Case studies of three young instrumentalists', *Music Education Research*, 2(1), 45–56.

41  *Ibid.*

42  Sloboda, J.A., Davidson, J.W., Howe, M.J.A, and Moore, D.G. (1996), 'The role of practice in the development of performing musicians', *British Journal of Psychology*, 87, 287–309.

43  Trainor, L.J., et al. (2012), 'Becoming musically enculturated: effects of music classes for infants on brain and behavior', *Annals of the New York Academy of Sciences*, 1252, 129–138

44  Hannon, E.E., and Trainor, L.J. (2007), 'Music acquisition: Effects of enculturation and formal training on development', *Trends in Cognitive Sciences*, 11(11), 466–472. Bigand, E., and Poulin-Charronnat, B. (2006), 'Are we "experienced listeners"? A review of the musical capacities that do not depend on formal musical training', *Cognition*, 100(1), 100–130. Trainor, L.J., and Trehub, S.E. (1994), 'Key membership and implied harmony in Western tonal music: Developmental perspectives', *Perception and Psychophysics*, 56(2), 125–132.

## Chapter 3: Music for adolescence

1  You need to have seen *Dirty Rotten Scoundrels*, starring Michael Caine and Steve Martin, to get that reference. Good film.

2  Bonneville-Roussy, A., Rentfrow, P.J., Xu, M.K., and Potter, J. (2013), 'Music through the ages: Trends in musical engagement and preferences from adolescence through middle adulthood', *Journal of Personality and Social Psychology*, 105(4), 703–717.

3  Juslin, P.N., et al. (2008), 'An experience sampling study of emotional reactions to music: Listener, music, and situation', *Emotion*, 8(5), 668–683.

4  DeNora, T. (1999), 'Music as a technology of the self', *Poetics*, 27, 31–56. DeNora, T. (2000), *Music in everyday life.* Cambridge: Cambridge University Press.

5  Gabrielsson, A. (transl. R. Bradbury) (2011), *Strong experiences with music*. Oxford: Oxford University Press.

6  North, A.C., Hargreaves, D.J., and Hargreaves, J.J. (2004), 'Uses of music in everyday life', *Music Perception*, 22(1), 41–77. North, A.C., and Hargreaves, D.J. (2009), 'The power of music', *The Psychologist*, 22(2), 1012–1015.

7  Allen, R., Walsh, R., and Zangwell, N. (2013), 'The same, only different: what can responses to music in autism tell us about the nature of musical emotions?', *Frontiers in Psychology*, 4, 156.

8  Juslin, P., and Västfjäll, D. (2008), 'Emotional responses to music: The need to consider underlying mechanisms', *Behavioral and Brain Sciences*, 31(5), 559–575.

9  Juslin, P.N., and Laukka, P. (2003), 'Communication of emotion in vocal expression and music performance: Different channels, same code?', *Psychological Bulletin*, 129(5), 770–814.

10  Lerdahl, F., and Jackendoff, R. (1983), *A generative theory of tonal music*. Cambridge, MA: MIT Press.

11  Salimpoor, V.N., et al. (2011), 'Anatomically distinct dopamine release during anticipation and experience of peak emotion to music', *Nature Neuroscience*, 14, 257–262.

12  Davies, J.B. (1978), *The Psychology of Music*. London: Hutchinson.

13  North, A.C., Hargreaves, D.J., and O'Neill, S.A. (2000), 'The importance of music to adolescents', *British Journal of Educational Psychology*, 70, 255–272.

14  Krause, A.E., North, A.C., and Hewitt, L.Y. (2013), 'Music listening in everyday life: Devices and choice'. *Psychology of Music*, DOI: 10.1177/0305735613496860.

15  Schwartz, K.D., and Fouts, G.T. (2003), 'Music preferences, personality style and developmental issues of adolescents', *Journal of Youth and Adolescence*, 32(3), 205–213.

16  Lonsdale, A.J., and North, A.C. (2011), 'Why do we listen to music? A uses & gratifications analysis', *British Journal of Psychology*, 102(1), 108–134.

17  Mullis, R.L., and Chapman, P. (2000), 'Age, gender, and self-esteem differences in adolescent coping style', *Journal of Social Psychology*, 140(4), 539–541.

18  Saarikallio, S. (2007), 'Music as mood regulation in adolescence', Ph.D. dissertation, University of Jyväskylä, Jyväskylä, Finland. Saarikallio, S., and Erkkilä, J. (2007), 'The role of music in adolescents' mood regulation', *Psychology of Music*, 35(1), 88–109.

19  Miranda, D., and Claes, M. (2009), 'Music listening, coping, peer affiliation and depression in adolescence', *Psychology of Music*, 37(2), 215–233.

20  Raviv, A., Bar-Tal, D., Raviv, A., and Ben-Horin, A. (1996), 'Adolescent
    idolization of pop singers: Causes, expressions, and reliance', *Journal of
    Youth and Adolescence*, 25(5), 631–650. Saarikallio, A., and Erkkilä, J. (2007),
    'The role of music in adolescents' mood regulation', *Psychology of Music*,
    35(1), 88–109.

21  Saarikallio, S., and Erkkilä, J. (2007), 'The role of music in adolescents'
    mood regulation', *Psychology of Music*, 35(1), 88–109.

22  North, A.C., and Hargreaves, D.J. (2003), 'Is music important? Two
    common misconceptions', *The Psychologist*, 16(8), 406–410.

23  Associated Press article from 1957 sourced from http://quoteinvestigator.
    com/2012/07/13/rock-degenerate/ (downloaded 3 September 2012).

24  Maguire, E.R., and Snipes, J.B. (1994), 'Reassessing the link between
    country music and suicide', *Social Forces*, 72(4), 1239-1243. Mulder, J., et al.
    (2007), 'Music Taste Groups and Problem Behavior', *Journal of Youth and
    Adolescence*, 36(3), 313–324.

25  Bleich, S., Zillmann, D., and Weaver, J. (1991), 'Enjoyment and
    consumption of defiant rock music as a function of adolescent
    rebelliousness', *Journal of Broadcasting and Electronic Media*, 35(3), 351–366.
    Hansen, C.H., and Hansen, R.D. (1990), 'Rock music videos and antisocial
    behavior', *Basic and Applied Social Psychology*, 11(4), 357–369. Johnson,
    J.D., Jackson, L.A., and Gatto, L. (1995), 'Violent attitudes and deferred
    academic aspiration: Deleterious effects of exposure to rap music', *Basic
    and Applied Social Psychology*, 16(1-2), 27–41.

26  Anderson, C.A., et al. (2003), 'The influence of media violence on youth',
    *Psychological Science in the Public Interest*, 4(3), 81–110.

27  Martin, G., Clarke, M., and Pearce, C. (1993), 'Adolescent suicide: Music
    preference as an indicator of vulnerability', *Journal of the American Academy
    of Child and Adolescent Psychiatry*, 32(3), 530–535.

28  Hansen, C.H., and Hansen, R.D. (1990), 'Rock music videos and antisocial
    behavior', *Basic and Applied Social Psychology*, 11(4), 357–369. Johnson,
    J.D., Jackson, L.A., and Gatto, L. (1995), 'Violent attitudes and deferred
    academic aspirations: Deleterious effects of exposure to rap music', *Basic
    and Applied Social Psychology*, 16(1-2), 27–41. Kalof, L. (1999), 'The effects
    of gender and music video imagery on sexual attitudes', *Journal of Social
    Psychology*, 139(3), 378–385.

29  Anderson, C.A., Carnagey, N.L., and Eubanks, J. (2003), 'Exposure to
    violent media: The effects of songs with violent lyrics on aggressive
    thoughts and feelings', *Journal of Personality and Social Psychology*, 84(5),
    960–971.

30  North, A.C., and Hargreaves, D.J. (2005), 'Brief report: Labelling effects on the perceived deleterious consequences of pop music listening', *Journal of Adolescence*, 28(3), 433–440.

31  Fischer, P., and Greitemeyer, T. (2006), 'Music and aggression. The impact of sexual-aggressive song lyrics on aggression-related thoughts, emotions and behavior toward the same and the opposite sex', *Personality and Social Psychology Bulletin*, 32(9), 1165–1176.

32  MacDonald, R.A.R., Hargreaves, D.J., and Miell, D. (eds.), *Musical identities*. Oxford: Oxford University Press.

33  O'Neill, S.A. (2002), 'The self-identity of young musicians', in R.A.R. MacDonald, D.J. Hargreaves and D. Miell (eds), *Musical identities* (pp. 79–96). Oxford: Oxford University Press.

34  Rentfrow, P.J. (2012), 'The role of music in everyday life: Current directions in the social psychology of music', *Social and Personality Psychology*, 6(5), 402–416.

35  Rentfrow, P.J., and Gosling, S.D. (2003), 'The do re mi's of everyday life: the structure and personality correlates of music preferences', *Journal of Personality and Social Psychology*, 84(6), 1236–1256.

36  Tarrant, M., North, A.C., and Hargreaves, D.J. (2000), 'English and American adolescents' reasons for listening to music', *Psychology of Music*, 28(2), 166–173.

37  Tekman, H.G., and Hortaçsu, N. (2002), 'Aspects of stylistic knowledge: What are different styles like and why do we listen to them?', *Psychology of Music*, 30(1), 28–47.

38  Berger, J., and Heath, C. (2008), 'Who Drives Divergence? Identity-Signaling, Outgroup Dissimilarity, and the Abandonment of Cultural Tastes', *Journal of Personality and Social Psychology*, 95(3), 593–607.

39  Tarrant, M., North, A.C., and Hargreaves, D.J. (2001), 'Social categorisation, self-esteem, and the estimated musical preferences of male adolescents', *Journal of Social Psychology*, 141(5), 565–581.

40  Zillmann, D., and Gan, S. (1997), 'Musical taste in adolescence', in D.J. Hargreaves, and A. North (eds), *The social psychology of music* (pp. 161–187). Oxford: Oxford University Press.

41  Knobloch, S., Vorderer, P., and Zillmann, D. (2000), 'The impact of music preferences on the perception of potential friends in adolescence', *Zeitschrift für Sozialpsychologie*, 31, 18–30.

42  Rodríguez-Bailón, R., Ruiz, J., and Moya, M. (2009), 'The Impact of Music on Automatically Activated Attitudes: Flamenco and Gypsy People', *Group Processes Intergroup Relations*, 12(3) 381–396.

43  Holbrook, M.B., and Schindler, R.M. (1989), 'Some exploratory findings on the development of musical tastes', *Journal of Consumer Research*, 16, 119–124.

44  Gabrielsson, A. (transl. R. Bradbury) (2011), *Strong Experiences with Music*. Oxford: Oxford University Press.

45  Rentfrow, P.J. (2012), 'The role of music in everyday life: Current directions in the social psychology of music', *Social and Personality Psychology*, 6(5), 402–416.

46  Salimpoor, V.N., et al. (2011), 'Anatomically distinct dopamine release during anticipation and experience of peak emotion to music', *Nature Neuroscience*, 14, 257–262.

47  Janata, P., Tomic, S.T., and Rakowski, S.K. (2007), 'Characterisation of music-evoked autobiographical memories', *Memory*, 15, 845–860.

48  Janata, P. (2009), 'The neural architecture of music-evoked autobiographical memories', *Cerebral Cortex*, 19(11), 2579–2594.

49  '(Sittin' on) the Dock of the Bay' by Otis Redding, 'Across the Universe' by The Beatles, 'Bachata Rosa' by Juan Luis Guerra, 'Mr Tambourine Man' by The Byrds, 'Piece of my Heart' by Big Brother and the Holding Company (featuring Janis Joplin on lead vocals). 'Bachata Rosa' is the odd one out.

50  'The Moors' by Weather Report, 'If You Want Me To Stay' by Sly Stone, 'Concrete Jungle' by The Wailers, 'September Gurls' by Alex Chilton's Big Star, 'Be My Baby' by The Ronettes, 'Every Day' by Buddy Holly.

## Chapter 4: The musical adult

1  Altenmüller, E., and Schlaug, G. (2012), 'Music, Brain and Health: Exploring Biological Foundations of Music's Health Effect', in R.A.R. MacDonald, G. Kreutz and L. Mitchell (eds.), *Music, Health, & Wellbeing*. Oxford: Oxford University Press.

2  Maguire, E.A., Woollett, K., and Spiers, H.J. (2006), 'London taxi drivers and bus drivers: A structural MRI and neuropsychological analysis', *Hippocampus*, 16(12), 1091–1101.

3  Driemeyer, J., et al. (2008), 'Changes in gray matter induced by learning— revisited', *PLOS ONE*, 3(7), e2669.

4  Schlaug, G., et al. (2009), 'Training-induced Brain plasticity in Young Children', *Annals of the New York Academy of Sciences*, 1169, 205–208.

5  Stewart, L. (2008), 'Do musicians have different brains?', *Clinical Medicine*, 8, 304–308. Barrett, K.C., Ashley, R., Strait, D.L., and Kraus, N. (2013) Art and Science: How Musical Training Shapes the Brain. *Frontiers in Auditory Cognitive Neuroscience*, 4, 713

6   Hyde, K.L., et al. (2009), 'The effects of musical training on structural brain development: a longitudinal study', *Annals of the New York Academy of Sciences*, 1169, 182–186. Hyde, K.L., et al. (2009), 'Musical Training Shapes Structural Brain Development', *Journal of Neuroscience*, 29(10), 3019–3025.

7   Schlaug, G., Jancke, L., Huang, Y., and Staiger, J.F. (1995), 'Increased corpus callosum size in musicians', *Neuropsychologia*, 33(8), 1047–1055.

8   Westerhausen, R., et al. (2006), 'Interhemispheric transfer time and structural properties of the corpus callosum', *Neuroscience Letters*, 409(2), 140–145. Patston, L.L.M, et al. (2007), 'The unusual symmetry of musicians: Musicians have equilateral interhemispheric transfer for visual information', *Neuropsychologia*, 45(9), 2059–2065.

9   Ridding, M.C., Brouwer, B., and Nordstrom, M.A. (2000), 'Reduced interhemispheric inhibition in musicians', *Experimental Brain Research*, 133, 249–253.

10  Bengtsson, S.L., et al. (2005), 'Extensive piano practicing has regionally specific effects on white matter development', *Nature Neurosciences*, 8, 1148–1150.

11  Halwani, G.F., Loui, P., Rueber, T., and Schlaug, G. (2011), 'Effects of practice and experience on the arcuate fasciculus: comparing singers, instrumentalists, and non-musicians', *Frontiers in Psychology*, 2, 156.

12  Stewart, L. (2008), 'Do musicians have different brains?', *Clinical medicine*, 8(3), 304–308.

13  Ragert, P., Schmidt, A., Altenmüller. E, and Dinse, H.R. (2004), 'Superior tactile performance and learning in professional pianists: evidence for meta-plasticity in musicians', *European Journal of Neuroscience*, 19(2), 473–478.

14  Watanabe, D., Savion-Lemieux, T., and Penhune, V.B. (2007), 'The effect of early musical training on adult motor performance: Evidence for a sensitive period in motor learning', *Experimental Brain Research*, 176(2), 332–340.

15  Amunts, K., et al. (1997), 'Motor cortex and hand motor skills: Structural compliance in the human brain', *Human Brain Mapping*, 5(3), 206–215.

16  Bangert, M., and Schlaug, G. (2006), 'Specialization of the specialized in features of external human brain morphology', *European Journal of Neuroscience*, 24(6), 1832–1834.

17  Pantev, C., Engelien, A., Candia, V., and Elbert, T. (2001), 'Representational Cortex in Musicians: Plastic Alterations in Response to Musical Practice', *Annals of the New York Academy of Sciences*, 930(1), 300–314.

18  Elbert, T., et al. (1995), 'Increased cortical representation of the fingers of the left hand in string players', *Science*, 270(5234), 305–307.

19  Schneider, P., et al. (2002), 'Morphology of Heschl's gyrus reflects enhanced activation in the auditory cortex of musicians', *Nature Neuroscience*, 5(7), 688–694.

20  Gaab, N., et al. (2005), 'Neural correlates of rapid spectrotemporal processing in musicians and nonmusicians', *Annals of the New York Academy of Sciences*, 1060, 82–88. Musacchia, G., Strait, D., and Kraus, N. (2008), 'Relationships between behavior, brainstem and cortical encoding of seen and heard speech in musicians and nonmusicians', *Hearing Research*, 241(1-2), 34–42.

21  Strait, D., and Kraus, N. (2011), 'Playing music for a smarter ear: cognitive, perceptual and neurobiological evidence', *Music Perception*, 29(2), 133–146.

22  Pantev, C., et al. (1998), 'Increased auditory cortical representation in musicians', *Nature*, 392(6678), 811–814.

23  Pantev, C., et al. (2001), 'Timbre-specific enhancement of auditory cortical representations in musicians', *Neuroreport*, 12(1), 169–174.

24  Strait, D.L., et al. (2012), 'Specialization among the specialized: auditory brainstem function is tuned in to timbre', *Cortex*, 48(3), 360-362.

25  Wong, P.C.M., et al. (2007), 'Musical Experience Shapes Human Brainstem Encoding of Linguistic Pitch Patterns', *Nature Neuroscience*, 10(4), 420–422.

26  Slevc, L.R., and Miyake, A. (2006), 'Individual differences in second language proficiency: Does musical ability matter?', *Psychological Science*, 17(8), 675–681.

27  Parbery-Clark, A., Strait, D.L., and Kraus, N. (2011), 'Context-dependent encoding in the auditory brainstem subserves enhanced speech-in-noise perception in musicians', *Neuropsychologia*, 49(12), 3338–3345.

28  Parbery-Clark, A., Tierney, A., Strait, D.L., and Kraus, N. (2012), 'Musicians have fine-tuned neural distinction of speech syllables', *Neuroscience*, 219, 111–119.

29  White-Schwoch, T., et al. (2013), 'Older adults benefit from music training early in life: biological evidence for long-term training-driven plasticity', *Journal of Neuroscience*, 33(45), 17667–17674.

30  Haueisen, J., and Knösche, T.R. (2001), 'Involuntary Motor Activation in Pianists Evoked by Music Perception', *Journal of Cognitive Neuroscience*, 13(6), 786–792.

31  Jakobson, L.S., Lewycky, S.T., Kilgour, A.R., and Stoesz, B.M. (2008), 'Memory for verbal and visual material in highly trained musicians', *Music Perception*, 26(1), 41–55. Ho, Y., Cheung, M., and Chan, A.S. (2003), 'Music Training Improves Verbal but Not Visual Memory: Cross-Sectional and Longitudinal Explorations in Children', *Neuropsychology*, 17(3), 439-450.

Franklin, M.S., et al. (2008), 'The effects of musical training on verbal memory', *Psychology of Music*, 36(3), 353–365.

32  Watanabe, D., Savion-Lemieux, T., and Penhune, V.B. (2007), 'The effect of early musical training on adult motor performance: evidence for a sensitive period in motor learning', *Experimental Brain Research*, 176(2), 332–340. Meister et al. (2005), 'Effects of long-term practice and task complexity in musicians and nonmusicians performing simple and complex motor tasks: Implications for cortical motor organization', *Human Brain Mapping*, 25(3), 345–352.

33  Zatorre, R.J. (2013), 'Predispositions and Plasticity in Music and Speech Learning: Neural Correlates and Implications', *Science*, 342 (6158), 585–589.

34  Stewart, L. (2011), 'Characterizing Congenital Amusia', *Quarterly Journal of Experimental Psychology*, 64(4), 625–638.

35  Cuddy, L.L., Balkwill, L.-L., Peretz. I., and Holden, R.R. (2005), 'Musical difficulties are rare: A study of "tone deafness" among university students', *Annals of the New York Academy of Science*, 1060, 311–324.

36  Sloboda, J.A., Wise, K.J., and Peretz, I. (2005), 'Quantifying tone deafness in the general population', *The Neurosciences and Music II: From Perception to Performance (Annals of the New York Academy of Sciences)*, 1060, 255–261.

37  Wise, K.J., and Sloboda, J.A. (2008), 'Establishing an empirical profile of self-defined "tone deafness": Perception, singing performance and self-assessment', *Musicae Scientiae*, 12, 3–23.

38  Anderson, S., et al. (2012), 'Congenital amusia: is there potential for learning? A study of the effects of singing interventions on pitch perception and production of those with congenital amusia', *Annals of the New York Academy of Sciences*. 1252, 345-353.

39  Loui, P., Guenther, F.H., Mathys, C., and Schlaug, G. (2008), 'Action-perception mismatch in tone-deafness', *Current Biology*, 18(8), R331–R332. Williamson, V.J., et al. (2012), 'Perception and action de-coupling in congenital amusia: Sensitivity to task demands', *Neuropsychologia*, 50(1), 172–180.

40  Peretz, I., et al. (2002), 'Congenital Amusia: a disorder of fine-grained pitch discrimination', *Neuron*, 33(2), 185–191.

41  Lebrun, M.-A., et al. (2012), 'Congenital amusia in childhood: A case study', *Cortex*, 48(6), 683–688.

42  Kalmus, H., and Fry, D.B. (1980), 'On tune deafness (dysmelodia): frequency, development, genetics and musical background', *Annals of Human Genetics*, 43(4), 369–382.

43  Henry, M.J., and McAuley, J.D. (2010), 'On the Prevalence of Congenital Amusia', *Music Perception*, 27(5), 413–418.

44  Omigie, D., Müllensiefen, D., and Stewart, L., (2013) 'The experience of music in congenital amusia', *Music Perception*, 30(1), 1-18.

45  McDonald, C., and Stewart, L. (2008), 'Uses and functions of music in congenital amusia', *Music Perception*, 25(4), 345–355.

46  Williamson, V.J., and Stewart, L. (2010), 'Memory for pitch in Congenital Amusia: Beyond a fine-grained pitch perception problem', *Memory*, 18(6), 657–669.

47  Loui, P., Alsop, D., and Schlaug, G. (2009), 'Tone-Deafness: a Disconnection Syndrome?', *Journal of Neuroscience*, 29(33), 10215–10220.

48  Peretz, I., Brattico, E., Järvenpää, M., and Tervaniemi, M. (2009), 'The amusic brain: in tune, out of key, and unaware', *Brain*, 132(5), 1277–1286. Omigie, D., Pearce, M., Williamson V.J., and Stewart, L. (2013), 'Electrophysiological correlates of melodic processing in congenital amusia', *Neuropsychologia*, 51(9),1749-1762.

49  Moreau, P., Jolicoeur, P., and Peretz, I. (2009), 'Automatic brain responses to pitch changes in congenital amusia', *Annals of the New York Academy of Sciences*, 1169, 191–194.

50  Omigie, D., Pearce, M.T., and Stewart, L. (2012), 'Tracking of pitch probabilities in congenital amusia', *Neuropsychologia*, 50(7), 1483–1493.

51  http://faculty.washington.edu/losterho/DemorestXOsterhout_2012.pdf

52  Egermann, H., Fernando, N., Chuen, L., and McAdams, S. (in preparation), 'Universal psychophysiological response to music – Comparing Western listeners to Congolese Pygmies'.

53  Demorest, S.M., Morrison, S.J., Beken, M.N., and Jungbluth, D. (2008), 'Lost in translation: an enculturation effect in music memory performance', *Music Perception*, 25, 213–223. Morrison, S.J., Demorest, S.M., and Stambaugh, L.A. (2008), 'Enculturation effects in music cognition: the role of age and music complexity', *Journal of Research in Music Education*, 56(2), 118–129.

54  Demorest, S.M., et al. (2010), 'Music comprehension among Western and Turkish listeners: FMRI investigation of an enculturation effect', *Social, Cognitive and Affective Neuroscience*, 5(2-3), 282–291. Demorest, S.M., and Osterhout, L.L. (2012), 'ERP responses to cross-cultural melodic expectancy violations', *Annals of the New York Academy of Sciences*, 1252, 152–157.

55 Wong, P.C., Chan, A.H., Roy, A., and Margulis, E.H. (2011), 'The bimusical brain is not two monomusical brains in one: evidence from musical affective processing', *Journal of Cognitive Neuroscience*, 23(12), 4082–4093.

56 http://www.guardian.co.uk/lifeandstyle/2012/oct/12/experience-head-injury-musical-prodigy?INTCMP=SRCH

57 Marcus, G. (2011), *Guitar Zero: The new musician and the science of learning*. New York: Penguin Press.

58 Mithen, S.J. (2005), *The Singing Neanderthals: the Origins of Music, Language, Mind and Body*. Cambridge, Massachusetts: Harvard University Press.

59 Mithen, S., and Parsons, L. (2008), 'The Brain as a Cultural Artefact', *Cambridge Archaeological Journal*, 18(3), 415–422.

60 Zatorre, R.J., Delhommeau, K., and Zarate, J.M. (2012), 'Modulation of auditory cortex response to pitch variation following training with microtonal melodies', *Frontiers in Psychology*, 3, 544. Lappe, C., Trainor, L.J., Herholz, S.C., and Pantev, C. (2011), 'Cortical Plasticity Induced by Short-Term Multimodal Musical Rhythm Training', *PLOS ONE*, 6(6): e21493.

61 Herholz, S.C., and Zatorre, R.J. (2012), 'Musical Training as a Framework for Brain Plasticity: Behavior, Function, and Structure', *Neuron*, 76(3), 486–502.

## Chapter 5: Music at work

1 A colleague and good friend of mine, Anneli Beronius Haake, has studied music and work for many years and I thank her for much of the inspiration for the first part of this chapter.

2 Antrim, D.K. (1943), 'Music in industry', *The Musical Quarterly*, XXIX(3), 275–290. Kirkpatrick, F.H. (1943), 'Music Takes the Mind Away', *Personnel Journal*, 22, 225–228.

3 Wyatt, S., and Langdon, J.N. (1937), 'Fatigue and boredom in repetitive work', Industrial Health Research Board report No. 77. London: Her Majesty's Stationery Office.

4 Fox, J.G., and Embrey, E.D. (1972), 'Music – an aid to productivity', *Applied Ergonomics*, 3(4), 202–205. Newman Jr, R.I, Hunt, D.L., and Rhodes, F. (1966), 'Effect of music on employee attitude and productivity in a skateboard factory', *Journal of Applied Psychology*, 50(6), 493–496.

5 Uhrbrock, R.S. (1961), 'Music on the job: its influence on worker morale and production', *Personnel Psychology*, 14(1), 9–38.

6 Smith, W.A.S. (1961), 'Effects of industrial music in a work situation requiring complex mental activity', *Psychological Reports*, 8, 159–162.

7   Oldham, G.R., et al. (1995), 'Listen while you work? Quasi-experimental relations between personal-stereo headset use and employee work response', *Journal of Applied Psychology*, 80(5), 547–564.

8   Lesiuk, T. (2005), 'The effect of music listening on work performance', *Psychology of Music*, 33(2), 173–191.

9   Haake, A.B. (2011), 'Individual music listening in workplace settings: an exploratory survey of offices in the UK', *Musicae Scientiae*, 15(1), 107–129.

10  Kämpfe, J., Sedlmeier, P., and Renkewitz, F. (2010), 'The impact of background music on adult listeners: A meta-analysis', *Psychology of Music*, 39(4), 424–448.

11  Berlyne, D.E. (1971), *Aesthetics and psychobiology*. New York: Meredith. Kahneman, D. (1973), 'Arousal and attention', in D. Kahneman (ed.), *Attention and effort* (pp. 28–49). Englewood Cliffs, NJ: Prentice Hall. Yerkes, R.M., and Dodson, J.D. (1908), 'The relation of strength of stimulus to rapidity of habit-formation', *Journal of Comparative Neurology and Psychology*, 18(5), 459–482.

12  Thompson, W.F., Schellenberg, E.G., and Letnic, A.K. (2012), 'Fast and loud music disrupts reading comprehension', *Psychology of Music*, 40, 698–706.

13  Csikszentmihalyi, M. (1990), *Flow: The Psychology of Optimal Experience*. New York: Harper & Row.

14  Thompson, W.F., Schellenberg, E.G., and Husain, G. (2001), 'Mood, arousal, and the Mozart effect', *Psychological Science*, 12(3), 248–251.

15  Furnham, A., and Bradley, A. (1997), 'Music While You Work: The Differential Distraction of Background Music on the Cognitive Test Performance of Introverts and Extraverts', *Applied Cognitive Psychology*, 11(5), 445–455.

16  Eysenck, H. (1967), *The biological basis of personality*. Springfield, IL: Thomas.

17  Cassidy, G., and MacDonald, R.A.R. (2007), 'The effect of background music and background noise on the task performance of introverts and extraverts', *Psychology of Music*, 35(3), 517–537.

18  Chamorro-Premuzic, T., and Furnham, A. (2007), 'Personality and music: Can traits explain how people use music in everyday life?', *Journal of British Psychology*, 98(2), 175–185.

19  Martí Pérez, J. (1997), 'When music becomes noise: Sound and music that people in Barcelona hear but don't want to listen to', *World of Music*, 39(2), 9–17.

20  Parente, J.A. (1976), 'Musical preference as a factor of music distraction', *Perceptual and Motor Skills*, 43, 337–338.

21 Greasley, A.E. (2008), 'Engagement with music in everyday life: An in-depth study of adults' musical preferences and listening behaviours' (Unpublished doctoral thesis, Keele University, Stoke-on-Trent, UK).

22 Cassidy, G.G., and MacDonald, R.A.R. (2010), 'The effects of music on time perception and performance of a driving game', *Scandinavian Journal of Psychology*, 51(6), 455–464.

23 Hartley, L.R., and Williams, T. (1977), 'Steady state noise and music and vigilance', *Ergonomics*, 20(3), 277–285.

24 Oakes, S., and North, A.C. (2006), 'The impact of background musical tempo and timbre congruity upon ad content recall and affective response', *Applied Cognitive Psychology*, 20(4), 505–520.

25 Ransdell, S.E., and Gilroy, L. (2001), 'The effects of background music on word processed writing', *Computers in Human Behavior*, 17(2), 141–148.

26 Kämpfe, J., Sedlmeier, P., and Renkewitz, F. (2011), 'The impact of background music on adult listeners: A meta-analysis', *Psychology of Music*, 39(4), 424–448.

27 Lanza, J. (1994), *Elevator music: A surreal history of Muzak, easy-listening and other moodsong*. New York: St Martin's Press.

28 Frith, S. (2002), 'Music and everyday life', *Critical Quarterly*, 44(1), 35–48.

29 Wearden, J.H., and Penton-Voak, I.S. (1995), 'Feeling the heat: body temperature and the rate of subjective time, revisited', *Quarterly Journal of Experimental Psychology*, 48(2), 129–41.

30 Hammond, C. (2012), *Time warped*. Edinburgh: Canongate Books Ltd.

31 Yalch, R.F., and Spangenberg, E.R. (2000), 'The effects of music in a retail setting on real and perceived shopping times', *Journal of Business Research*, 42(2), 139–147.

32 Yalch, R.F., and Spangenberg, E. R. (1990), 'Effects of store music on shopping behavior', *Journal of Consumer Marketing*, 7(2), 55–63.

33 Kellaris, J.J., and Kent, R.J. (1992), 'The influence of music on consumers' temporal perceptions: Does time fly when you're having fun?', *Journal of Consumer Psychology*, 1(4), 365–376.

34 North, A.C., and Hargreaves, D.J. (2008), *The social and applied psychology of music*. Oxford: Oxford University Press.

35 Smith, P.C., and Curnow, R. (1966), '"Arousal Hypothesis" and the Effects of Music on Purchase Behavior', *Journal of Applied Psychology*, 50, 255–256.

36 Milliman, R.E. (1982), 'Using Background Music to Affect Behavior of Supermarket Shoppers', *Journal of Marketing*, 46 (Summer), 86–91.

37 Caldwell, C., and Hibbert, S.A. (1999), 'Play That One Again: The effect of music tempo on consumer behaviour in a Restaurant', in *European Advances*

*in Consumer Research*, Volume 4 (eds. Bernard Dubois, Tina M. Lowrey, L.J. Shrum, and Marc Vanhuele), pp. 58–62.

38  Guéguen, N., Jacob, C., Lourle, M., and Le Guellec, H. (2007), 'Effect of background music on consumer's behavior: A field experiment in an open-air market', *European Journal of Scientific Research*, 16(2), 268–272.

39  North, A.C., Hargreaves, D.J., and McKendrick, J. (1999), 'Music and on-hold waiting time', *British Journal of Psychology*, 90, 161–164.

40  Lai, C.-J., et al. (2011), 'Effect of Background Music Tempo and Playing Method on Shopping Website Browsing', *Smart Innovation, Systems and Technologies*, 10, 439–447.

41  Areni, C.S., and Kim, D. (1993), 'The influence of background music on shopping behaviour: Classical versus Top Forty music in a wine store', in *Advances in Consumer Research*, Volume 20 (eds. L. McAlister and M.L. Rothschild), pp. 336–340.

42  North, A.C., Shilcock, A., and Hargreaves, D.J. (2003), 'The effect of musical style on restaurant customers' spending', *Environment and Behavior*, 35, 712–718.

43  Wilson, S. (2003), 'The effect of music on perceived atmosphere and purchase intentions in a restaurant', *Psychology of Music*, 31(1), 93–112.

44  North, A.C., Hargreaves, D.J., and McKendrick, J. (1999), 'The effect of music on instore wine selections', *Journal of Applied Psychology*, 84(2), 271–276.

45  Jacob, C., Guéguen, N., Boulbry, G., and Sami, S. (2009), '"Love is in the air": congruence between background music and goods in a florist', *The International Review of Retail, Distribution and Consumer Research*, 19(1), 75–79.

46  MacInnis, D.J., and Park, C.W. (1991), 'The Differential Role of Characteristics of Music on High- and Low-involvement Consumers' Processing of Ads', *Journal of Consumer Research*, 18, 161–173.

47  Oakes, S. (2007), 'Evaluating Empirical Research into Music in Advertising: A Congruity Perspective', *Journal of Advertising Research*, 47(1), 38–50.

48  Beverland, M., Lim, E.A.C., Morrison, M., and Terziovski, M. (2006), 'In-store music and consumer–brand relationships: relational transformation following experiences of (mis)fit', *Journal of Business Research*, 59 (9), 982–989.

49  Zander, M.F. (2006), 'Musical influences in advertising: how music modifies first impressions of product endorsers and brands', *Psychology of Music*, 34 (4), 465–480.

## Chapter 6: Music at play

1 North, A.C., Hargreaves, D.J., and Hargreaves, J.J. (2004), 'Uses of music in everyday life', *Music Perception*, 22(1), 41–77.

2 Krause, A.E., North, A.C., and Hewitt, L.Y. (2013), 'Music listening in everyday life: Devices and choice'. *Psychology of Music*, DOI: 10.1177/0305735613496860.

3 Besson, M., and Schön, D. (2001), 'Comparison between language and music', *Annals of the New York Academy of Sciences*, 930, 232–258.

4 Camurri, A., et al. (2004), 'Multimodal Analysis of Expressive Gesture in Music and Dance Performances', *Gesture-Based Communication in Human-Computer Interaction*, 2915, 20–39. Marin, M.M., and Bhattacharya, J. (2010), 'Music induced emotions: Some current issues and crossmodal comparisons', in J. Hermida and M. Ferrero (eds), *Music Education* (pp. 1–38). Hauppauge, NY: Nova Science Publishers.

5 Hagen, E.H., and Bryant, G.A. (2003), 'Music and dance as a coalition signalling system', *Human Nature*, 14(1), 21–51.

6 Witek, M.A.G. (2009), 'Groove Experience: Emotional and Physiological Responses to Groove-Based Music', *Proceedings of the 7th Triennial Conference of the European Society for the Cognitive Sciences of Music, ESCOM*, University of Jyvaskyla. Senn, O., and Kilchenmann, L. (2011), 'The secret ingredient – State of affairs and future directions in groove studies', in Antonio Baldassarre (ed.), *Musik, Raum, Akkord, Bild – Festschrift for Dorothea Baumann's 65th Birthday*, Bern: pp. 799–810.

7 Winkler, I., et al. (2009), 'Newborn infants detect the beat in music', *Proceedings of the National Academy of Sciences*, 106, 2468–2471.

8 Honing, H., et al. (2012). 'Rhesus monkeys (*Macaca mulatta*) detect rhythmic groups in music, but not the beat', *PLOS ONE*, 7(12), e51369.

9 Patel, A.D., Iversen, J.R., Bregman, M.R., and Schulz, I. (2009), 'Experimental evidence for synchronization to a musical beat in a nonhuman animal', *Current Biology*, 19, 827–830.

10 Fitch, W.T. (2013), 'Rhythmic cognition in humans and animals: distinguishing meter and pulse perception', *Frontiers in Systems Neuroscience*, 31, 7:68.

11 Schachner, A., Brady, T.F., Pepperberg, I.M., and Hauser, M.D. (2009), 'Spontaneous motor entrainment to music in multiple vocal mimicking species', *Current Biology*, 19(10), 831–836.

12 Hattori, Y., Tomonaga, M., and Matsuzawa, T. (2013), 'Spontaneous synchronized tapping to an auditory rhythm in a chimpanzee', *Scientific Reports 3*, 1566. Cook, P., Rouse, A., Wilson, M., and Reichmuth, C. (2013),

'A California Sea Lion (*Zalophus californianus*) Can Keep the Beat: Motor Entrainment to Rhythmic Auditory Stimuli in a Non Vocal Mimic', *Journal of Comparative Psychology*.

13  Luck, G., Saarikallio, S., Thompson, M., Burger, B., and Toiviainen, P. (2012), 'Hips don't lie: Multi-dimensional ratings of opposite-sex dancers' perceived attractiveness', in E. Cambouropoulos, C. Tsougras, P. Mavromatis and K. Pastiadis (eds), *Proceedings of 12th International Conference on Music Perception and Cognition* (Thessaloniki, Greece).

14  Zillmann, D., and Bhatia, A. (1989), 'Effects of associating with musical genres on heterosexual attraction', *Communication Research*, 16(2), 263–288.

15  Guéguen, N., Jacob, C., and Lamy, L. (2010), '"Love is in the air": Effects of songs with romantic lyrics on compliance with a courtship request', *Psychology of Music*, 38(3), 303–307.

16  Guéguen, N., Meineri, S., and Fischer-Lokou, J. (2013), 'Men's music ability and attractiveness to women in a real-life courtship context', *Psychology of Music*, published online 1 May 2013.

17  North, A.C., Tarrant, M., and Hargreaves, D.J. (2004), 'The effects of music on helping behaviour: a field study', *Environment and Behaviour*, 36(2), 266–275.

18  Lamy, L., Fischer-Lokou, J., and Guéguen, N. (2009), 'Induced reminiscence of love and chivalrous helping', *Current Psychology*, 28(3), 202–209.

19  LeDoux, J.E. (2000), 'Emotion circuits in the brain', *Annual Review of Neuroscience*, 23, 155–184.

20  Koelsch, S., et al. (2006), 'Investigating emotion with music: an fMRI study', *Human Brain Mapping*, 27(3), 239–250. Blood, A.J., and Zatorre, R.J. (2001), 'Intensely pleasurable responses to music correlate with activity in brain regions implicated in reward and emotion', *Proceedings of the National Academy of Sciences*, 98(2), 11818–11823.

21  Griffiths, T.D., Warren, J.D., Dean, J.L., and Howard, D. (2004), '"When the feeling's gone": a selective loss of musical emotion', *Journal of Neurology, Neurosurgery & Psychiatry*, 75, 344–345.

22  Gosselin, N., et al. (2005), 'Impaired recognition of scary music following unilateral temporal lobe excision', *Brain*, 128(3), 628–640.

23  Eldar, E., et al. (2007), 'Feeling the real world: limbic response to music depends on related content', *Cerebral Cortex*, 17(12), 2828–2840.

24  Boltz, M.G. (2001), 'Musical soundtracks as a schematic influence on the cognitive processing of filmed events', *Music Perception*, 18:427–454.

25   Phan, K.L., Wager, T.D., Taylor, S.F., and Liberzon, I. (2002), 'Functional neuroanatomy of emotion: a meta-analysis of emotion activation studies in PET and fMRI', *Neuroimage*, 16(2), 331–348.

26   Cohen, A.J. (2001), 'Music as a source of emotion in film', in Juslin, P.N., Sloboda, J.A. (eds.), *Music and emotion*. New York: Oxford University Press. pp. 249–272.

27   Austin, A., Moore, E., Chordia, P., and Gupta, U. (2010), 'Characterization of Movie Genre Based on Music Score', in *Proceedings of the 35th IEEE Conference of Acoustics, Speech, and Signal Processing*, 421–424.

28   Baumgartner, T., Lutz, K., Schmidt, C.F., and Jäncke, L. (2006), 'The emotional power of music: how music enhances the feeling of affective pictures', *Brain Research*, 23, 1075(1), 151–164

29   Huron, D. (2011), 'Why is sad music pleasurable? A possible role for prolactin', *Musicae Scientiae*, 15(2), 146–158.

30   Koelsch, S. (2012), *Brain and music*. Wiley.

31   http://filmsound.org/gustavo/leitmotif-revisted.htm

32   Hargreaves, D.J., and North, A.C. (2008), *The Social and Applied Psychology of Music*. Oxford: Oxford University Press.

33   The British Association of Sport and Exercise Sciences statement on the use of music in exercise: http://www.bases.org.uk/write/Documents/SES_EXPERT_3.pdf

34   Crust, L., and Clough, P.J. (2006), 'The influence of rhythm and personality in the endurance response to motivational asynchronous music', *Journal of Sports Sciences*, 24(2), 187–195.

35   Karageorghis, C.I., Terry, P.C., and Lane, A.M. (1999), 'Development and initial validation of an instrument to assess the motivational qualities of music in exercise and sport: The Brunel Music Rating Inventory', *Journal of Sports Sciences*, 17(9), 713–724.

36   Karageorghis, C.I., and Priest, D.L. (2012), 'Music in the exercise domain: A review and synthesis (Part I)', *International Review of Sport and Exercise Psychology*, 5(1): 44–66.

37   Hall, K.G., and Erickson, B. H. (1995), 'The effects of preparatory arousal on sixty-meter dash performance', *The Applied Research in Coaching and Athletics Annual*, 10, 70–79.

38   Priest, D.L., and Karageorghis, C.I. (2008), 'A qualitative investigation into the characteristics and effects of music accompanying exercise', *European Physical Education Review*, 14(3), 347–366.

39   Karageorghis, C.I., et al. (2009), 'Psychophysical and ergogenic effects of synchronous music during treadmill walking', *Journal of Sport & Exercise Psychology*, 31(1), 18–36.

40   Karageorghis, C.I., and Priest, D.L. (2012), 'Music in the exercise domain: a review and synthesis (Part I)', *International Review of Sport and Exercise Psychology*, 5(1), 44–66.

41   van der Vlist, B., Bartneck, C., and Mäueler, S. (2011), 'moBeat: Using interactive music to guide and motivate users during aerobic exercising', *Applied Psychophysiology and Biofeedback*, 36(2), 135–145.

42   Karageorghis, C.I., and Priest, D.L. (2012), 'Music in the exercise domain: A review and synthesis (Part II)', *International Review of Sport and Exercise Psychology*, 5(1), 67–84.

43   Dyrlund, A.K., and Wininger, S.R. (2008), 'The effects of music preference and exercise intensity on psychological variables', *Journal of Music Therapy*, 45(2), 114-134.

44   Karageorghis, C.I., and Priest, D.L. (2012), 'Music in the exercise domain: a review and synthesis (Part I)', *International Review of Sport and Exercise Psychology*, 5(1), 44–66.

45   The British Association of Sport and Exercise Sciences statement on the use of music in exercise: http://www.bases.org.uk/write/Documents/SES_EXPERT_3.pdf

46   Karageorghis, C., Jones, L., and Stuart, D.P. (2008), 'Psychological effects of music tempi during exercise', *International Journal of Sports Medicine*, 29(7), 613–619.

47   Crust, L., and Clough, P.J. (2006), 'The influence of rhythm and personality in the endurance response to motivational asynchronous music', *Journal of Sports Sciences*, 24(2), 187–195.

48   Karageorghis, C.I., et al. (2011), 'Ergogenic and psychological effects of synchronous music during circuit-type exercise', *Psychology of Sport and Exercise*, 11(6), 551–559.

49   http://www.theguardian.com/lifeandstyle/the-running-blog/2013/may/10/haile-gebrselassie-interview

50   http://www.theaustralian.com.au/arts/music/music-the-fuel-for-performance-overdrive-by-olympic-athletes/story-fn9d2mxu-1226424849410

51   Gluch, P.D. (1993), 'The use of music in preparing for sport performance', *Contemporary Thought*, 2, 33–53.

52   Jarraya, M., et al. (2012), 'The effects of music on high-intensity short-term exercise in well trained athletes', *Asian Journal of Sports Medicine*, 3(4), 233–238

53 http://www.guardian.co.uk/football/2013/feb/03/can-music-help-footballers-play-better?CMP=twt_fd

54 Brownley, K.A., McMurray, R.G., and Hackney, A.C. (1995), 'Effects of music on physiological and affective response to graded treadmill exercise in trained and untrained runners', *International Journal of Psychophysiology*, 19(3), 193–201. Mohammadzadeh, H., Tartibiyan, B., and Ahmadi, A. (2008), 'The effects of music on the perceived exertion rate and performance of trained and untrained individuals during progressive exercise', *Facta Universitatis: Series Physical Education & Sport*, 6, 67–74.

55 Terry, P.C., Karageorghis, C.I., Saha, A.M., and D'Auria, S. (2012), 'Effects of synchronous music on treadmill running among elite triathletes', *Journal of Science and Medicine in Sport*,15(1), 52-57.

56 Bishop, D.T., Karageorghis, C.I., and Loizou, G. (2007), 'A grounded theory of young tennis players' use of music to manipulate emotional state', *Journal of Sport and Exercise Psychology*, 29(5), 584–607.

57 Bishop, D. (2010), '"Boom Boom How": Optimising performance with music', *Sport and Exercise Psychology Review*, 6, 35-47.

## Chapter 7: Music and memory

1 Kang, H.J., and Williamson, V.J. (2013), 'Background music can facilitate second language learning', *Psychology of Music*. DOI: 10.1177/0305735613485152

2 Baddeley, A.D., Eysenck, M., and Anderson, M.C. (2009), *Memory*. Hove: Psychology Press. Baddeley, A.D. (2007), *Working memory, thought and action*. Oxford: Oxford University Press.

3 http://www.world-memory-statistics.com/disciplines.php

4 http://www.worldmemorychampionships.com/memory-achievements/

5 Hughes, E. (1915), 'Musical memory in piano playing and piano study', *The Musical Quarterly*, 1, 592–603.

6 Hallam, S. (1997), 'The development of memorisation strategies in musicians: Implications for education', *British Journal of Music Education*, 14(1), 87–97.

7 Ginsborg, J. (2002), 'Classical singers learning and memorising a new song: An observational study', *Psychology of Music*, 30(1), 58–101.

8 Chaffin, R., Lisboa, T., Logan, T., and Begosh, K.T. (2010), 'Preparing for Memorized Cello Performance: The Role of Performance Cues', *Psychology of Music*, 38, 3–30.

9 Noice, H., Chaffin, R., Jeffrey, J., and Noice, A. (2008), 'Memorization by a jazz pianist: A case study', *Psychology of Music*, 36(1), 63–79.

10  Williamon, A., Valentine, E., and Valentine, J. (2002), 'Shifting the focus of attention between levels of musical structure', *European Journal of Cognitive Psychology*, 14(4), 493–520. Williamon, A. (2002), 'Memorising music', in J. Rink (ed.), *Musical Performance: A Guide to Understanding* (pp. 113-126). Cambridge: Cambridge University Press. Chaffin, R., and Imreh, G. (2002), 'Practicing perfection: Piano performance as expert memory', *Psychological Science*, 13, 342–349.

11  Chaffin, R., and Imreh, G. (1997), '"Pulling teeth and torture": Musical memory and problem solving', *Thinking & Reasoning*, 3(4), 315–336. Chaffin, R., and Imreh, G. (2002), 'Practicing perfection: Piano performance as expert memory'. *Psychological Science*, 13, 342–349.

12  Williamon, A., and Valentine, E. (2002), 'The role of retrieval structures in memorizing music', *Cognitive Psychology*, 44(1), 1–32. Williamon, A. and Egner, T. (2004), 'Memory structures for encoding and retrieving a piece of music: An ERP investigation', *Cognitive Brain Research*, 22(1), 36–44.

13  Halpern, A.R, and Müllensiefen, D. (2008), 'Effects of timbre and tempo change on memory for music', *Quarterly Journal of Experimental Psychology*, 61(9), 1371–1384.

14  Standing, L. (1973), 'Learning 10,000 pictures', *Quarterly Journal of Experimental Psychology*, 25(2), 207–222.

15  Levitin, D.J. (1994), 'Absolute memory for musical pitch: Evidence from the production of learned melodies', *Perception & Psychophysics*, 56(4), 414–423.

16  Frieler, K., et al. (2013), 'Absolute Memory for Pitch: A Comparative Replication of Levitin's 1994 Study in Six European Labs', *Musicae Scientiae*, Special issue: Replication in music psychology, 7(3), 334–349.

17  Dowling, W.J., and Bartlett, J.C. (1981), 'The importance of interval information in long-term memory for melodies', *Psychomusicology*, 1(1), 30–49. Dowling, W.J., Kwak, S., and Andrews, M.W. (1995), 'The time course of recognition of novel melodies', *Perception & Psychophysics*, 57(2), 197–210.

18  Stalinski, S.M., and Schellenberg, E.G. (2013), 'Listeners Remember Music They Like', *Journal of Experimental Psychology: Learning, Memory, and Cognition*, 39(3), 700–716.

19  Weiss, M.W., Trehub, S.E., and Schellenberg, E.G. (2012), 'Something in the Way She Sings: Enhanced Memory for Vocal Melodies', *Psychological Science*, 23(10), 1074–1078.

20  Krumhansl, C. (2010), 'Plink! Thin slices of music', *Music Perception*, 27(5), 337–354.

21  Rubin, D.C. (1995), *Memory in oral traditions: The cognitive psychology of epic, ballads, and counting-out rhymes*. New York: Oxford University Press.

22  Dowling, W.J., Bartlett, J.C., Halpern, A.R., and Andrews, M.W. (2008), 'Melody Recognition at Fast and Slow Tempos: Effects of Age, Experience, and Familiarity', *Perception and Psychophysics*, 70(3), 496–502.

23  Schulkind, M.D., Hennis, L.K., and Rubin, D.C. (1999), 'Music, emotion, and autobiographical memory: They're playing your song', *Memory & Cognition*, 27(6), 948–955.

24  Finke, C., Esfahani, N.E., and Ploner, C.J. (2012), 'Preservation of musical memory in an amnesic professional cellist', *Current Biology*, 22(15), R591–2.

25  Samson, S., Dellacherie, D., and Platel, H. (2009), 'Emotional power of music in patients with memory disorders: clinical implications of cognitive neuroscience', *The Neurosciences and Music III: disorders and plasticity (Annals of the New York Academy of Sciences)*, 1169, 245–255: Baird, A., and Samson, S. (2009), 'Memory for music in Alzheimer's disease: Unforgettable?', *Neuropsychological Review*, 19(1), 85–101.

26  Schulkind, M.D. (2009), 'Is memory for music special?', *Annals of the New York Academy of Science*, 1169, 216–24.

27  Schacter, D.L. (1987), 'Implicit Memory: History and Current Status', *Journal of Experimental Psychology: Learning, Memory, and Cognition*, 13(3), 501–518. Hassin, R.R. (2013), 'Yes It Can: On the Functional Abilities of the Human Unconscious', *Perspectives on Psychological Science*, 8(2), 195–207.

28  De Gelder, B., De Haan, E.H.F., and Heywood, C.A. (2001), *Out of mind: Varieties of unconscious processes*. London: Oxford University Press. Cavaco, S., et al. (2004), 'The scope of preserved procedural memory in amnesia', *Brain*, 127(8): 1853–1867.

29  Liikkanen L. (2012), 'Musical Activities Predispose to Involuntary Musical Imagery', *Psychology of Music*, 40(2), 236–256.

30  Brown, S. (2006), 'The perceptual music track: The phenomenon of constant musical imagery', *Journal of Consciousness studies*, 13(6), 25–44.

31  Sacks, O. (2007), *Musicophilia: Tales of music and the brain*. New York: Alfred A. Knopf.

32  Kellaris, J.J. (2008), 'Music and consumers', in C.P. Haugtvedt, P. Herr and F.R. Kardes (eds.), *Handbook of consumer psychology* (pp. 837–856). New York: Taylor & Francis.

33  Levitin, D.J. (2006), *This is your brain on music*. New York: Dutton.

34  Halpern, A.R., and Bartlett, J.C. (2011), 'The persistence of musical memories: A descriptive study of earworms', *Music Perception*, 28(4), 425–443. Beaman, C.P., and Williams, T.I. (2010), 'Earworms (stuck song

syndrome): Towards a natural history of intrusive thoughts', *British Journal of Psychology*, 101(4), 637–653.

35  Williamson, V.J., and Jilka, S.R. (2013), 'Experiencing earworms: An interview study of Involuntary Musical Imagery', *Psychology of Music*, DOI: 10.1177/0305735613483848

36  Müllensiefen, D., et al., 'Individual differences in spontaneous involuntary musical imagery', *Music Perception* (in press 2013)

37  Wammes, M., and Baruš, I. (2009), 'Characteristics of spontaneous musical imagery', *Journal of Consciousness Studies*, 16(1), 37–61.

38  Floridou, G., Williamson, V.J., and Müllensiefen, D. (2012), 'Contracting earworms: The roles of personality and musicality', in E. Cambouropoulos, C. Tsougras, K. Mavromatis, K. Pastiadis (eds), *Proceedings of ICMPC-ESCOM 12* (Thessaloniki, Greece), 302–310.

39  Williamson, V.J., and Müllensiefen, D. (2012), 'Earworms from three angles', in E. Cambouropoulos, C. Tsougras, K. Mavromatis, K. Pastiadis (eds), *Proceedings of ICMPC-ESCOM 12* (Thessaloniki, Greece), 1124–1133.

40  Williamson, V.J., et al. (2012), 'How do earworms start? Classifying the everyday circumstances of Involuntary Musical Imagery', *Psychology of Music*, 40(3), 259–284.

41  Kvavilashvili, L., and Mandler, G. (2004), 'Out of one's mind: A study of involuntary semantic memories', *Cognitive Psychology*, 48(1), 47–94. Berntsen, D. (2009), *Involuntary Autobiographical Memories: An Introduction to the Unbidden Past*. Cambridge: Cambridge University Press.

42  Schlagman, S., and Kvavilashvili, L. (2008), 'Involuntary autobiographical memories in and outside the laboratory: How different are they from voluntary autobiographical memories?', *Memory and Cognition*, 36(5), 920–932.

## Chapter 8: Music and lifelong well-being

1  Sloboda, J. (2005), *Exploring the musical mind: Cognition, Emotion, Ability, Function*. Oxford: Oxford University Press.

2  Saarikallio, S. (2012), 'Cross cultural approaches to music and health', in R.A.R Macdonald, G. Kreutz and L. Mitchell (eds.) *Music, Health and Wellbeing* (pp. 477–490). Oxford: Oxford University Press.

3  http://staff.bath.ac.uk/ecsscw/But_what_is_Wellbeing.pdf

4  Macdonald, R.A.R, Kreutz, G., and Mitchell, L. (eds.) (2012), *Music, Health and Wellbeing*. Oxford, Oxford University Press.

5  Bruscia, K.E. (1998), *Defining Music Therapy* (2nd edn). Gilsum: Barcelona Publishers.

6  Gold et al. (2011), 'Music therapy or music medicine?', *Psychotherapy and Psychosomatics*, 80, 304.

7  Lane, D. (2011), 'Music as Medicine, Music and the Brain' (podcast), available at: http://www.loc.gov/podcasts/musicandthebrain/podcast_lane.html

8  Cepeda, M.S., Carr, D.B., Lau, J., and Alvarez, H. (2006), 'Music for pain relief', Cochrane Database of Systematic Reviews, Issue 2. Art. No.: CD004843. DOI: 10.1002/14651858.CD004843.pub2.

9  Ayoub, C.M., et al. (2005), 'Music and ambient operating room noise in patients undergoing spinal anesthesia', *Anesthesia & Analgesia*, 100(5), 1316–1319.

10  Salimpoor, V.N., et al. (2011), 'Anatomically distinct dopamine release during anticipation and experience of peak emotion to music', *Nature Neuroscience*, 14, 257–262.

11  Salimpoor, V.N., et al. (2013), 'Interactions Between the Nucleus Accumbens and Auditory Cortices Predict Music Reward Value', *Science*, 216–219.

12  McKinney C.H., et al. (1997), 'Effects of guided imagery and music (GIM) therapy on mood and cortisol in healthy adults', *Health Psychology*, 16(4), 390–400. Koelsch, S., et al. (2011), 'Effects of Music Listening on Cortisol Levels and Propofol Consumption during Spinal Anesthesia', *Frontiers in Psychology*, 2, 58.

13  Lane, D. (1991), 'The effect of a single music therapy session on hospitalized children as measured by salivary immunoglobulin A, speech pause time, and a Patient Opinion Likert Scale', PhD Thesis available at http://rave.ohiolink.edu/etdc/view?acc_num=case1055429377

14  Doheny, L., et al. (2012), 'Exposure to biological maternal sounds improves cardiorespiratory regulation in extremely preterm infants', *The Journal of Maternal-Fetal and Neonatal Medicine*, 25(9), 1591–1594.

15  Loewy, J., et al. (2013), 'The Effects of Music Therapy on Vital Signs, Feeding, and Sleep in Premature Infants', *Pediatrics*, 131(5), 902–918.

16  Tramo, M., et al. (2011), 'Effects of music on physiological and behavioral indices of acute pain and stress in premature infants: Clinical trial and literature review', *Music and Medicine*, 3(2), 72–83.

17  McMahon, E., Wintermark, P., and Lahav, A. (2012), 'Auditory brain development in premature infants: the importance of early experience', *Annals of the New York Academy of Sciences*, 1252, 17–24.

18  Neal, D.O., and Lindeke, L.L. (2008), 'Music as a nursing intervention for preterm infants in the NICU', *Neonatal Network*, 27(5), 319–327.

19   Standley, J.M. (2002), 'A meta-analysis of the efficacy of music therapy for premature infants', *Journal of Pediatric Nursing*, 17(2), 107–113.

20   Standley, J.M. (2003), 'The effect of music-reinforced nonnutritive sucking on feeding rate of premature infants', *Journal of Pediatric Nursing*, 18(3), 169–173. Standley, J.M. (2000), 'The effect of contingent music to increase non-nutritive sucking of premature infants', *Pediatric Nursing*, 26(5), 493–499.

21   Yildiz, A., and Arikan, D. (2012), 'The effects of giving pacifiers to premature infants and making them listen to lullabies on their transition period for total oral feeding and sucking success', *Journal of Clinical Nursing*, 21(5–6), 644–656.

22   Allen, R., and Heaton, P.F. (2010), 'Autism, music, and the therapeutic potential of music in alexithymia', *Music Perception*, 27(4), 251–261. Heaton, P.F. (2009), 'Assessing musical skills in autistic children who are not savants', *Philosophical Transactions of the Royal Society B: Biological Sciences*, 364(1522), 1443–1447.

23   Hess, K.L., Morrier, M.J, Heflin, L.J, and Ivey, M.L. (2008), 'Autism treatment survey: services received by children with autism spectrum disorders in public school classrooms', *Journal of Autism and Developmental Disorders*, 38(5), 961–971.

24   Kim, J., Wigram, T., and Gold, C. (2008), 'The effects of improvisational music therapy on joint attention behaviors in autistic children: a randomized controlled study', *Journal of Autism and Developmental Disorders*, 38(9), 1758–1766.

25   Lim, H.A. (2010), 'Effect of "developmental speech and language training through music" on speech production in children with autism spectrum disorders', *Journal of Music Therapy*, 47(1), 2–26.

26   Wan, C.Y., et al. (2011), 'Auditory-Motor Mapping Training as an Intervention to Facilitate Speech Output in Non-Verbal Children with Autism: A Proof of Concept Study', *PLOS ONE*, 6(9), e25505.

27   Phillips-Silver, J. (2009), 'On the meaning of movement in music, development and the brain', *Contemporary Music Review*, 28(3), 293–314.

28   Srinivasan, S.M., and Bhat, A.N. (2013), 'A review of "music and movement" therapies for children with autism: embodied interventions for multisystem development', *Frontiers in Integrative Neuroscience*, 7, 22.

29   Jackson, N.A. (2003), 'A survey of music therapy methods and their role in the treatment of early elementary school children with ADHD', *Journal of Music Therapy*, 40(4), 302–323.

30 Pelham, W.E. Jr, et al. (2011), 'Music and Video as Distractors for Boys with ADHD in the Classroom: Comparison with Controls, Individual Differences, and Medication Effect', *Journal of Abnormal Child Psychology*, 39(8), 1085–1098.

31 Fan Zhang et al. (2012), 'Music therapy for attention deficit hyperactivity disorder (ADHD) in children and adolescents (Protocol)', Cochrane Database of Systematic Reviews 2012, Issue 8. Art. No.: CD010032. DOI: 10.1002/14651858.CD010032.

32 http://www.nhs.uk/Conditions/Dyslexia/Pages/Introduction.aspx

33 Patel, A.D. (2012), 'Language, music, and the brain: A resource-sharing framework', in P. Rebuschat, M. Rohrmeier, J. Hawkins, and I. Cross (eds.), *Language and Music as Cognitive Systems* (pp. 204–223). Oxford: Oxford University Press. Patel, A.D. (2008), *Music, Language, and the Brain*. New York: Oxford University Press.

34 Hornickel, J., and Kraus, N. (2013), 'Unstable Representation of Sound: A Biological Marker of Dyslexia', *The Journal of Neuroscience*, 33(8), 3500–3504.

35 Butzlaff, R. (2000), 'Can music be used to teach reading?', *Journal of Aesthetic Education*, 34(3/4), 167–178.

36 Forgeard, M., et al. (2008), 'The relation between music and phonological processing in normal-reading children and children with dyslexia', *Music Perception*, 25(4), 383–390

37 Overy, K., Nicolson, R.I., Fawcett, A.J., and Clarke, E.F. (2003), 'Dyslexia and music: Measuring musical timing skills', *Dyslexia*, 9(1), 18–36.

38 Tallal, P., Miller, S., and Fitch, R.H. (1993), 'Neurological basis of speech: A case of the pre-eminence of temporal processing', *Annals of the New York Academy of Science*, 682, 27–47.

39 Overy, K. (2000), 'Dyslexia, Temporal Processing and Music; The potential of music as an early learning aid for dyslexic children', *Psychology of Music*, 28(2), 218–229.

40 Slater, J., Tierney, A., and Kraus, N. (2013), 'At-risk elementary school children with one year of classroom music instruction are better at keeping a beat'. *PLOS ONE*. 8(10): e77250.

41 Cogo-Moreira, H., et al. (2012), 'Music education for improving reading skills in children and adolescents with dyslexia', Cochrane Database of Systematic Reviews Issue 8. Art. No.: CD009133. DOI: 10.1002/14651858. CD009133.pub2.

42 http://www.prismlab.org/research_page/research

43 http://www.cochrane.org/cochrane-reviews

44 Mansky, P.J., and Wallerstedt, D.B. (2006), 'Complementary medicine in palliative care and cancer management', *Cancer Journal*, 12(5), 425–431.

45 Aldridge, D., Gustorff, G., and Hannich, H.-J. (1990), '"Where am I?" Music therapy applied to coma patients', *Journal of the Royal Society of Medicine*, 83(6), 345–346.

46 Aldridge, D. (1996), *Music therapy research and practice in medicine*. London: Jessica Kingsley.

47 Bradt, J., Dileo, C., and Grocke, D. (2010), 'Music interventions for mechanically ventilated patients', Cochrane Database of Systematic Reviews 2010, Issue 12. Art. No.: CD006902. DOI: 10.1002/14651858. CD006902.pub2.

48 Mackay, J., and Mensah, G.A. (2004). *The atlas of heart disease and stroke*. Geneva: World Health Organization.

49 Särkämö, T., et al. (2008), 'Music listening enhances cognitive recovery and mood after middle cerebral artery stroke', *Brain*, 131(3), 866–876.

50 Tsai, P.L., et al. (2013), 'Listening to classical music ameliorates unilateral neglect after stroke', *American Journal of Occupational Therapy*, 67(3), 328–35.

51 Bodak, R. (2012), 'Using music to increase spatial awareness in two right hemisphere stroke patients with chronic unilateral neglect'. Unpublished PhD thesis, Goldsmiths, University of London.

52 Thaut, M.H., et al. (1996), 'Rhythmic auditory stimulation in gait training for Parkinson's disease patients', *Movement Disorders*, 11(2), 193–200.

53 Nombela, C., Hughes, L.E., Owen, A.M., and Grahn, J.A. (2013), 'Into the groove: can rhythm influence Parkinson's disease?', *Neuroscience and Biobehavioural Reviews*, Sep 3. pii: S0149-7634(13)00193-0

54 Bradt, J., et al. (2010), 'Music therapy for acquired brain injury', Cochrane Database of Systematic Reviews 2010, Issue 7. Art. No.: CD006787. DOI: 10.1002/14651858.CD006787.pub2.

55 Muto, T., et al. (2007), 'Interactive cueing with walk-Mate for Hemiparetic Stroke Rehabilitation', *Journal of NeuroEngineering and Rehabilitation*, 9, 58

56 Schlaug, G., et al. (2010), 'From singing to speaking: facilitating recovery from nonfluent aphasia', *Future Neurology*, 5(5), 657–665.

57 Conklyn, D., et al. (2012), 'The Effects of Modified Melodic Intonation Therapy on Nonfluent Aphasia: A Pilot Study', *Journal of Speech, Language, and Hearing Research*, 55(5), 1463–1471.

58 Zipse, l., Norton, A., Marchina, S., and Schlaug, G. (2012), 'When right is all that is left: plasticity of right-hemisphere tracts in a young aphasic patient' *Annals of the New York Academy of Sciences*, 1252, 237–245.

59  Stahl, B., et al. (2013), 'How to engage the right brain hemisphere in aphasics without even singing: evidence for two paths of speech recovery', *Frontiers in Human Neuroscience*, 7, 35.

60  Lai, H.L., and Good, M. (2005), 'Music improves sleep quality in older adults', *Journal of Advanced Nursing*, 49(3), 234–244. Cappuccio, F.P., et al. (2011), 'Sleep duration predicts cardiovascular outcomes: a systematic review and meta-analysis of prospective studies', *European Heart Journal*, 32(12), 1484–1492.

61  Bradt, J., Dileo, C., Grocke, D., and Magill, L. (2011), 'Music interventions for improving psychological and physical outcomes in cancer patients', Cochrane Database of Systematic Reviews, Issue 8. Art. No.: CD006911. DOI: 10.1002/14651858.CD006911.pub2.

62  Bradt, J., and Dileo, C. (2009), 'Music for stress and anxiety reduction in coronary heart disease patients', Cochrane Database of Systematic Reviews, Issue 2. Art. No.: CD006577. DOI: 10.1002/14651858. CD006577.pub2.

63  Cucherat, M. (2007), 'Quantitative relationship between resting heart rate reduction and magnitude of clinical benefits in post-myocardial infarction: a meta-regression of randomized clinical trials', *European Heart Journal*, 28(24), 3012–3019.

64  Lane, D. (2011), 'Music as Medicine, Music and the Brain' (podcast), available at: http://www.loc.gov/podcasts/musicandthebrain/podcast_lane.html

65  Lin, S.-T. et al. (2011), 'Mental Health Implications of Music: Insight from Neuroscientific and Clinical Studies', *Harvard Review of Psychiatry*, 19(1), 34–46.

66  Maratos, A., Crawford, M.J., and Procter, S. (2011), 'Music therapy for depression: it seems to work, but how?', *British Journal of Psychiatry*, 199(2), 92–93.

67  Mössler, K., Chen, X., Heldal, T.O., and Gold, C. (2011), 'Music therapy for people with schizophrenia and schizophrenia-like disorders', Cochrane Database of Systematic Reviews, Issue 12. Art. No.: CD004025. DOI: 10.1002/14651858.CD004025.pub3.

68  Vink, A.C., Bruinsma, M.S., and Scholten, R.J.P.M. (2003), 'Music therapy for people with dementia', Cochrane Database of Systematic Reviews, Issue 4. Art. No.: CD003477. DOI: 10.1002/14651858.CD003477.pub2.

69  Golda, C., Solli, H.P., Krüger, V., and Lie, S.A. (2009), 'Dose–response relationship in music therapy for people with serious mental disorders:

Systematic review and meta-analysis', *Clinical Psychology Review*, 29(3), 193–207.

70 Clair, A. (2011), 'Music Therapy, Alzheimer's and Post-Traumatic Stress' (podcast), available at: http://www.loc.gov/podcasts/musicandthebrain/podcast_clair.html

71 Maratos, A., Crawford, M.J., and Procter, S. (2011), 'Music therapy for depression: it seems to work, but how?', *British Journal of Psychiatry*, 199(2), 92–3. DeNora, T. (2003), *Beyond Adorno: Rethinking Music Sociology*. Cambridge: Cambridge University Press.

72 Brandes, V., et al. (2010), 'Receptive music therapy for the treatment of depression: a proof-of-concept study and prospective controlled clinical trial of efficacy', *Psychotherapy and Psychosomatics*, 79(5), 321–322.

73 Cuddy, L.L., et al. (2012), 'Memory for Melodies and Lyrics in Alzheimer's Disease', *Music Perception*, 29(5) 479–491.

74 Simmons-Stern, N.R., Budson, A.E., and Ally, B.A. (2010), 'Music as a memory enhancer in patients with Alzheimer's disease', *Neuropsychologia*, 48(10), 3164–3167.

75 Moussard, A., Bigand, E., Belleville, S., and Peretz, I. (2012), 'Music as an Aid to Learn New Verbal Information in Alzheimer's Disease', *Music Perception*, 29(5), 521–531.

76 Guétin, S., et al. (2011), 'Effect of Music Therapy on Anxiety and Depression in Patients with Alzheimer's Type Dementia: Randomised, Controlled Study', *Dementia and Geriatric Cognitive Disorders*, 28(1), 36–46.

77 Clair, A. (2011), 'Music Therapy, Alzheimer's and Post-Traumatic Stress' (podcast), available at: http://www.loc.gov/podcasts/musicandthebrain/podcast_clair.html

78 Nair, B., et al. (2010), 'The effect of Baroque music on behavioural disturbances in patients with dementia', *Australasian Journal on Ageing*, 30(1), 11–15.

79 Kwekkeboom K.L. (2003), 'Music versus distraction for procedural pain and anxiety in patients with cancer', *Oncology Nursing Forum*, 30(3), 433–440.

# Index

acquired savant syndrome 108
ADHD 209–10
ADS (adult directed speech) 23, 24, 27
adolescence
    best music of one's life 71–5
    experiments with music 59–63
    moods and emotions 54–9
    music for 53–75
    problem thoughts/behaviours 63–6
adult directed speech *see* ADS)
agency 60
Alzheimer's 220–1
    and musical memory 189
AMMT 209, 216
amnesia 187
amnesic cellist ('PM') 188–9
Amunts, Katrin 90
amusia 97–104
    acquired 100
    brain differences 103–4
    congenital 100–1
    diagnosis 99–101
    manifestations 99
    in words of ones with 101–3
amygdala 152–3, 154, 190–1
animals
    movement to beat 141–5
    and music 6
aphasia 216
Arctic Monkeys 116
arcuate fasciculus (AF) 86–7, 104
Areni, Charles 134
arousal 118–19
    mood and 120
    personality and 122–3
arousal state 34–5
*Artist, The* (film) 151, 157

assembly lines 112–13
athletes, music use 162–4
Attention Deficit Hyperactivity
    Disorder (ADHD) 209–10
attention level 118–19
auditory cortex 91, 108–9
auditory evoked potential 92
Auditory-Motor Mapping Training
    (AMMT) 209, 216
Auerbach, Sigmund 82–3
autism spectrum 208–9
autonomic relaxation response 202, 203, 218, 219

baby talk 23–5
Bach, J.S. 175
background music
    effects 118–21, 125–6
    personality and 121–4
    preference and choice 124–5, 127
Baddeley, Alan 2
Balogh, Suzy 162
Baruš, Imants 193
beat
    detection in newborns 18–20, 142–3
    implied 142
    induction 20
    movement to 141–5
Beatles, The 116
Beheim-Schwarzbach, Dorothée 83
Bejo, Bérénice 157
Besson, Mireille 40
Beverland, Michael 137
Bhatia, Azra 148
Blunt, James 116
Bradley, Anna 122–4

brain
    activation signatures 74
    bimusical 106–7
    body maps 88–90
    changes through music 80–2
    deep stimulation 58
    differences in amusia 103–4
    'ghosting' 94–5
    injury 212–17
    music learning and 82–97
    plasticity 80–1, 108
    reward system 202–3
    structure 85–7
brands 137–8
*Bridges of Madison County, The* (film)
    155

cancer patients 217–18
'canned' music 127
Cassidy, Eva 128, 129
Chandrasekharan, Bharath 39
Changizi, Mark 5–6
Charles, Ray 58, 63
childhood, music in 31–52
chimpanzee, beat synchronisation
    144
choices, instant 136–7
chunking 174
Claes, Michel 62, 66
Cochrane reports 212, 213–14, 215,
    218, 221
cockatoo, beat synchronisation 143–4
cocoon, auditory 117
cognition, music effect on
        performance 126
cognitive ageing 184
cognitive engagement 119–20
coma 213–14
commercial world, music in 128–38
computer games 121–2
concentration, music effect on
        performance 127
concrete content 153–4
conditioned head turn procedure 27
consumer, music and 130–5
contour detection, in newborns 20–3
coping, music and 61–2, 64–6
corpus callosum 85–6
cortical homunculus 88
cortisol 203
cross-cultural music 106

crying 24–5
Cuddy, Lola 98
Curnow, Ross 131

dance
    music and 140–7
    for romance 145–7
    signals 146–7
Darwin, Charles 5
Davidson, Jane 46
Davies, John Booth 58
Day, Doris 194
dementia 220–1, 222
    *see also* Alzheimer's
DeNora, Tia 54
depression, music and 62, 219–20, 221
*Desert Island Discs* 184
Desjardins, Renée 26
Di Bernardo, Christina 95–6
distinctiveness, optimal 70
'dose effect' 41–2
Dowling, Jay 179
Dujardin, Jean 157
dyslexia 210–12

earworms 191–5
Eldar, Eran 153–4
emotion
    defined 55–6
    as function of music 60
    mood vs. 55
    music and 54–9, 126, 152–5, 190,
        222–3
emotional jolt 72–3
emotional state, communication 26
enculturation of music 52, 57
    effect 106
Eneko (author's nephew) 208–9
epilepsy 189
episodic autobiographical memory
    72
equestrian therapy 209
ergogenic music 158–9
expectation 57–8
Experience Sampling Method (ESM)
    studies 140
extraverts 122–4
Eysenck, Hans 122

factory, music in 112–14
fatigue 159

fear, music and 152
'fight or flight' 56, 152
film music 151–8
Finke, Carsten 188
flow state 118–19
foetal memory 15
Ford, Henry 112
formant frequencies 26
Forrest, Andrew 2
fragile X syndrome 208
Frith, Simon 125
frontal cortex 108, 190–1
functional music 127
Furnham, Adrian 122–4

Gabrielsson, Alf 54
Gan, Su-lin 70
Gattis, Meredith 28
Gebrselassie, Haile 162
gender, and music in exercise 161
Giffords, Gabrielle 216, 217
Granier-Deferre, Carolyn 16
groove music 142
group identity 66, 69–71
Guéguen, Nicolas 149–50

Haake, Anneli Beronius 116–17
Haka war dance and cry 145
Haley, Bill 186
Hallam, Susan 42
Halpern, Andrea 177
Halwani, Gus 86–7
Hargreaves, David 54, 63, 68
hearing in noise (HIN) 38–40
hearing skills 38–40, 91–4
heart disease patients 217–18
herpes simplex encephalitis 186
HIN 38–40
hippocampus 81, 95
Hitch, Graham 2
Honing, Henkjan 142–3
Hornickel, Jane 42
Huron, David 58, 155–6

idée fixe 157
identity 60, 66–71
    group 66, 69–71
    self- 67–9
IDS (infant directed speech) 23–9
    benefits to adults 24–5
    for learning 25–9

Infant Behaviour Questionnaire 51
infant directed speech see IDS
instrument, choosing 43–5
intelligence
    music and 32–5
    music lessons and 35–7
interpersonal relationships 60, 62–3
introverts 122–3
involuntary musical imagery 191–5

Jachendoff, Ray 58
Jackson, Michael 194
Jacob, Céline 136
James, William 18, 56
James–Lange theory 55–6
Janata, Petr 73–4
Jaws films 157
juggling 81
Juslin, Patrik 55, 57

Kämpfe, Juliane 126
Karageorghis, Costas 159
Kim, David 134
Kitamura, Christine 28
Kraus, Nina 35, 38–9, 42
Krause, Amanda 140
Krumhansl, Carol 182–3

Lahav, Amir 205–6
Lai, Chien-Jung 133
Lam, Christa 28
Lange, Carl 56
language learning 27–9
language processing 40–2
Laukka, Petri 57
leisure, music at 139–65
leitmotifs 156–7
Lennon, John 68
Lerdahl, Fred 58
Lesiuk, Teresa 115
Levitin, Daniel 178
life memories, music-evoked 73–4
limbic system 152, 155
listening
    biased by 105–6
    music-focused 139–40
listening skills 38–40, 91–4
Loewy, Joanne 206
Luck, Geoff 146–7

MacDonald, Raymond 68

Mampe, Birgit 22
Marcus, Gary 108
Martin, Dean 63
match making 147–8
meaning, music and 156–8
medial prefrontal cortex (MPFC) 74
melodic intonation therapy (MIT)
        216–17
memory
    defined 169–70
    episodic 170, 190
    episodic autobiographical 72
    foetal 15
    implicit 170–1, 189–90, 221
    involuntary 194
    learning 173–5
    music effect on performance
        126–7
    musicians vs. non-musicians 95–6
    retrieval 175–6
    semantic 170
    see also life memories; musical
        memory
messages, in music 137–8
Meyer, Leonard B. 57–8
Miell, Dorothy 68
Milliman, Ronald 132–3
mimicry, by babies 22, 25–6
mind popping 194
Miranda, Dave 62, 66
mismatch negativity (MMN) 19–20
MIT 216–17
Mithen, Steven 108
MMN 19–20
mnemonics 171
Montreal Battery for the Evaluation
        of Amusia 99
mood
    and arousal 120
    emotion vs. 55
    improvement 34–5
    music and 54–9, 120
    regulation with music 60–1
Moreno, Sylvain 40
'motherese' see IDS
motivation
    external 46–7, 48
    internal 46–7
    maintaining 46–7
motor control skills 87–91
motor cortex 88, 90, 109

motor response 94–5
movement 87–91
    music and 131–3, 158–61
    stroke patients 215–16
    synchronised 163
movement therapy 209
Mozart, Wolfgang Amadeus 11–12
Mozart effect 33–5, 118–19, 120
Müllensiefen, Daniel 177
mundane behaviour, music effect on
        performance 126
music
    at work see work music
    definition 4–5
    as frozen in time 71–2
    functions 60
    origin 5–6
    sad 155–6
    'vitamin' model of 197, 222
music activity classes 49–51
music learning, in adulthood 107–9
music lessons 43–9
    instrument choice 43–5
    and intelligence 35–7
    motivation maintenance 46–7
    practice 47–9
    teacher choice 45–6
    transfer benefits 37–42
music medicine 200, 201–2
    in adults 213–23
music therapy 200–2
    in adults 213–23
    in children 208–12
    in premature babies 205–7
musical fit 135–7
musical memory 171–96
    boosting 179–81
    capacity 183–4
    learning 174–5
    and liking 179–80
    longevity 184
    new music 178–9
    retrieval 175–6
    survival 185–91
    tune naming 182–3
    vocal vs. instrumental music 181
musical mirror 57
musical performance ability, as 'super
        skill' 37–8
musical tastes, cohesion/
        crystallisation 71

Nazzi, Thiery 21
neglect, unilateral 214
*Neighbours* (TV programme) theme 16
neuroticism 193
neurotransmitter 202–3
newborns
    contour detection 20–3
    rhythm 18–20, 142–3
North, Adrian 55, 63, 140
nostalgic familiarity 58
*Notebook, The* (film) 155

obsessive-compulsive traits 193
office, music in 114–18
Oldham, Greg 114
Omigie, Diana 100
online store, music tempo and 133
oral traditions 184
Overy, Katie 211

Pantev, Christo 90–1, 92
'Parental Advisory' sticker 64
Parente, Joseph 125
parents, and effective practice 48
Parkinson's patients 215
Parsons, Larry 108
Patel, Aniruddh 143–4
peer bonding 69–70
Peretz, Isabel 99
personality, background music and 121–4
photographs, memory for 177–8
pianists, motor ability 87–8
pick up line 149–51
Pileri, Stefania 95–6
pitch
    change detection in language 40–1
    losing sense of 99
    processing in speech 93
Plato 57
play *see* leisure
plink study 182–3
Post Traumatic Stress Disorder (PTSD) 219
practice 47–9
    deliberate 47
pre-exercise music 159–60
prega-phone 12, 14

premature babies
    feeding 207
    music and 204–7
prenatal music 12–18
    and intelligence in newborns 17
    and musical skills 17
Presley, Elvis 63–4
Priest, David-Lee 159
problem behaviour, music and 63–6
productivity, music and 113
prolactin 156
proprioception 88
prosocial behaviour, music and 151
psycho-physiological arousal 118–19
    mood and 120
    personality and 122–3
PTSD 219

RAS 215, 216
Rauscher, Frances 33–4
Raviv, Amiram 62
reading, and music 211–12
reading ability 41–2
relaxation response, autonomic 202, 203, 218, 219
reminiscence bump 184
rhesus monkeys, and beat detection 143
rhythm 211
rhythmic auditory stimulation (RAS) 215, 216
romance
    dance for 145–7
    music for 147–51
Rubin, David 184
rumination 193, 195

Saarikallio, Suvi 60–1, 63, 66–7, 68
Sacks, Oliver 107, 193
Sakkalou, Elena 28
Salimpoor, Valarie 58
Samson, Séverine 189
Särkämö, Teppo 214
Schellenberg, Glenn 36, 180
Schlaug, Gottfried 85
sea lion, beat synchronisation 144
self-identity 67–9
self-regulation 47
Sinatra, Frank 64
singers, arcuate fasciculus 87
Sloboda, John 55, 98, 197, 222

'smart music listening' 118, 120, 125, 127
Smith, Patricia Cain 131
'Snowball' (cockatoo) 143–4
somatosensory cortex 88
Spangenberg, Eric 130
speaking 216–17
speech perception 93–4
spending, music and 132, 134–5
sport, music and 158–64
Stalinski, Stephanie 180
Standing, Lionel 177–8
Standley, Jayne 207
Strait, Dana 39, 42, 92
string players, motor control 90–1
stroke patients 214–16
structural bars 175–6
superior temporal gyrus 82–3
*Superman* films 157

taxi drivers 81
teacher, choosing 45–6
tears 155–6
tempo of music
      and exercise outcome 160–1
      and online store purchases 133
timbre 99
time, absorption by music 129–30
time-on-task 115
tone deafness, *see* amusia
Toscanini, Arturo 172–3
Trainor, Laurel 26, 50–1
transliminality 192–3
Tulving, Endel 170
tunes, naming 182–3
Twain, Mark 194

uniqueness effect 183

Venezuelan work songs 111
ventilated patients 213–14
verbal learning 208–9
Virtual Musical Instrument (VMI) 212
vision 95–6
visuo-motor skills 96
'vitamin' model of music 197, 222
vocalisations, by animals 141–2, 144–5

Vogt, Cécile 83
Vogt, Oskar 83
vowel discrimination 26–7

Wagner, Richard 156
waiting 129
Walk-Mate 215–16
Wammes, Mike 193
Wan, Catherine 208–9
Wearing, Clive 186–8
Wearing, Deborah 186–8
Weiss, Michael 181
well-being, music and 197–223
      in children 207–12
      definition of well-being 199
      in infants 204–7
      mechanisms 202–4
      mental well-being in adults 218–21
      physical well-being in adults 212–18
      type of music 221–3
      *see also* music medicine; music therapy
white matter pathways 86, 104
Williamon, Aaron 175–6
Wingate test 162
Winkler, István 19
Winston, Robert 4
Wise, Karen 98
womb, music in *see* prenatal music
Wong, Patrick 93, 107
work music 111–38
      commercial world 128–38
      helpfulness 126–7
      as hindrance 114
      history 112–14
      in office 114–18
      time absorption 129–30
      *see also* background music
World Memory Championships 173

Yalch, Richard 130
Yerkes–Dodson (Y–D) curve 118–19, 122

Zander, Mark 137–8
Zatorre, Robert 58
Zillmann, Dolf 70, 148